IMAGES
of America

MORTON GROVE

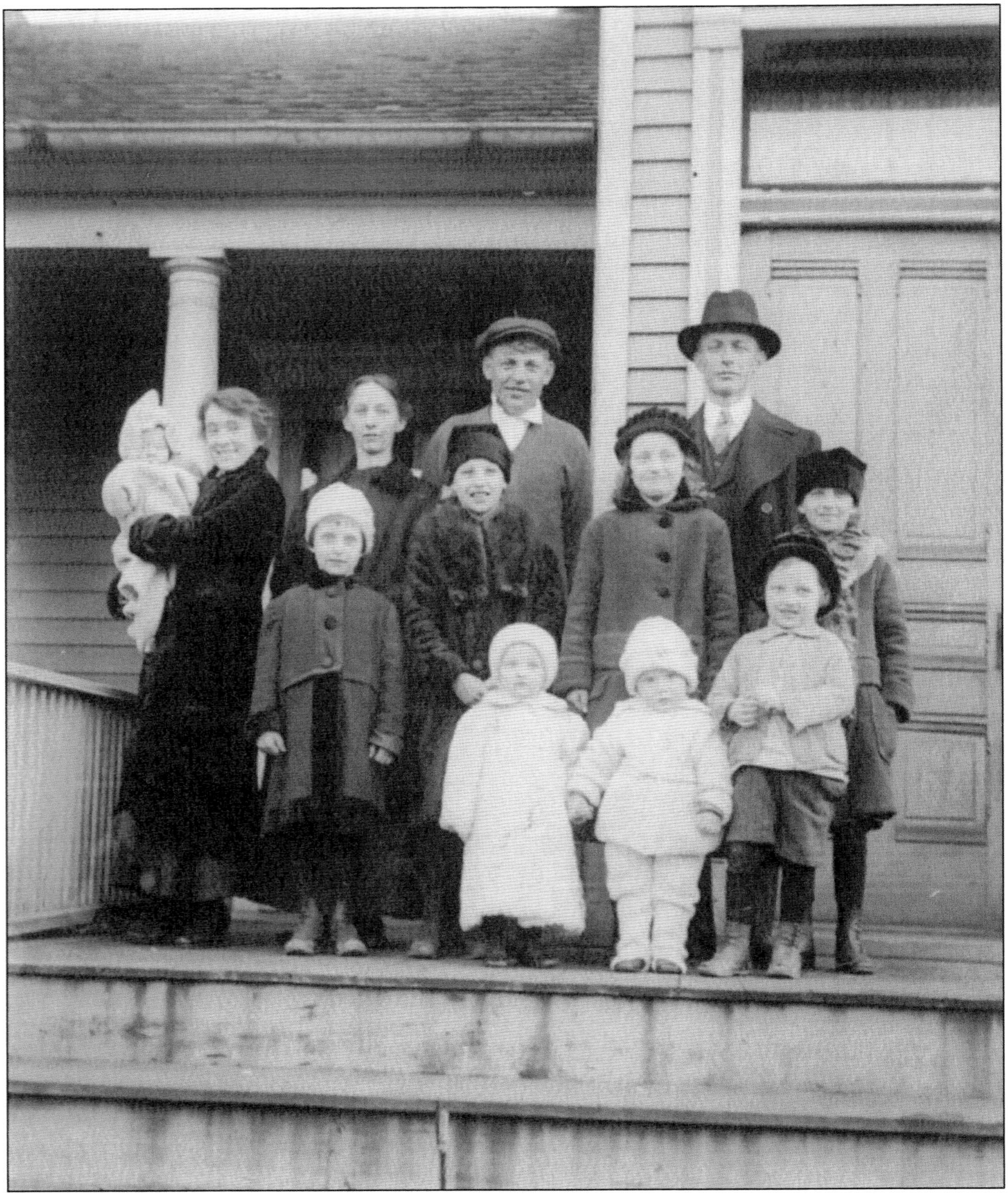

The Haupt and Yehl families are pictured on the porch of their farmhouse at 6025 Lincoln Avenue in 1916. From left to right are (first row) Bernice Yehl, Harold Haupt, and Howard Yehl; (second row) Ruth Yehl, Magdalen Yehl, Helen Paroubek, and Frances Yehl; (third row) Marian Haupt, Anna (née Seelhammer) Haupt, Elizabeth (née Haupt) Yehl, Mathias Yehl, and Peter Haupt. This farmhouse was moved to Harrer Park in 1984 and now serves as the Morton Grove Historical Museum.

On the Cover: Here, a baseball game occurs during recess at Grove School in approximately 1910. The one-room Morton Grove Public School was established in 1897 and expanded twice, in 1923 and 1926. In 1976, work started to convert the school into its current use as Village Hall and headquarters for the Morton Grove Police Department. It was renamed the Richard T. Flickinger Municipal Center in 1988 in honor of the recently deceased mayor.

IMAGES
of America

MORTON GROVE

Mary Busch and Tim Mayse-Lillig
for the Morton Grove Historical Society

ARCADIA
PUBLISHING

ISBN 978-0-7385-9881-9

Published by Arcadia Publishing
Charleston, South Carolina

Printed in the United States of America

Library of Congress Control Number: 2012949206

For all general information, please contact Arcadia Publishing:
Telephone 843-853-2070
Fax 843-853-0044
E-mail sales@arcadiapublishing.com
For customer service and orders:
Toll-Free 1-888-313-2665

Visit us on the Internet at www.arcadiapublishing.com

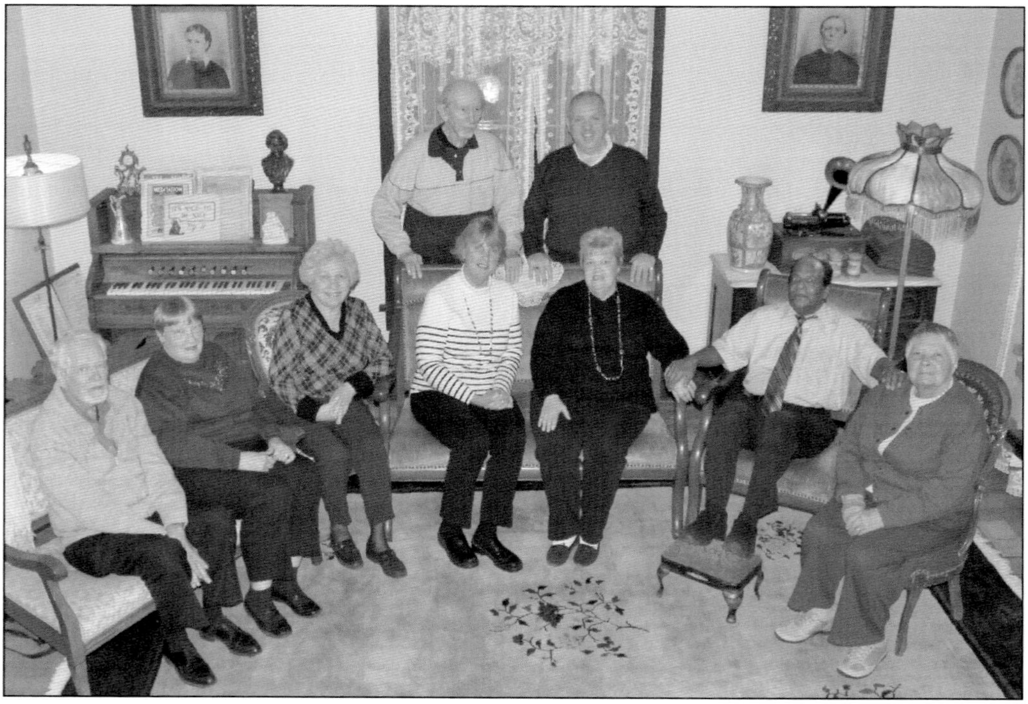

This pictorial volume chronicles the development of Morton Grove and the contributions made by its diverse residents over time. It is respectfully dedicated to all of the supporters, volunteers, members, board of directors, and officers of the Morton Grove Historical Society, both past and present. Pictured in the parlor of the Haupt-Yehl House (Morton Grove Historical Museum) is the current Morton Grove Historical Society's board of directors. From left to right are (seated) Milton Langer, Nancy Morrison, Mary Jane Calin, Lorraine Strybel, Donna Hedrick (president), George Kochikaran, and Sylvia Jurians; (standing) John Slater (treasurer) and Mark Matz. Not pictured are Ruth Budish and Maria Adames-Cordero (secretary). (Courtesy of Maria Toth.)

Contents

Acknowledgments

Morton Grove holds a unique place in the northern suburbs of Chicago. It is a small village that represents a wide spectrum of people from many diverse cultures and backgrounds. Now a modern suburb of that great city to its southeast, it is truly a microcosm of the America we know today.

The idea that "it takes a village" applies easily to the writing, editing, image selection, and the numerous other tasks required to publish a book. As an idea that grew from discussions at meetings of the Morton Grove Historical Society, the abstract concept of having a story written about our own village became a genuine probability. The Historical Society reached out to the Morton Grove Park District, who, with the historical society, operates the Morton Grove Historical Museum and Educational Center. With their approval, the book became a reality.

Museum curator Mary Busch and assistant curator Tim Mayse-Lillig took up the challenge of coauthoring the book on the behalf of the Morton Grove Historical Society, with the full support of the Morton Grove Park District. To assist the authors in this endeavor, a committee of volunteers was formed by the historical society, which was comprised of president Donna Hedrick, directors Milton Langer, Mark Matz, and Lorraine Strybel, along with Ray Minkus. The help of the professional team at Arcadia Publishing provided the structure and technical assistance to pull this project together.

Finally, the people of Morton Grove need to be recognized for their contribution. This book is the story of their lives and times, illustrated by the images that they left behind. Their photographic legacy has provided us with an abundant source of material, allowing this book to be published. In particular, those earlier historians who compiled books on Morton Grove for its 75th jubilee and centennial celebration in 1970 and 1995 have proven to be invaluable examples of historical research and documentation. It is our hope that this book will serve as a testimony to those who came before and as inspiration to those who will come later.

The dedication, acknowledgments, and introduction were written on behalf of the Morton Grove Historical Society by its director, Mark V. Matz. Unless attributed otherwise, all images appear courtesy of the Morton Grove Historical Society.

INTRODUCTION

This historical record of Morton Grove mirrors those of many communities across our country. The verbal, written, and photographic record of the people who lived on the land that now encompasses our village is a window looking into their history. In this volume is a chronicle beginning with the Native Americans and French traders. What follows is the story of early European farmers and their descendants, who lived, worked and developed businesses to support their growing community. As it transitioned from an agrarian-based society to the modern suburban community of today, the tale continues with the contributions made by the many residents with a variety of diverse cultures who have called the village of Morton Grove their home.

A significant amount of the village is and will remain undeveloped land as part of the Forest Preserve District of Cook County's system, which totals about 20 percent of the village today. While full of trees now, this landscape was much different when people first started to make their homes here. What early inhabitants first witnessed were prairies that resembled vast seas of native tall grasses and wildflowers on the flatland left by retreating glaciers. Illinois is nicknamed "the Prairie State," a phrase first coined in the 1840s, with the word *prairie* coming from a French word for "meadow."

By the time Morton Grove was incorporated in 1895, most of the natural prairies were gone. There were original oak, hickory, and maple forests along the river. Trees were precious commodities, with several becoming early landmarks and guideposts, as the native population formed them into trail-marker trees by bending and fastening saplings to mark points of interest. The village is fortunate to have Indian marker trees remaining, some estimated to be over 200 years old.

Water is a vital component of development. The Chicago River provided this for the area, along with rich prairie soil that attracted farmers. A source for freshwater and fishing, the river also supplied the power to operate the area's first sawmill in the 1830s, adding to the advantages of living in the area. An early name of the community was Miller's Mill, derived from that early business located just south of Dempster Street on the banks of the North Branch of the Chicago River.

The lumber milled by Miller's business was transported along Miller's Mill Road until the business closed in the 1860s. This road was originally a Native American trail and is now Lincoln Avenue.

Local truck farmers who traveled to the South Water Street Market in Chicago to sell their produce also provided cucumbers to the booming pickle industry that began in the late 1870s. The Globe Pickle Company was the first to do business in town, followed by the Squire Dingee and Henning Pickle companies. The Poehlmann Brothers Company arrived in the 1890s, established greenhouses, and quickly grew into the world's largest floral business, achieving worldwide recognition for taking the first-place prize for their roses at the St. Louis World's Fair in 1904. Poehlmann Brothers Company employed 300 to 500 people back then and operated in Morton Grove until 1931.

When the railroad came through in 1872 and purchased the rights to the Miller's sawmill property, a new era began. This new flag stop soon became a highly desirable location for commerce and industry. Named by the Chicago, Milwaukee & St. Paul Railway, the community was called Morton after Levi Parsons Morton, who provided financing to the railroad company. Morton was a vice president of the United States, ambassador to France, served in the US House of Representatives, and became the governor of New York just eight days after the village was incorporated as Morton Grove on December 24, 1895.

With the turn of the 19th to the 20th century, the village continued to grow and prosper as it welcomed home those who fought in World War I and looked ahead to the jazz age. A small airfield existed from 1919 to 1932 on farmland north of Dempster Street. In the Roaring Twenties, the village had a number of popular destinations for entertainment. Big-time nightclub managers of the era brought in the top talent of the day, like Guy Lombardo, Ted Lewis, Fred Waring, and Duke Ellington.

The Great Depression and lifting of Prohibition changed the mood of the country, and Morton Grove adjusted by working to meet the challenges of an uncertain economy. A new Village Hall was built in the late 1930s as the Works Progress Administration funded public building projects throughout the county. Another world war was looming, and many men and women were called to serve their country as priorities were shifting again to meet a new challenge after December 7, 1941. Bell & Gossett was just beginning operations in Morton Grove that year, and today, they continue building pumps under new ownership at their original plant on Austin Avenue. After World War II ended, along with the rationing and personal sacrifices made by the residents to help win the war, a new era of growth and prosperity was about to begin.

Morton Grove faced the baby boom with optimism. Those returning from the war needed homes for their growing families, and getting a new car to help them become more mobile was a top priority. People seeking new opportunities for a better life ventured out of Chicago into the suburbs, where they found older municipalities to their liking. The Edens Expressway opened up a path to the village and helped to foster the building boom that followed. The population of Morton Grove grew from 2,010 in 1940 to 3,926 in 1950 and soared a decade later to 20,533 in 1960. Housing styles changed from original farmhouses and brick bungalows to ranches and split-levels followed by condominium buildings and townhouses. The village has reached its physical limits, now bordered by other communities and forest preserves with the population in 2010 being 23,270 residents. The village embraced many changes over its history as it rose from a small agricultural community to a mix of many diverse cultures and businesses found here today.

Morton Grove has been recognized nationally for its qualities. The village was named by *Family Circle* magazine as "One of the Ten Best Towns for Families" in 2007 because it combined big-city opportunities with suburban charm. *Bloomberg Businessweek* named Morton Grove as the "Best Place to Raise Kids in Illinois" and ranked the village as the "No. 3 Place in the Country" for the same reason.

Morton Grove continues to be a great place to live, work, and raise a family. From its earliest days when Native Americans and French traders lived off the land, with the arrival of European settlers who grew their crops in the rich soil, to those entrepreneurs who started a variety of essential and innovative businesses, and right up through today as residents with richly diverse backgrounds add their own legacy, the village remains proud of its past while focused on the future.

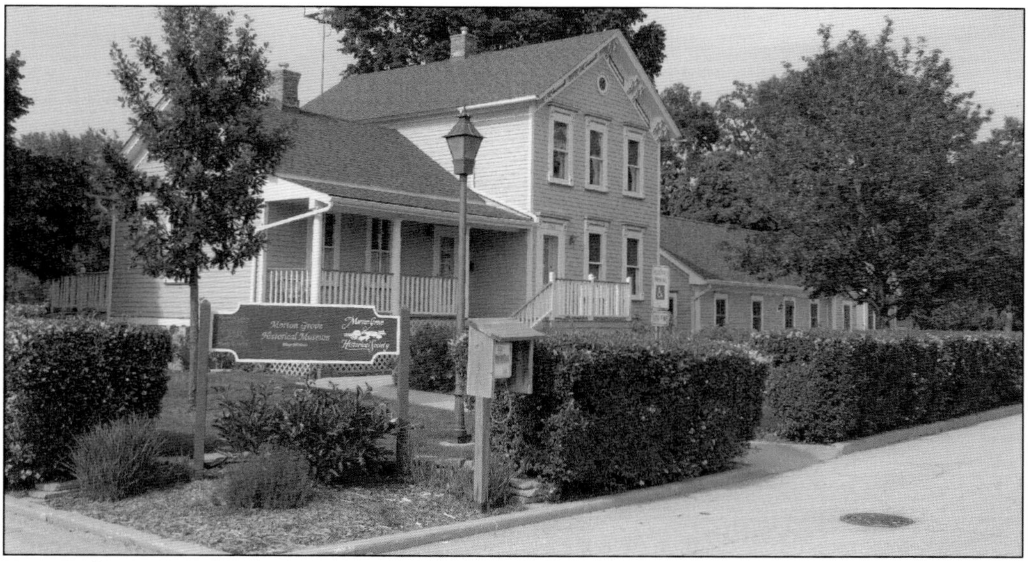

Here is the Morton Grove Historical Museum and Education Center. (Courtesy of Denise Wurl, Bluestem Studio LLC.)

One

Natural Landscapes and Native Americans

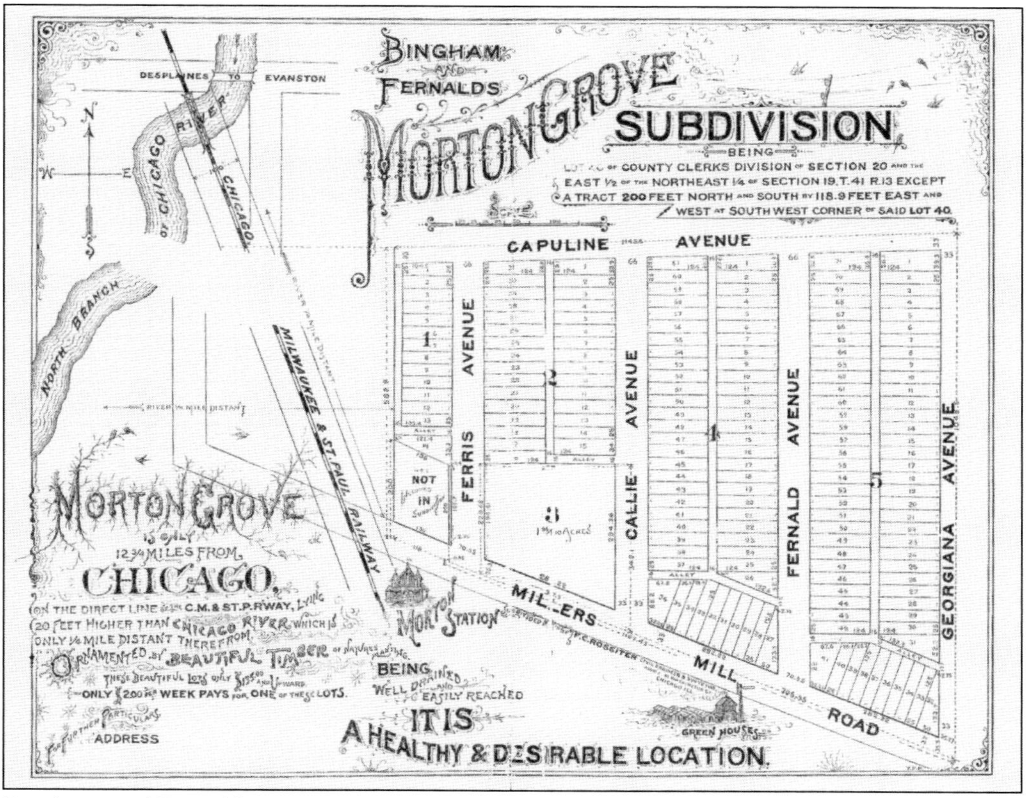

Bingham and Fernald's Morton Grove Subdivision map of 1891 illustrates the features of the landscape and proximity to Chicago which attracted early residents, preceding the village's incorporation in 1895. This well-drained land, 20 feet higher than the North Branch of the Chicago River and the convenience of the Chicago, Milwaukee & St. Paul Railway station contributed to the sale of lots in Morton Grove's first subdivision.

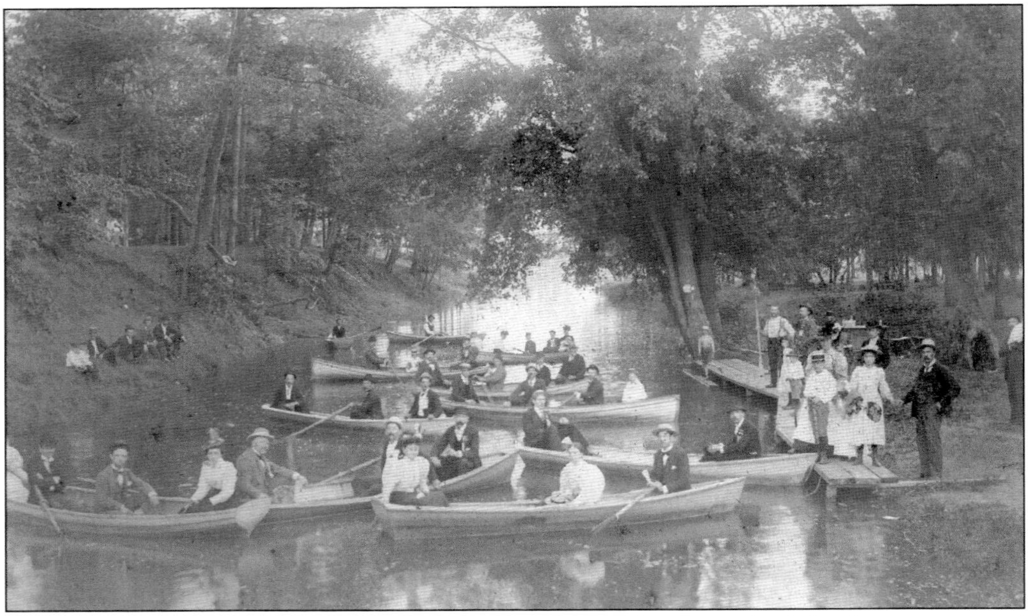

Boaters are pictured on the North Branch of the Chicago River, north of the dam constructed for this rowboat concession in St. Paul Park in the early 1900s. This picnic ground was owned and operated by George C. Klehm, the fourth president of the Cook County Board in 1886–1887, who donated this 95-acre park to the Forest Preserve District of Cook County shortly after its inception in the mid-1910s. As many as five trains, with 15 coaches each, stopped on the sidetrack of the Morton Grove train station to accommodate large groups who rented the picnic grounds. A shelter with a kitchen, bandstand, dance floor and a carousel along the river attracted groups to what was known as one of the largest, most beautiful and best-equipped pleasure parks in the vicinity of Chicago at that time.

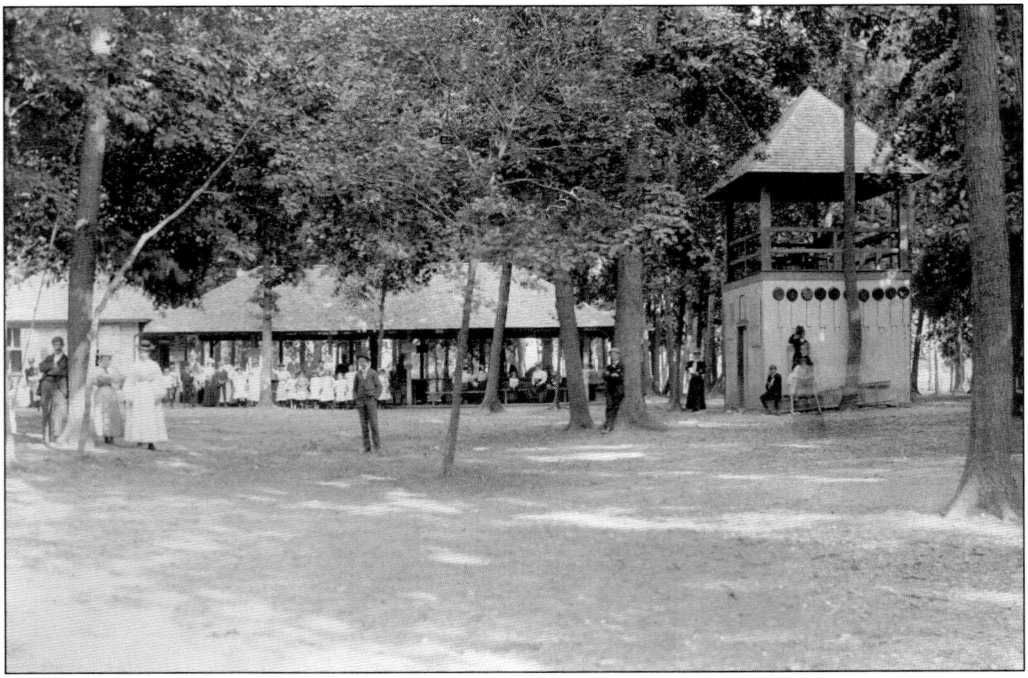

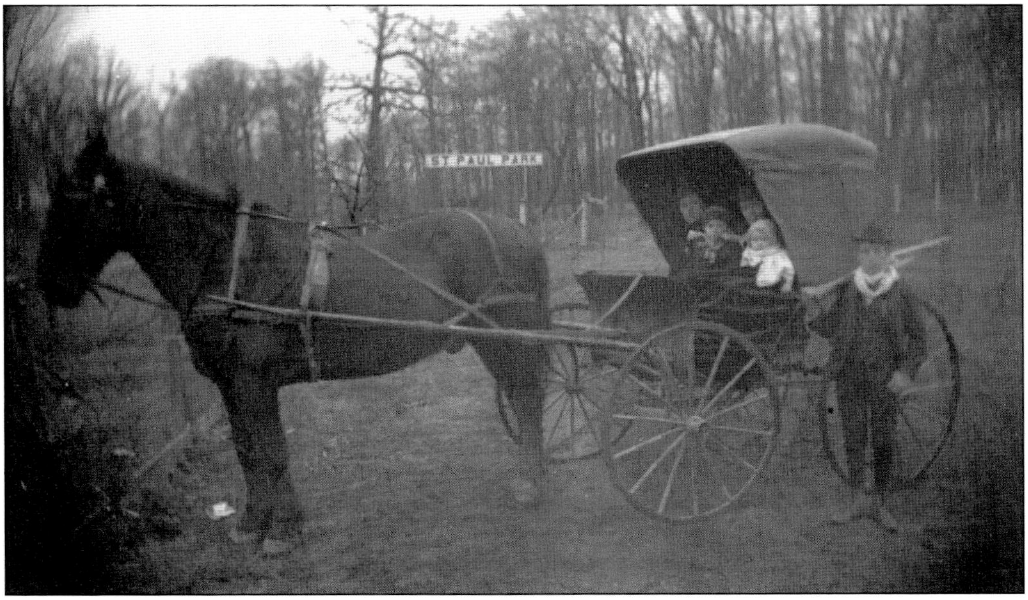

A local family is pictured in front of the entrance to St. Paul Park. In 1919, shortly after George C. Klehm donated this property to the Forest Preserve District of Cook County, he received a letter from its chief forester, Ransom Kennicott. The district intended to publish data on newly acquired lands, seeking information on every rock, tree, stream, story, and tradition. Klehm submitted a six-page letter detailing artifacts of early settlement and describing flora and fauna, stating, "They are a fertile field for the student of botany and wild animal life."

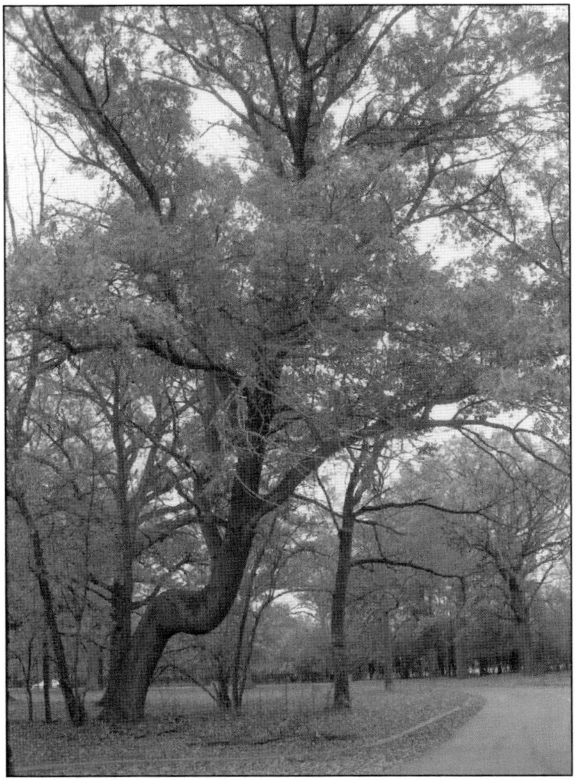

The Village of Morton Grove's Natural Resource Commission partnered with the Morton Grove Historical Society to recognize Champion and Heritage trees throughout the village since 2008. Six trees each year have been selected from community nominations, which represent early landscapes. Oaks, hickories, ironwoods, and sugar maples estimated to be over 200 years old have been documented. This red oak located in the Forest Preserve District of Cook County's Miami Woods is representative of the oak-hickory forests of this region. It is also believed to be an Indian marker tree, significant to our Native American past.

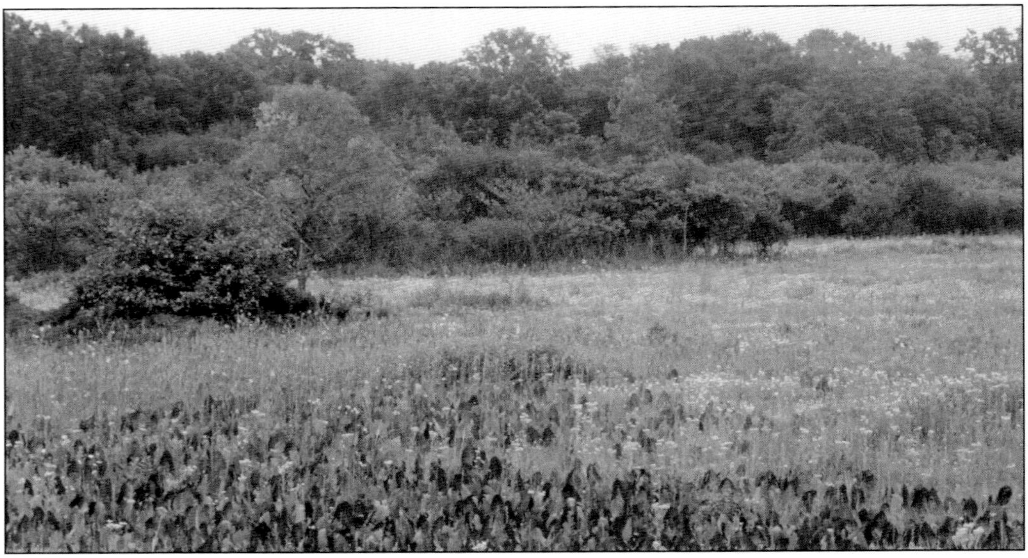

This 1982 photograph of Miami Woods Prairie, taken near the junction of Caldwell and Waukegan Roads, gives one a sense of the landscape that graced our region for thousands of years. Not long ago, beautiful prairies, woodlands, and wetlands covered most of what we now call Morton Grove. The Forest Preserve District of Cook County had the foresight to save some of these lands, beginning in 1916. Twenty percent of the land in Morton Grove is part of this preserve system. The North Branch Prairie Project, founded in 1977 by a group of dedicated volunteers, work to restore health to Miami, Wayside, and Linne-Railroad prairies. In time, they learned that the oak woodlands were equally precious and in need of expert care. This group, now called the North Branch Restoration Project, celebrates 35 years on leading edge restoration ecology. (Courtesy of Stephen Packard.)

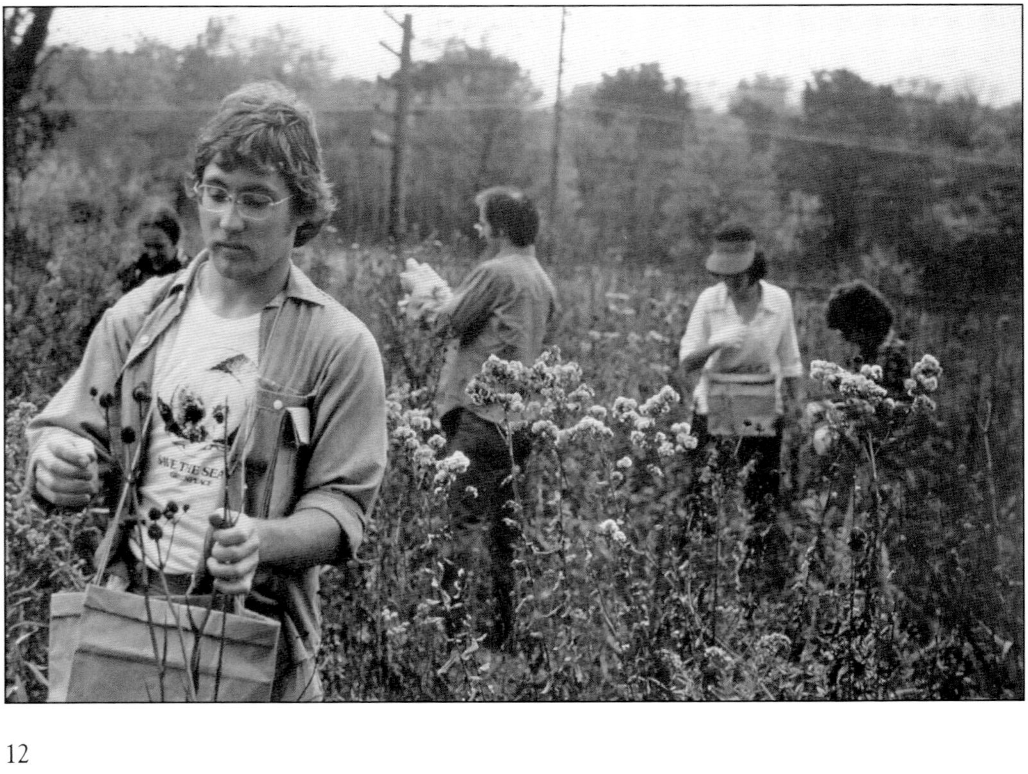

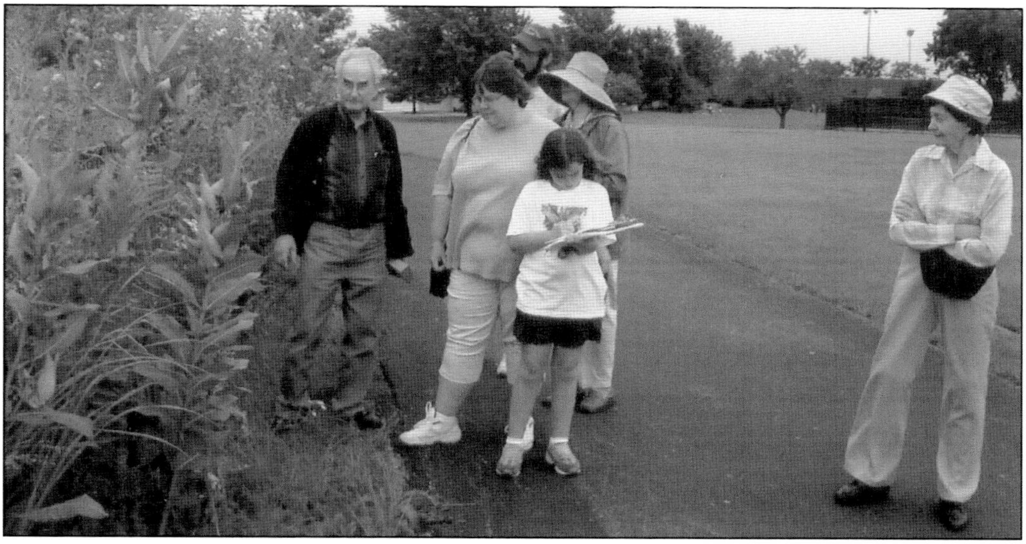

Local conservationists John and Mary Helen Slater, along with Journalist Mary Ellen Cohon, led the campaign in 1973 to preserve a 1.5-acre prairie remnant in what is now the Morton Grove Park District's Prairie View Park. Regional experts confirmed plant populations in response to community involvement inspired by a letter from Jack Bates, a descendant of the Gables who settled this land in the 1840s. This tract of land had never been plowed, according to Bates. Pictured from left to right on a tour in 2004 are (foreground) Preston Spinks, Mary Walsh, Sophia Sidlowski, Mary Helen Slater; (background) Steve Sidlowski and Gayle Kenney Dompke. The aerial photograph below illustrates the relationship of the prairie remnant to the park and residential development, dedicated as a historic site by the Morton Grove Historical Society in 1975 and protected as an Illinois Nature Preserve in 1979.

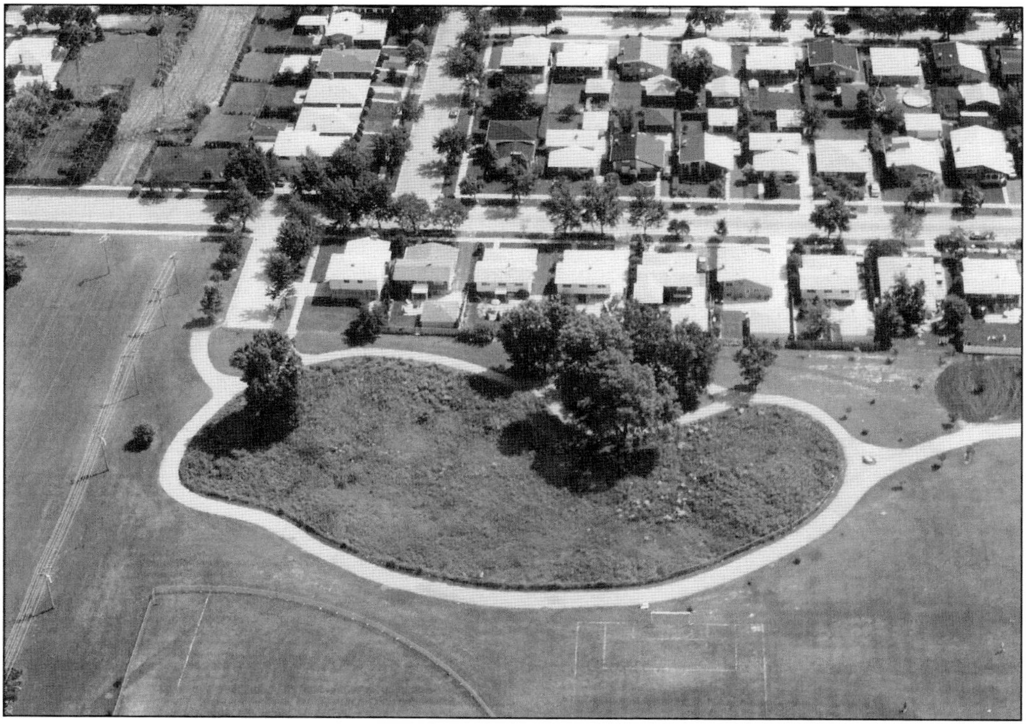

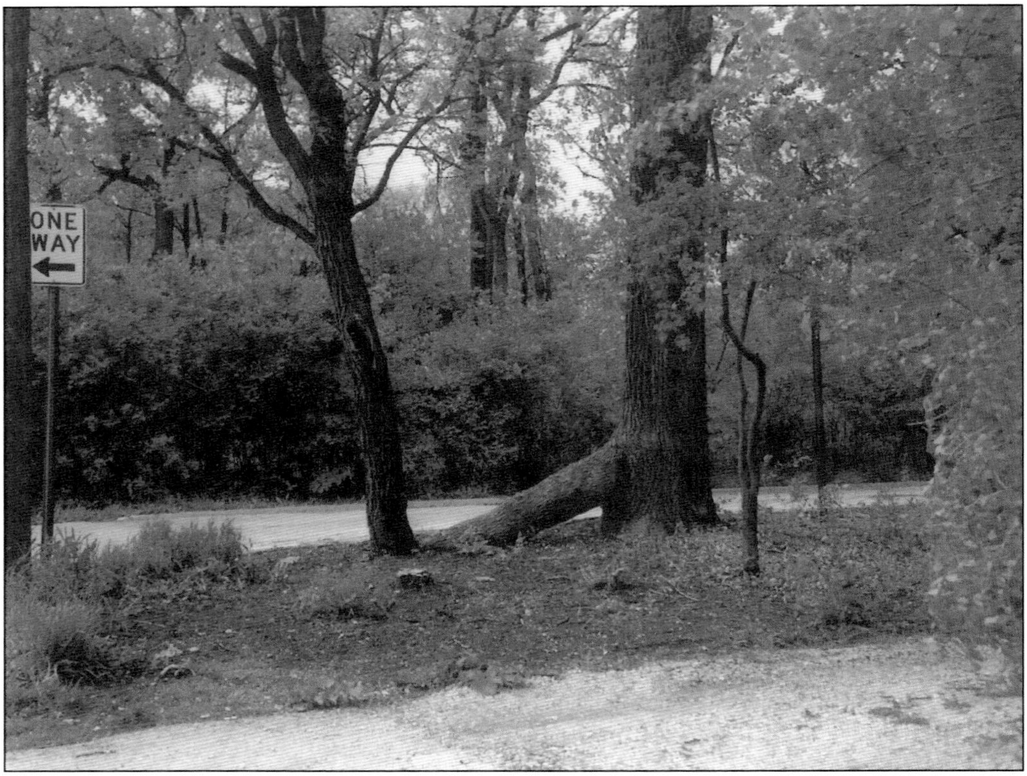

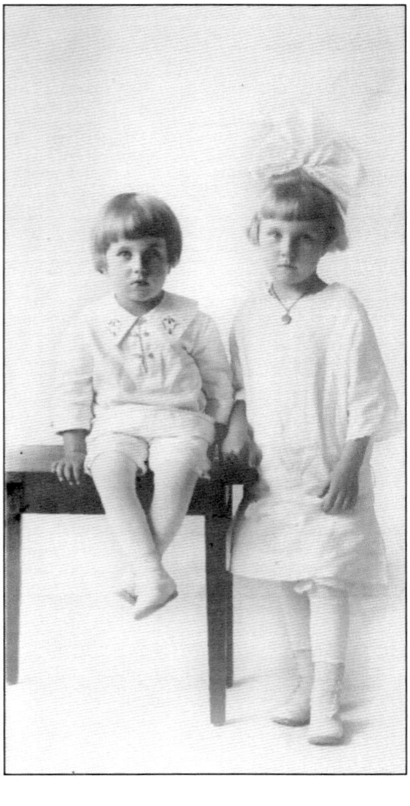

Many sources document the Indian trails historically present in Morton Grove. Indian marker trees, such as this white oak located at Beckwith Road and Nashville Avenue, are living proof. These trees, believed to be shaped by Native Americans and used as early road signs, pointed the way to villages, places to ford the river, and freshwater springs. George Wible and Jayne (née Wible) Barry, pictured in 1912, grew up with this tree on their family property. Stories were passed down from their grandparents Barbara and Nicholas Hoffman, of those who continued to follow these trail systems after they settled here in 1868. Barbara was known to place baskets of food next to this tree for travelers displaced from their homeland.

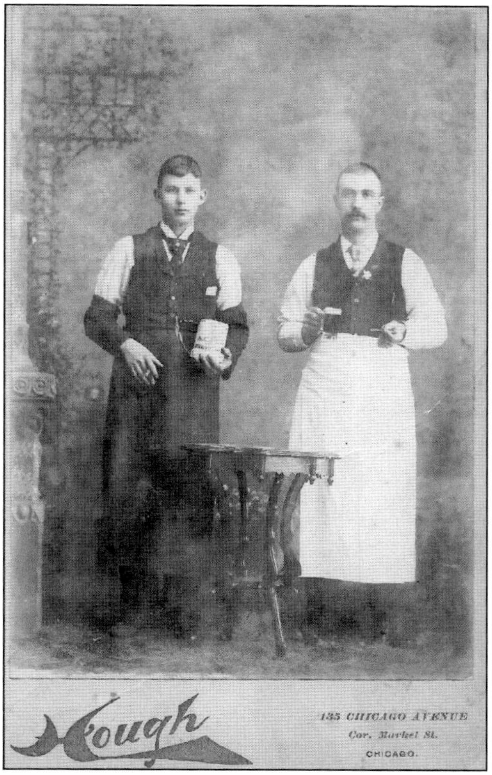

Dan Lumpp is pictured with his brother-in-law Willie Welle in this formal portrait taken at the Hough studio in Chicago. Dan operated a general merchandise store and saloon in the early 1900s located at Railroad Avenue and Miller's Mill Road (now Lehigh and Lincoln Avenue). The collection of Native American points shown here was donated to the Morton Grove Historical Museum by Anna May Schmitt Jacobs, the granddaughter of Dan Lumpp. Lumpp gave free beer to anyone who brought in an artifact for his collection. Adjacent to the tracks that were laid for the Chicago, Milwaukee & St. Paul Railway in 1872, locals frequently found arrowheads that had been unearthed during construction.

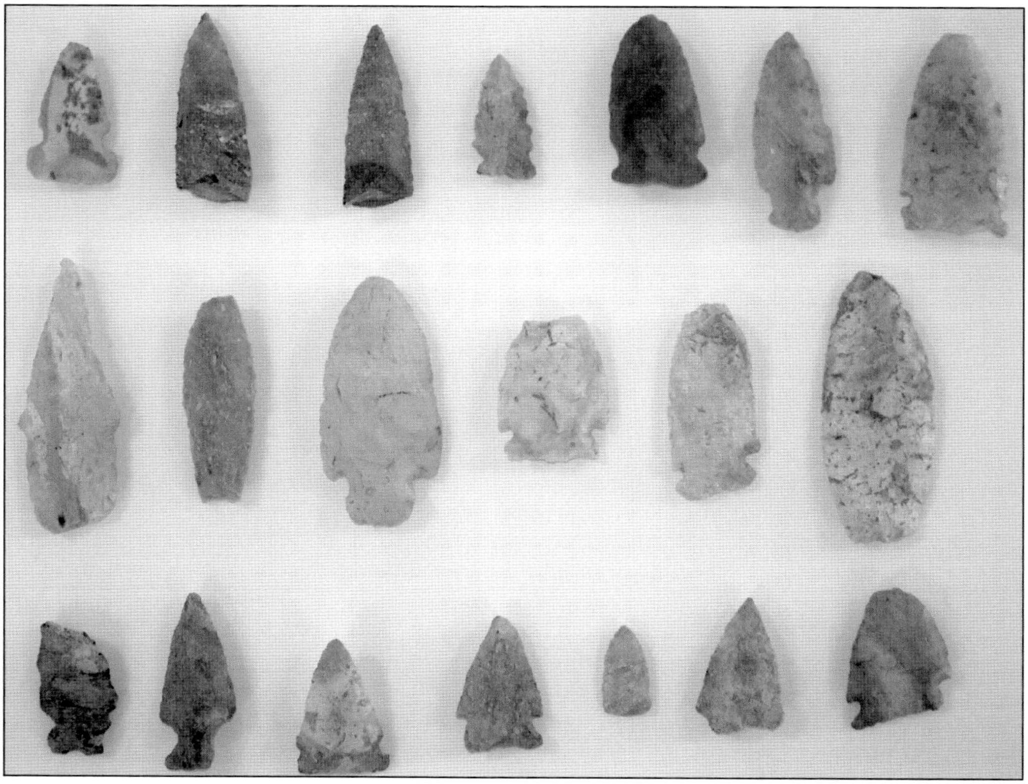

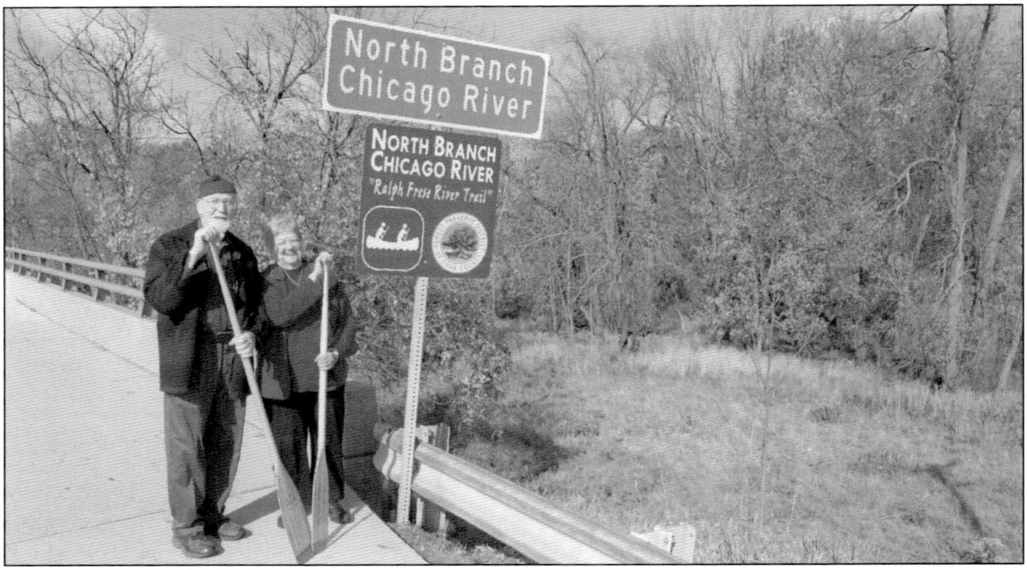

Ralph and Rita Frese are pictured on the Dempster Street bridge next to the sign marking the trail named in Ralph's honor. Ralph, pictured below at the Main Street Morton Grove exhibit opening, was a fourth-generation blacksmith and used his skills as a teenager during the Depression to forge a hook and carrier to tow his canoe upstream with his bicycle. Discovering the natural beauty and history of local waterways at an early age, he became an advocate for conservation through the Cook County Clean Streams Committee formed in 1953 and has provided valuable experiences in paddling through the Chicagoland Canoe Base for over 50 years. Building canoes with Boy Scouts, organizing the annual Des Plaines River Canoe Marathon in 1958, founding the annual New Year's Day Canoe Paddle in 1985, contributing to the 300th anniversary reenactment of the Jolliet-Marquette expedition of 1673, and receiving the National Rivers Hall of Fame Award through the Chicago Maritime Society are but a few of the reasons that this stretch has been named in his honor. (Above, courtesy of Alethea Busch Photography.)

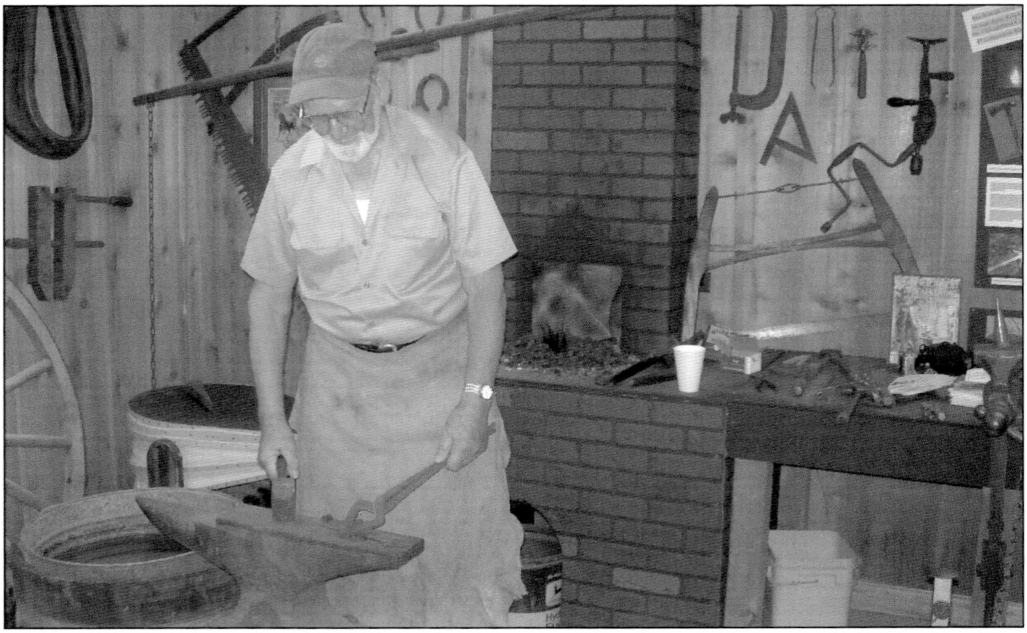

Two

Truck Farming and the Floral Industry

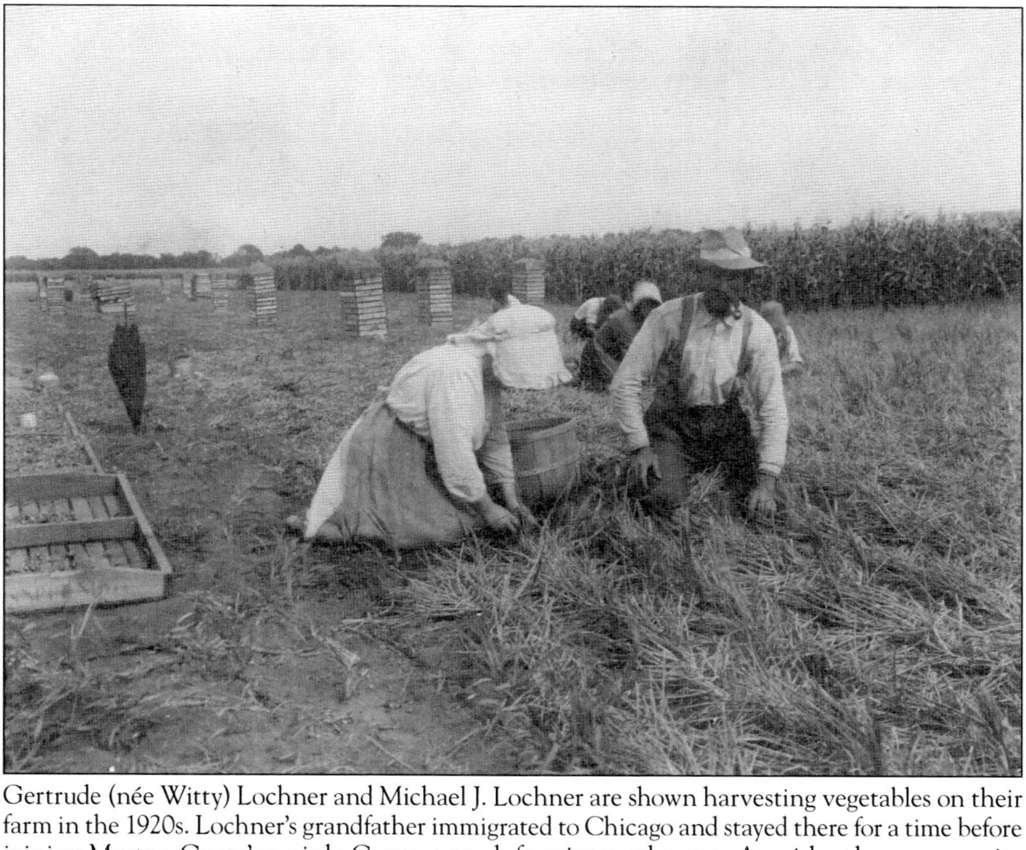

Gertrude (née Witty) Lochner and Michael J. Lochner are shown harvesting vegetables on their farm in the 1920s. Lochner's grandfather immigrated to Chicago and stayed there for a time before joining Morton Grove's mainly German truck farming settlement. As with other community leaders, the Lochners sold produce on South Water Street in Chicago and to local companies. As the local floral industry grew, they operated their own greenhouse and small businesses. (Courtesy of the Lochner family.)

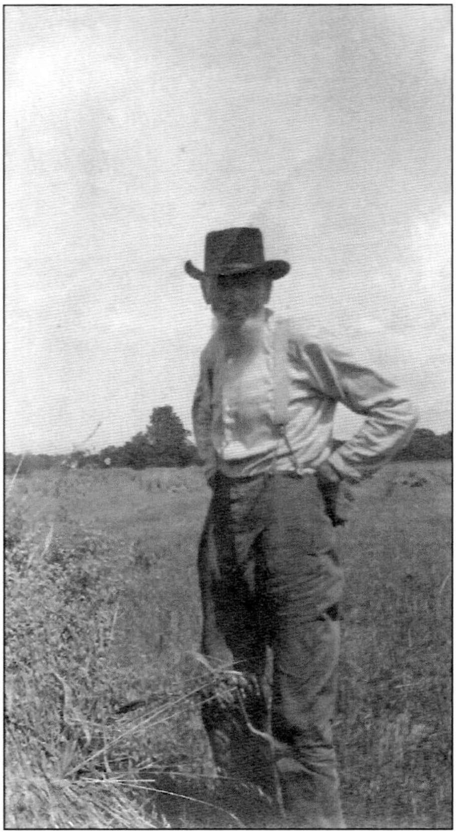

Michael M. Lochner, born in 1836 in Wuerzburg, Baiern, came to America with his family at the age of eight. In 1865, he married Theresa Baumann, whose family farmed the Baumanville area (now Lincoln Square in Chicago). Lochner is pictured on the land they raised 13 children on and where he and his wife continued to live after the Forest Preserve District of Cook County purchased their land. (Courtesy of the Lochner family.)

Carl Suhr is pictured plowing his fields on his farm located northeast of Church Street and Austin Avenue in Morton Grove in 1918. Suhr is using a steel moldboard plow developed by Illinois blacksmith John Deere in the late 1830s. This allowed farmers to till the heavy soils of the prairie more effectively.

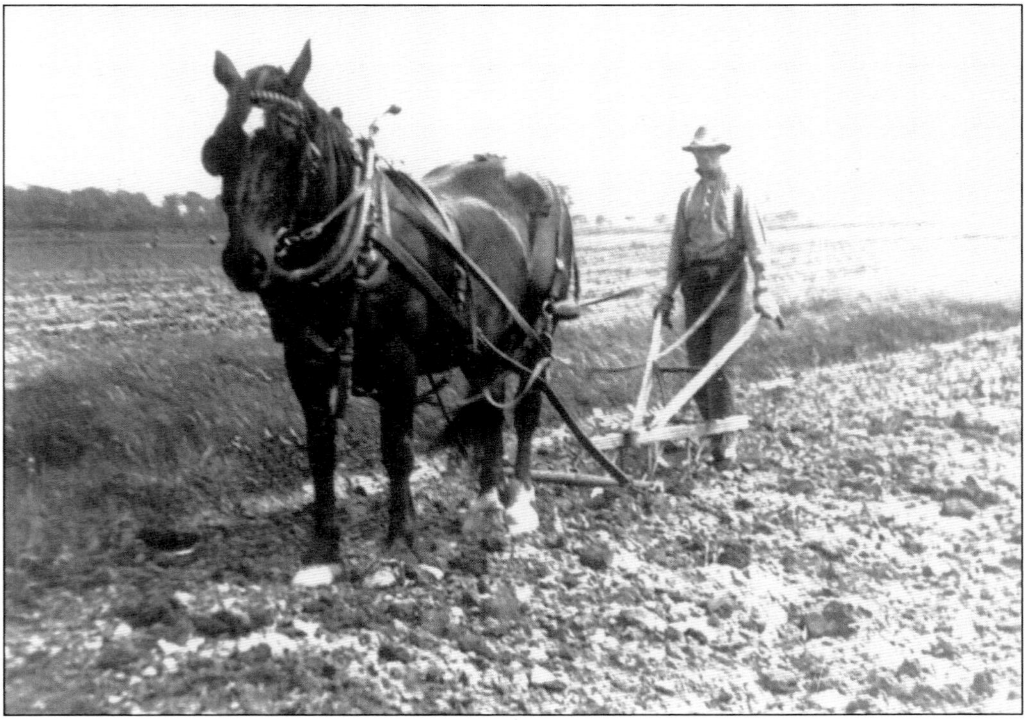

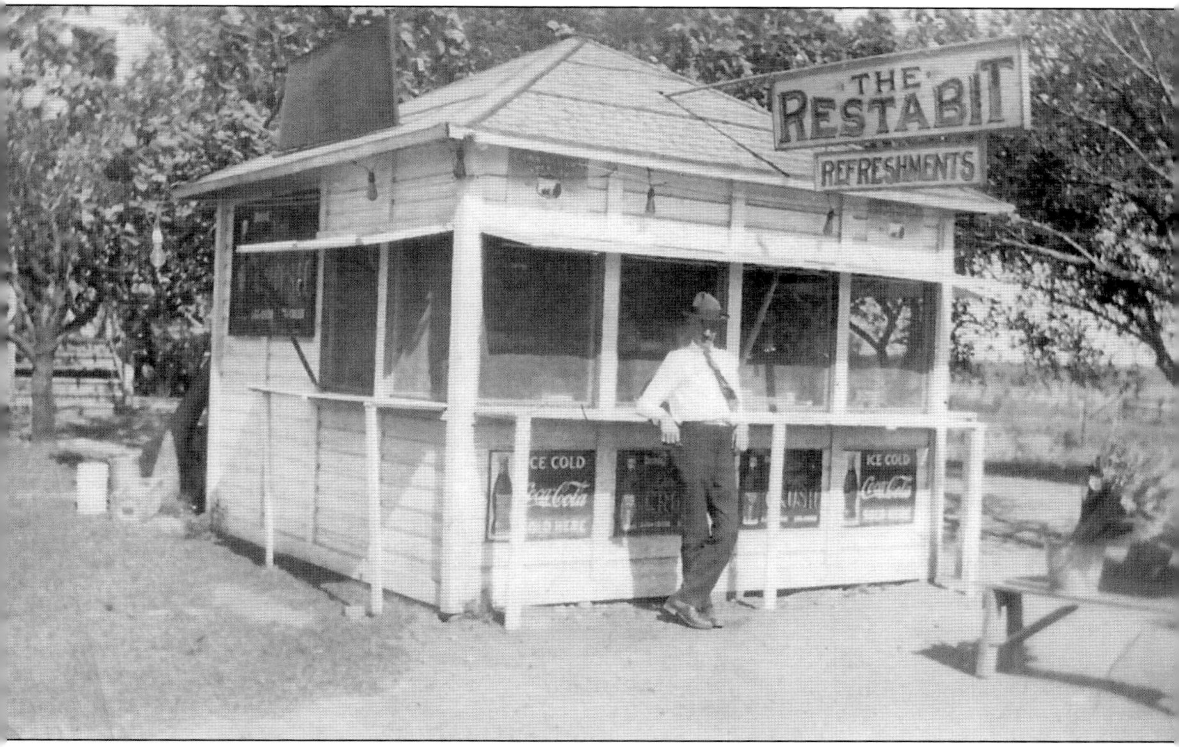

Michael J. Lochner, son of Michael M. Lochner, married Gertrude Witty in 1897, built a house across the road from the family homestead, and continued farming 30 acres. He is pictured in front of the Restabit refreshment stand along Dempster Street, where the family sold hamburgers, hot dogs, and ice cream next to their vegetable stand. His daughter Gertrude recalls onions being grown as their main crop contracted to Vaughn's Seed Company and pickles being sold to Henning's Pickle Company. Grain for the cattle, cows, and hogs were also important to their farm. Gertrude's love of wildflowers soon led the family business in a new direction. During the height of the Great Depression, Gertrude's brothers Richard and Michael built the Lochners' greenhouses after they sold the family farm, holding on to five or six acres. This family business would prosper until it closed down in 2005. (Courtesy of the Lochner family.)

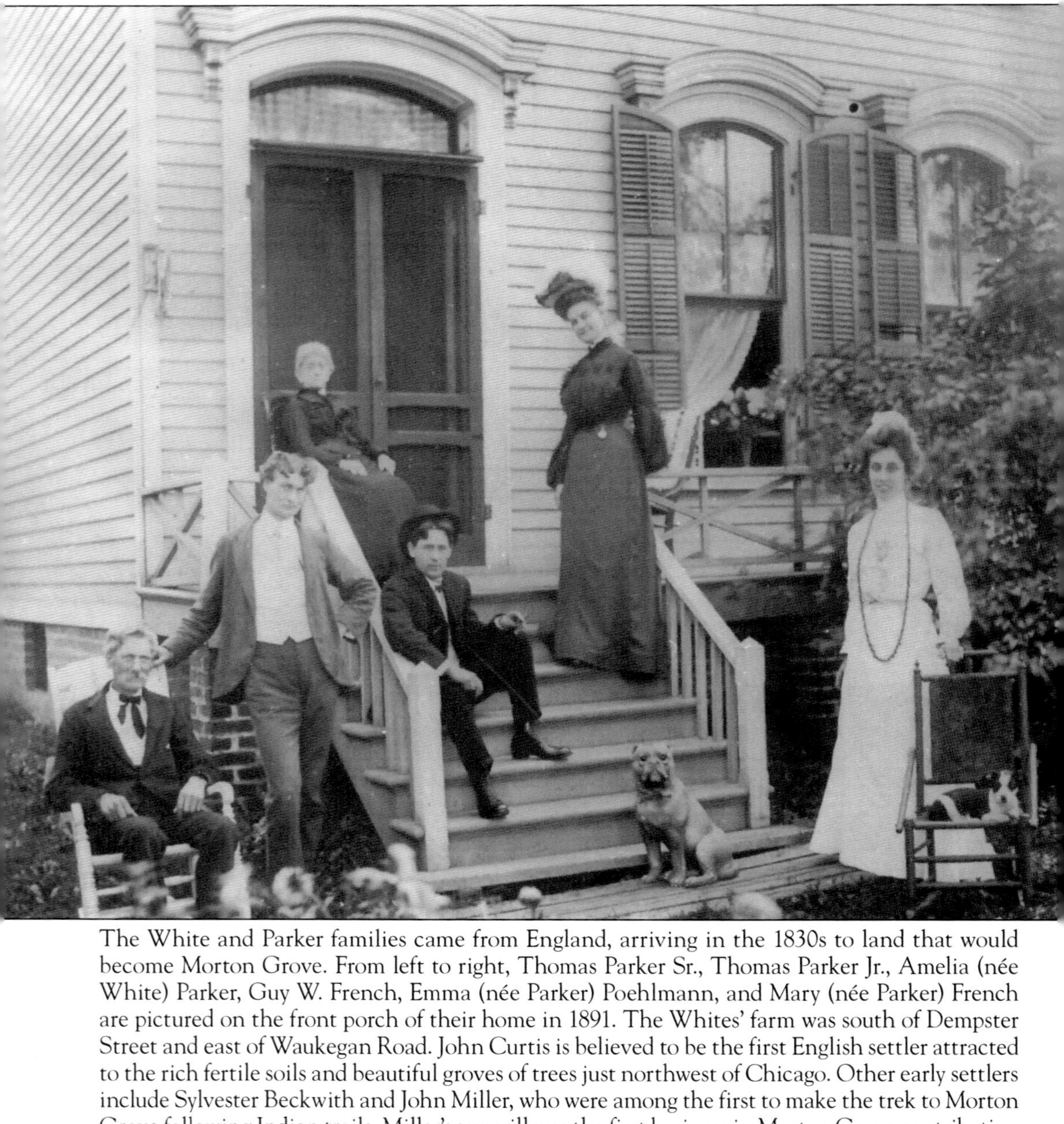

The White and Parker families came from England, arriving in the 1830s to land that would become Morton Grove. From left to right, Thomas Parker Sr., Thomas Parker Jr., Amelia (née White) Parker, Guy W. French, Emma (née Parker) Poehlmann, and Mary (née Parker) French are pictured on the front porch of their home in 1891. The Whites' farm was south of Dempster Street and east of Waukegan Road. John Curtis is believed to be the first English settler attracted to the rich fertile soils and beautiful groves of trees just northwest of Chicago. Other early settlers include Sylvester Beckwith and John Miller, who were among the first to make the trek to Morton Grove following Indian trails. Miller's sawmill was the first business in Morton Grove contributing lumber to the old Northwestern plank road, which is Milwaukee Road today.

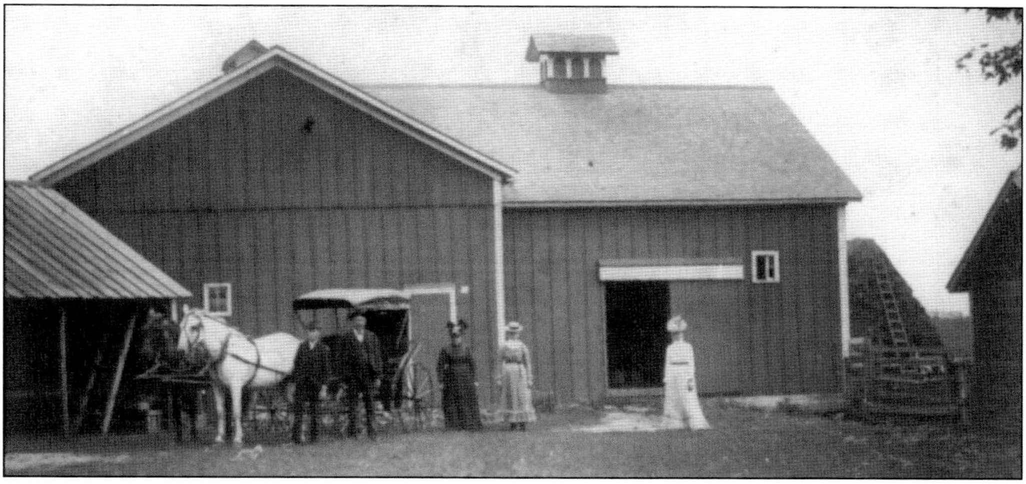

George, Henry, Anna (née Schwinge), Laura, and Rosa Engel are pictured on their family farm near the intersection of Harlem Avenue and Shermer Road, an area of Morton Grove annexed in the 1950s. Henry's parents, Christopher and Dorothy (née Lubbert) Engel, emigrated from Mecklenberg, Germany, in 1852, purchasing land from Peter Hoffman, the well-known Cook County coroner. Henry was born in this farmhouse in 1857 and married Anna in 1882. Their son George married Louise Kath in 1917, and they continued farming the land and raising horses, cows, ducks, geese, chickens, and pigs. Sylvia Engel recalls her father, George, getting up at 2:00 a.m. to deliver produce to the South Water Street Market in Chicago. Many families depended on meat and dairy products provided by the Engels during the Depression. Members of the Engel family are pictured with early bicycles.

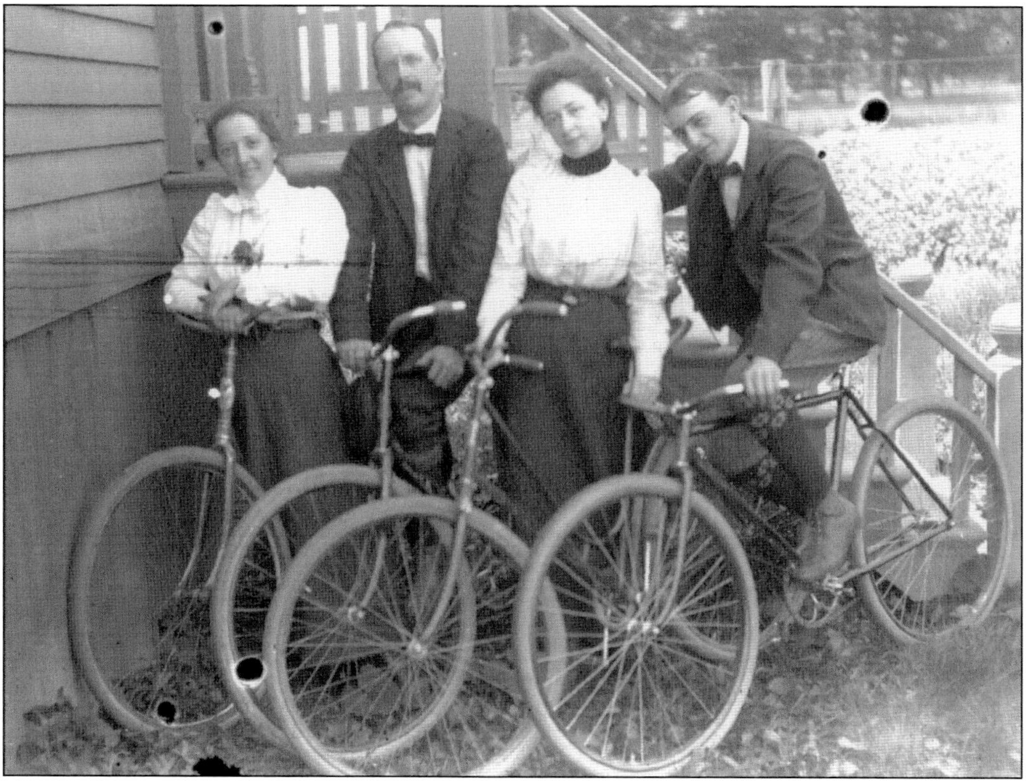

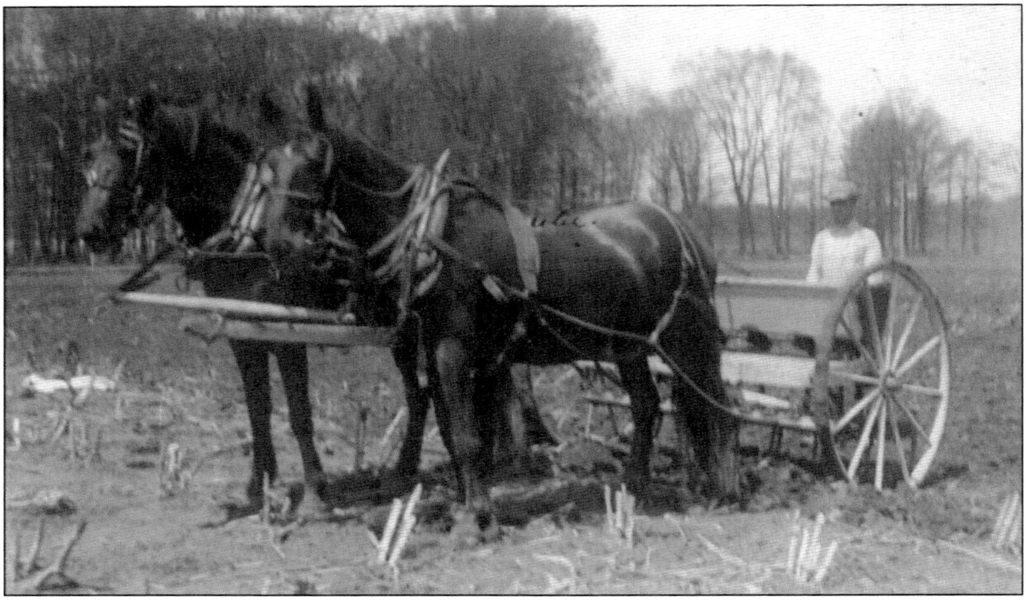

In 1842, Carl Huscher brought his family from Germany to a farm situated at the future corner of Dempster Street and Waukegan Road. His grandson Fred L. Huscher is pictured seeding his farmland located north and south of Dempster Street, west of Austin Avenue. Over the following decades, the Huscher family owned businesses significant to the early development of Morton Grove, including Huscher Coal and Ice and the Dells.

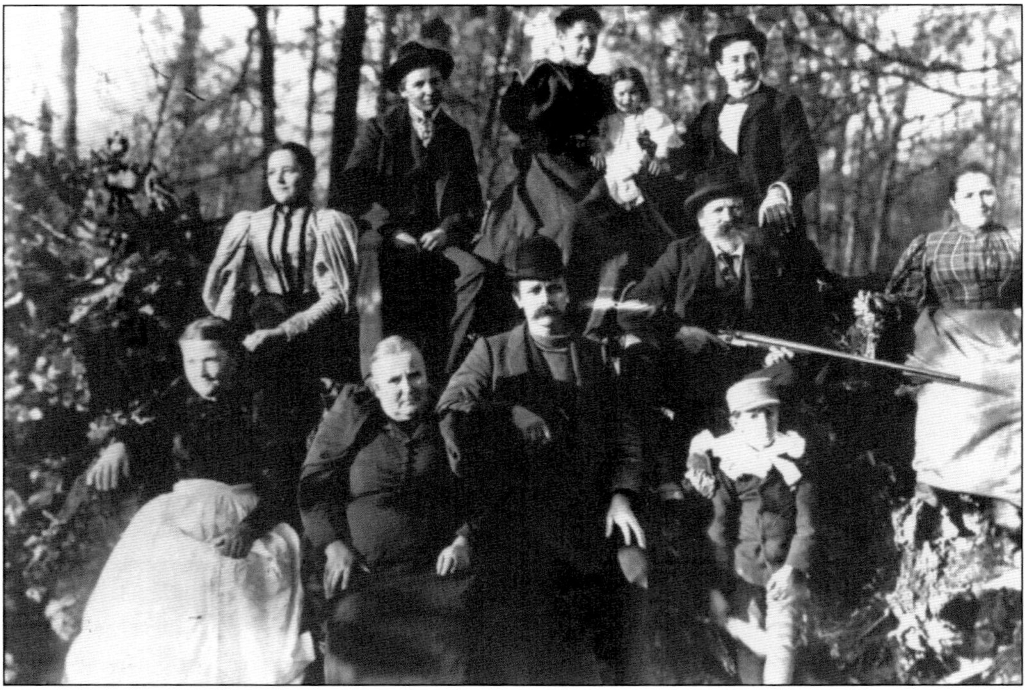

The Huscher and Sonne families are shown at the Huscher's woods near Dempster Street and Austin Avenue in the early 1890s. Pictured from left to right are (first row) Ernestine Bigler, Marie Huscher, Charles Huscher, and Fred L. Huscher; (second row) Freida (née Huscher) Sonne, unidentified, Fred Huscher, and Emma Huscher; (third row) two unidentified, and William Sonne.

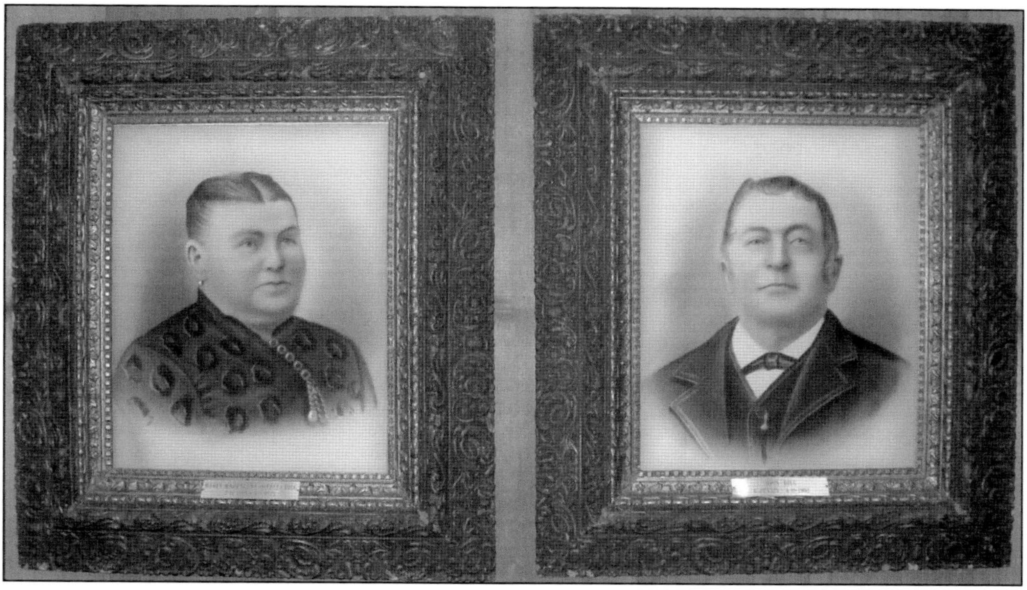

Portraits of early pioneers John and Maria Magdelena (née Gabel) Dilg are typical of this time period. John Dilg, who arrived in Chicago in 1850, married the daughter of George Gabel. Gabel came to Chicago in 1843 from Württemberg, Germany, purchasing land for farming and opening an Indian trading post in 1847 on what is now 9101 Waukegan Road, providing lodging to people traveling between Chicago and Milwaukee. In 1856, he sold the property to his son-in-law John. John and Maria Magdelena raised 13 children together. Their son Henry and generations of Dilg family members continued to operate the "Homestead" as a general store and meeting place for nearly 100 years. The original homestead can be seen in the photograph of the Ed Roberts' Colonial Restaurant and Hotel, which went through many modifications and changes in ownership before its demolition in 1999.

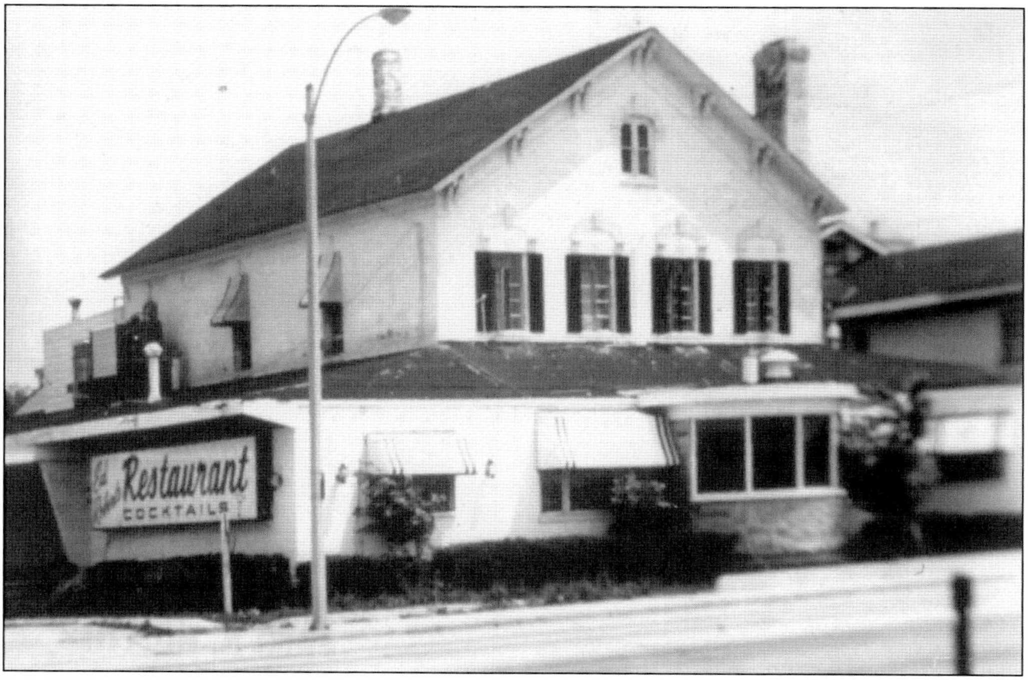

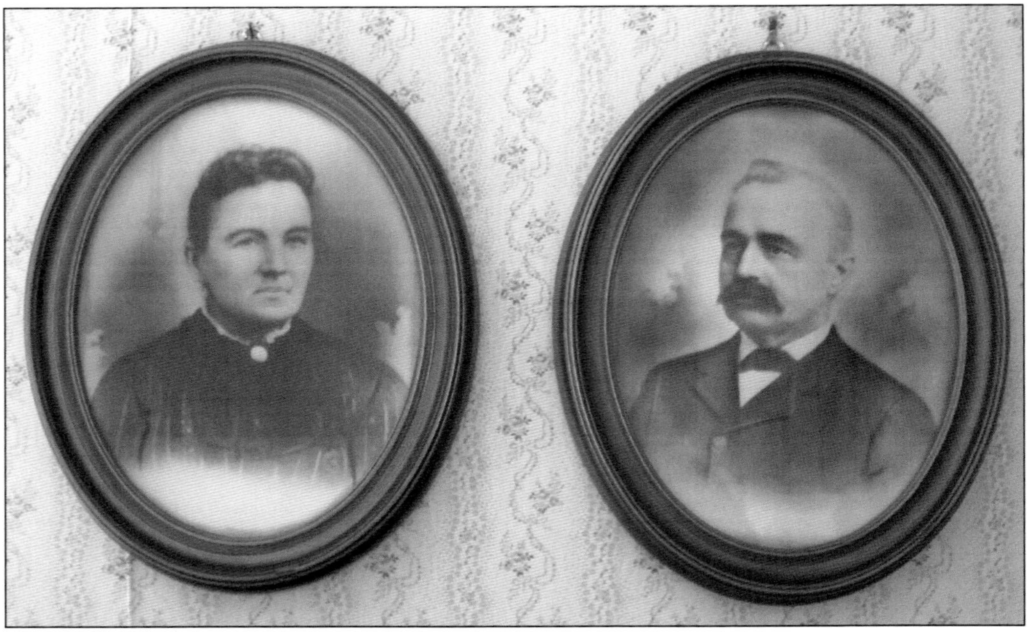

Nicholas Hoffman emigrated from Coblenz, Germany, in 1859, purchasing land in 1868 from early English pioneer Sylvester Beckwith. Settling on this land, which was located near Beckwith Road and Lehigh Avenue today, Nicholas and Barbara (née Wilhelm) Hoffman (pictured above), raised 13 children, farmed the land, and grazed sheep, along with raising a variety of farm animals. The family home was later moved across the road by oxen and placed on the northeast corner of Beckwith Road and Nashville Avenue, adjacent to the Indian trail marker tree that was recognized by the family. Nicholas Hoffman is pictured below on the family farm.

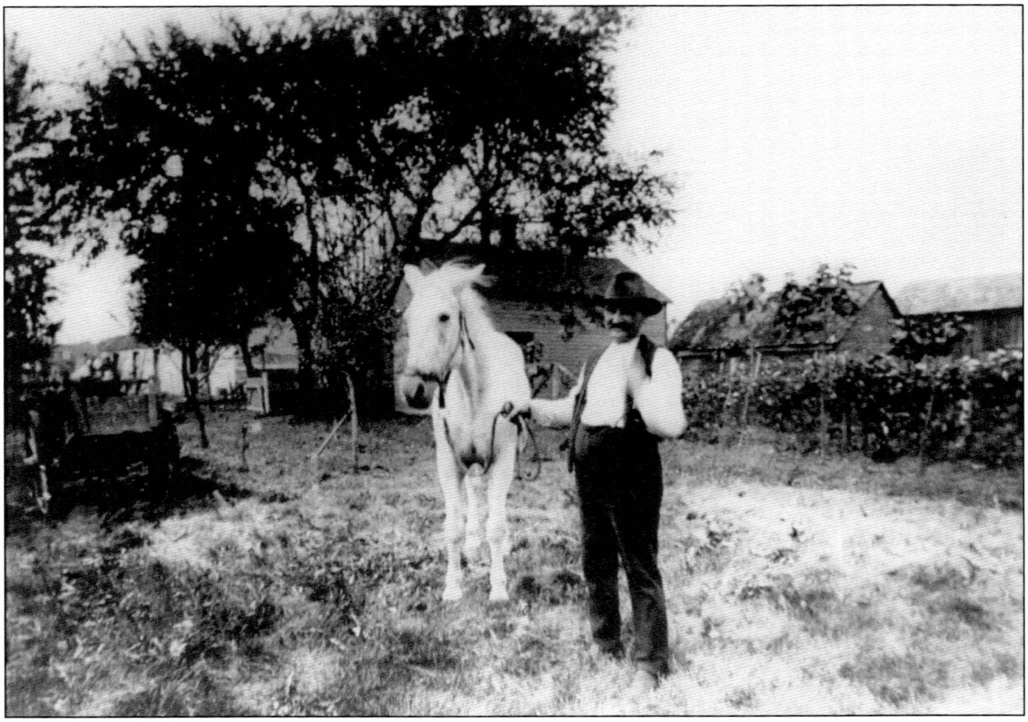

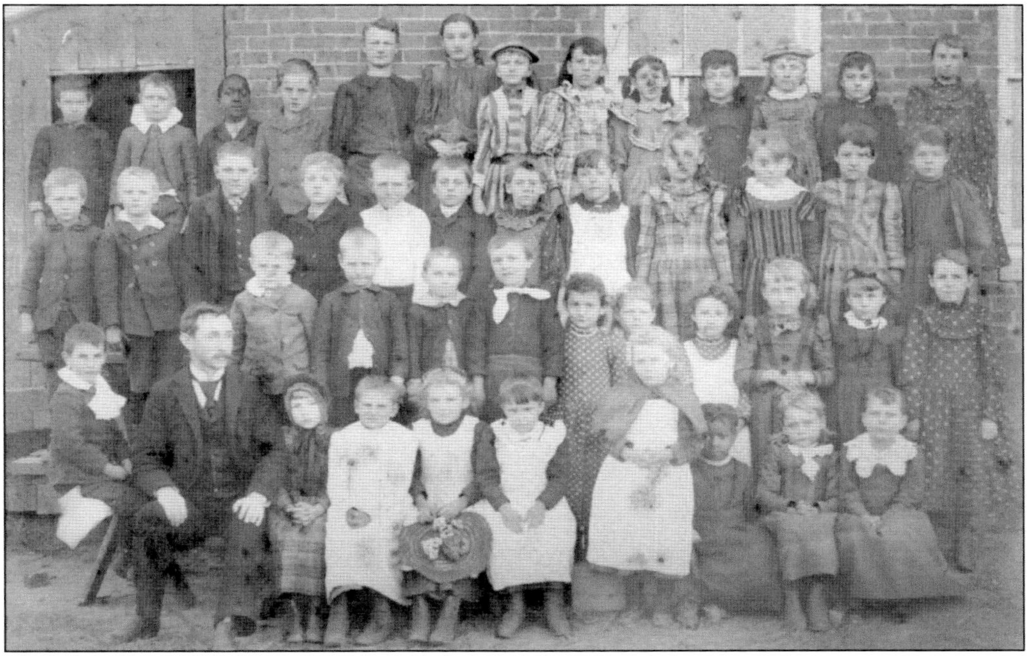

In 1860, Morton Grove's first school, known as District No. 2, was built at the southwest corner of Waukegan and Beckwith Roads. This one-room structure was the second rural school in Cook County and served a large area including many surrounding towns. This building, commonly known as the Little Red Schoolhouse, served as a school until 1927 when Golf Elementary School was built. The old school was sold and used as various businesses until it was demolished in 1992. An attempt to declare the building a historic site was unsuccessful, due to the structural changes that had been made throughout the intervening decades. The class portrait from the 1890s shows children and their one teacher arranged outside of the building. The informal photograph from 1910 shows students and teachers in the adjoining schoolyard.

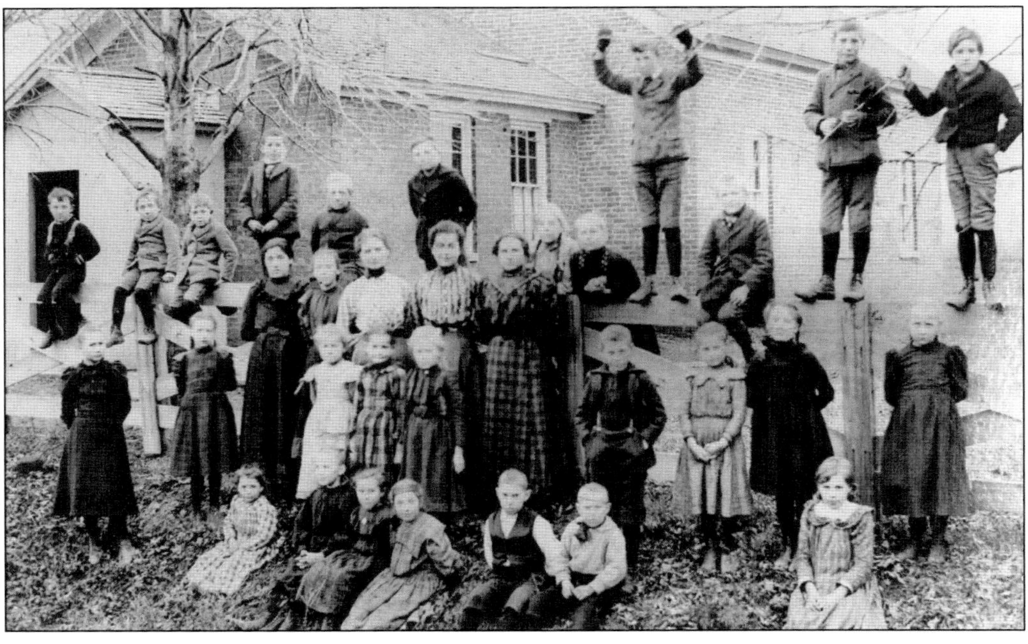

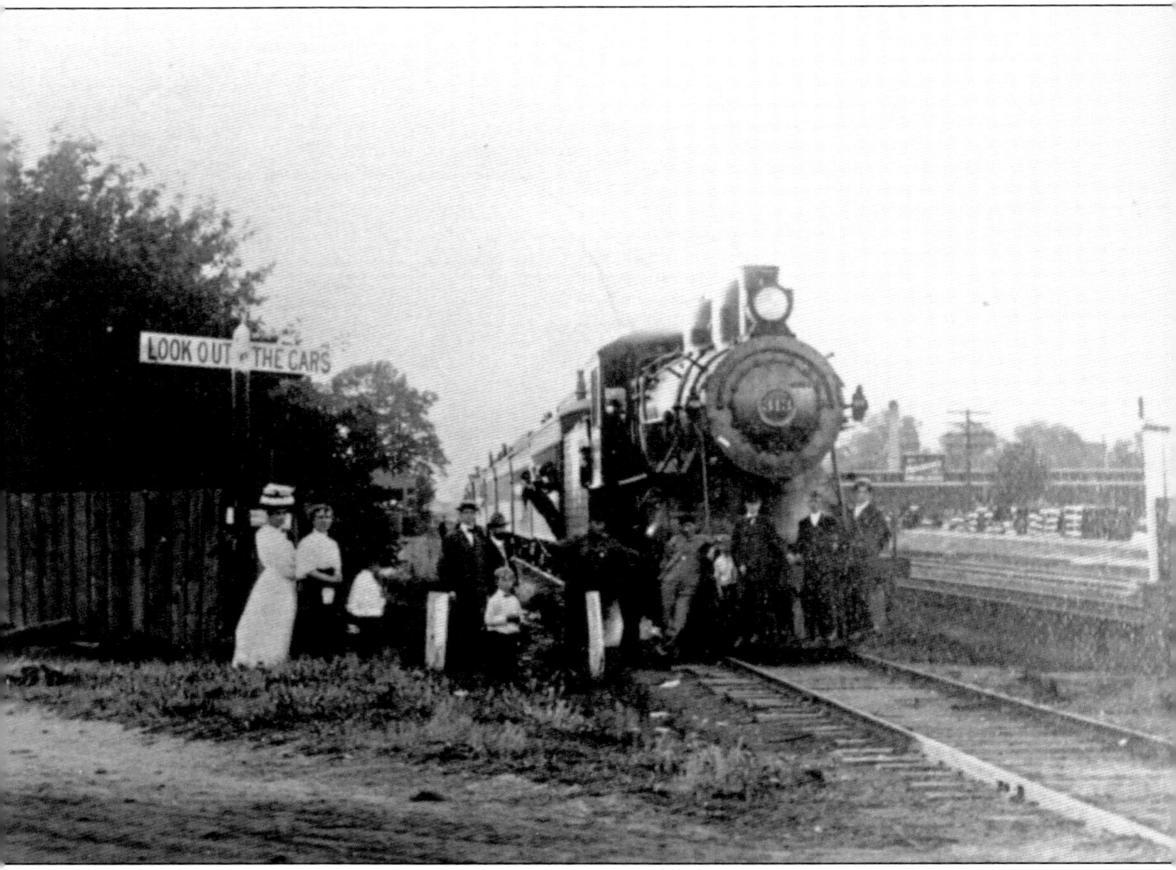

Miller's Mill, a sawmill built by John Miller in 1834 on the banks of the North Branch of the Chicago River, about 300 feet south of Dempster Street and 75 feet west of Lincoln Avenue, was in operation up until the early 1860s. In 1866, the Miller family sold this property to a neighbor, Medard Lochner, and by the early 1870s, this land was purchased as a right-of-way by the Chicago, Milwaukee & St. Paul Railway Company. In 1872, the first tracks were laid between Chicago and Milwaukee, and the first steam locomotive passed over the single track in what is now Morton Grove, just one year after the Great Chicago Fire and the Great Peshtigo Fire in Wisconsin. The double track was laid in 1892 in anticipation of the World's Columbian Exposition. This railway put Morton Grove on the map, allowing the floral and pickle industries to flourish and become known nationwide. Henning Pickle Company can be seen in the background.

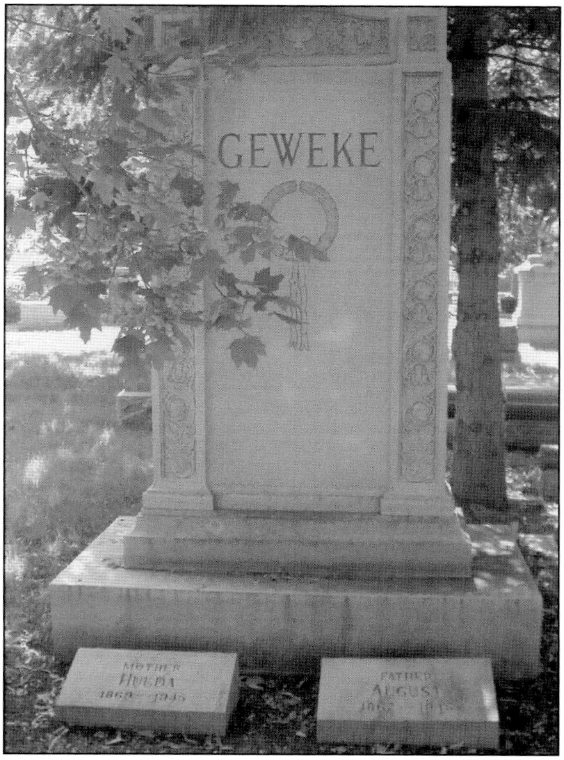

St. Matthew's Lutheran Cemetery, located south of Dempster Street on Shermer (Telegraph) Road, was one of the first cemeteries in Niles Centre. Early settlers buried here include members of the Dilg, Engel, Suhr, Schwinge, Teegen, Minx, Kath, Steil, Schroeder, and Geweke families. The first documented burial in 1859 was Heinrich W. Geweke. Alma and Amanda Geweke, also buried here, married brothers in the Kath family and were cousins to the Engels, who settled near Harlem Avenue and Shermer Road. Christopher Engel emigrated from Mecklenberg, Germany, in 1852 and is noted as a founder of St. Matthew's Lutheran Church, built in 1897 just south of this cemetery.

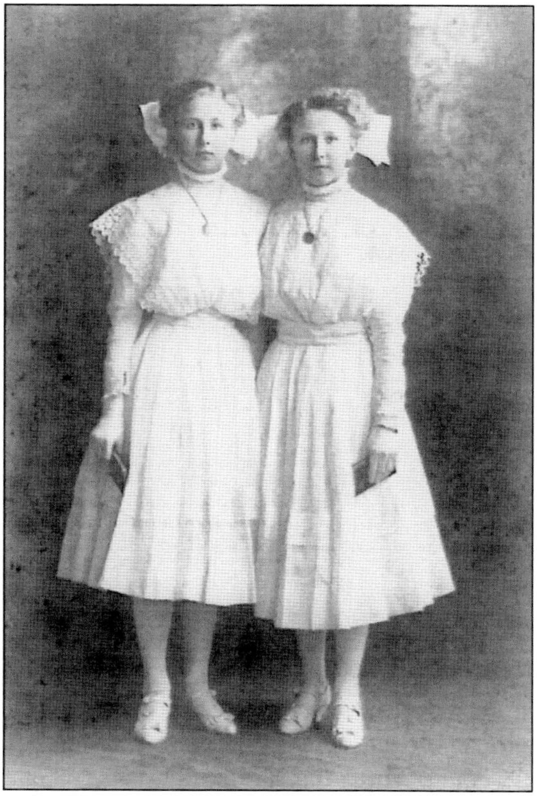

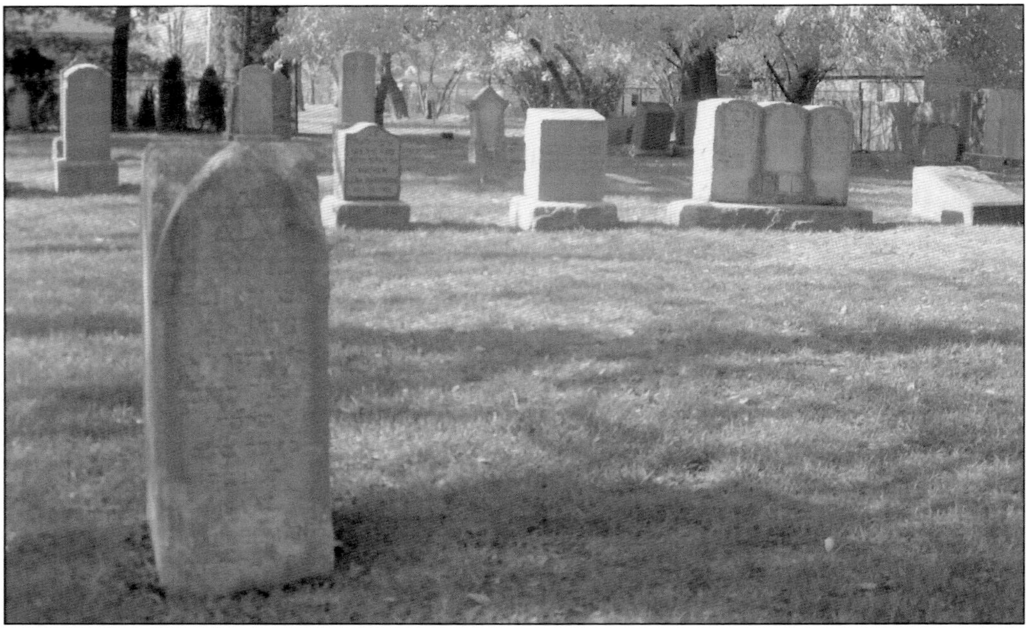

In the latter half of the 1800s, groups of Jews immigrated to Chicago from Drohiczen, a small town in White Russia (Belarus). The Kehilath Jacob Anshe Drohiczen is Morton Grove's only cemetery. After the last burial in 1937, the gravestones were neglected, and the cemetery was abandoned. Many attempts have been made to restore the cemetery since the 1960s. It is currently being managed by the Jewish Federation of Metropolitan Chicago.

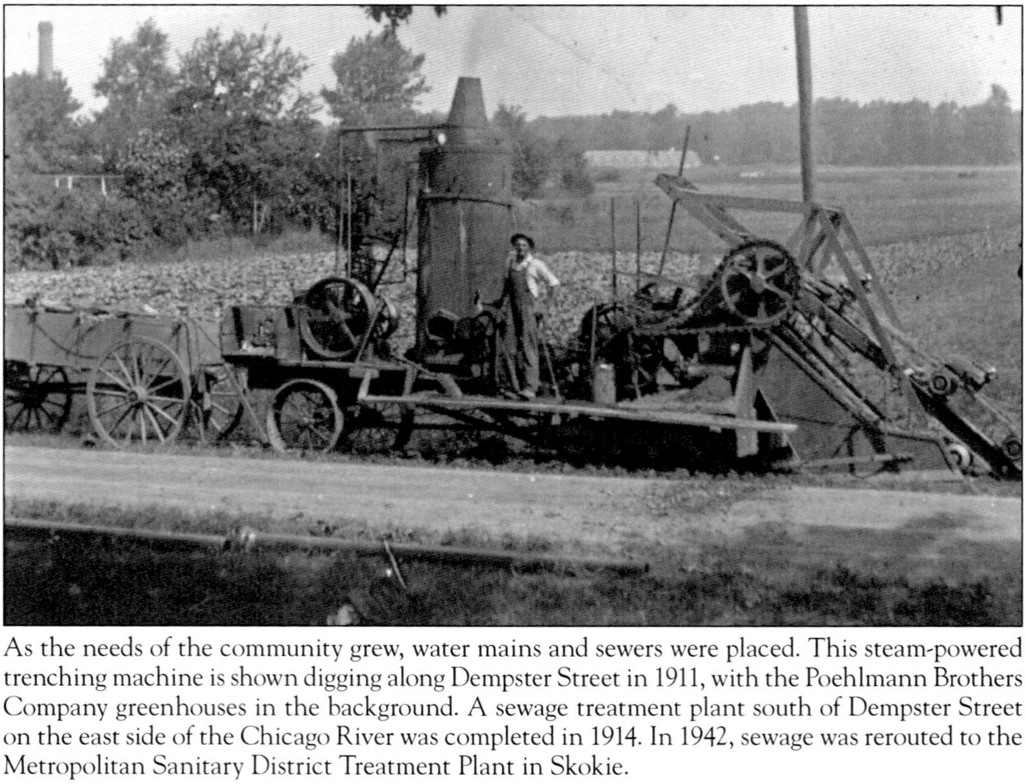

As the needs of the community grew, water mains and sewers were placed. This steam-powered trenching machine is shown digging along Dempster Street in 1911, with the Poehlmann Brothers Company greenhouses in the background. A sewage treatment plant south of Dempster Street on the east side of the Chicago River was completed in 1914. In 1942, sewage was rerouted to the Metropolitan Sanitary District Treatment Plant in Skokie.

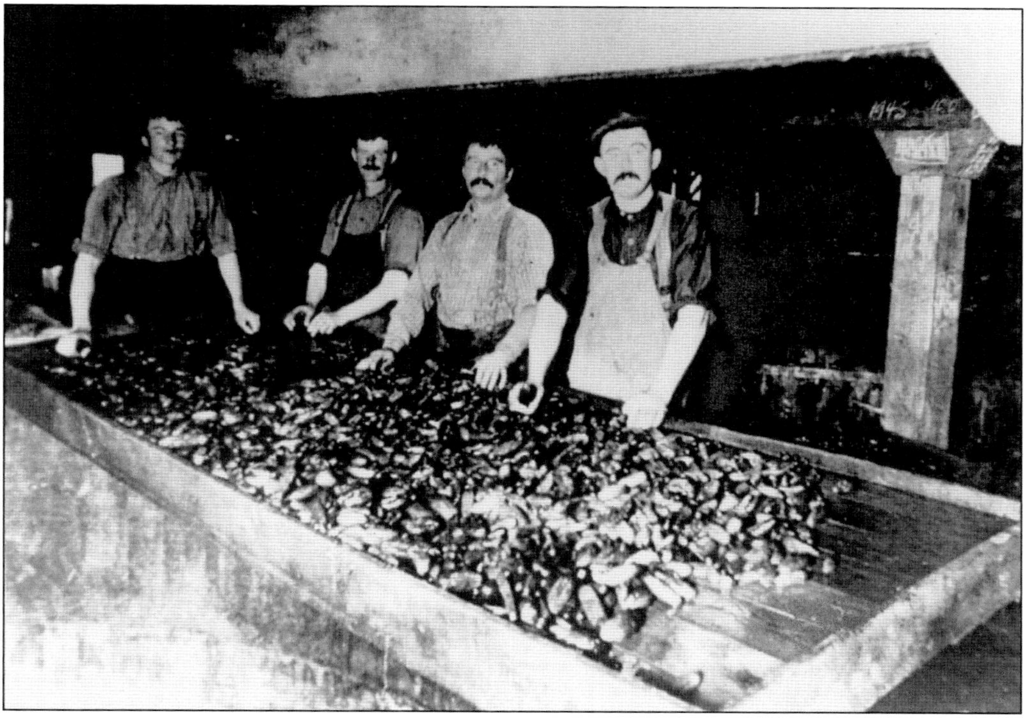

With the possibility of delivering products by train, truck farming led to the processing of produce. Beginning in the late 1870s, Globe Pickle Company, Squire Dingee, and Henning Pickle Company all processed cucumbers grown locally. Here, Jake Baumhardt (third from left) and Emil Eiser (far right) are pictured on the right sorting pickles. Residents who were children at the time recalled their interaction with the factory workers, who would sometimes throw pickles to the children.

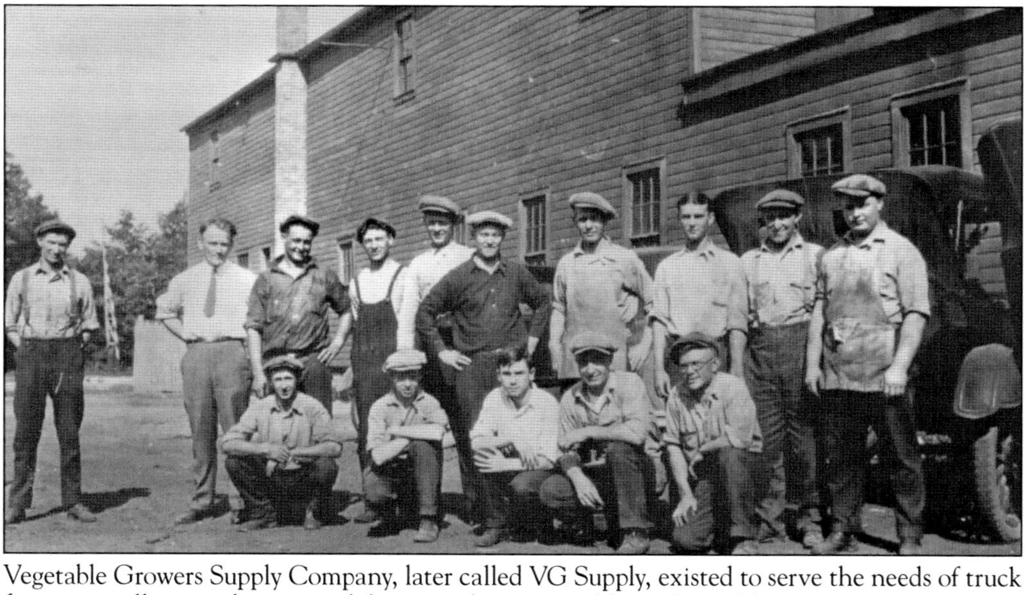

Vegetable Growers Supply Company, later called VG Supply, existed to serve the needs of truck farmers, smaller greenhouses, and those supplying vegetables to the pickling companies of Morton Grove. Later, it transitioned to providing gardening products for suburban homeowners. The company's employees and trucks are pictured here outside of the store.

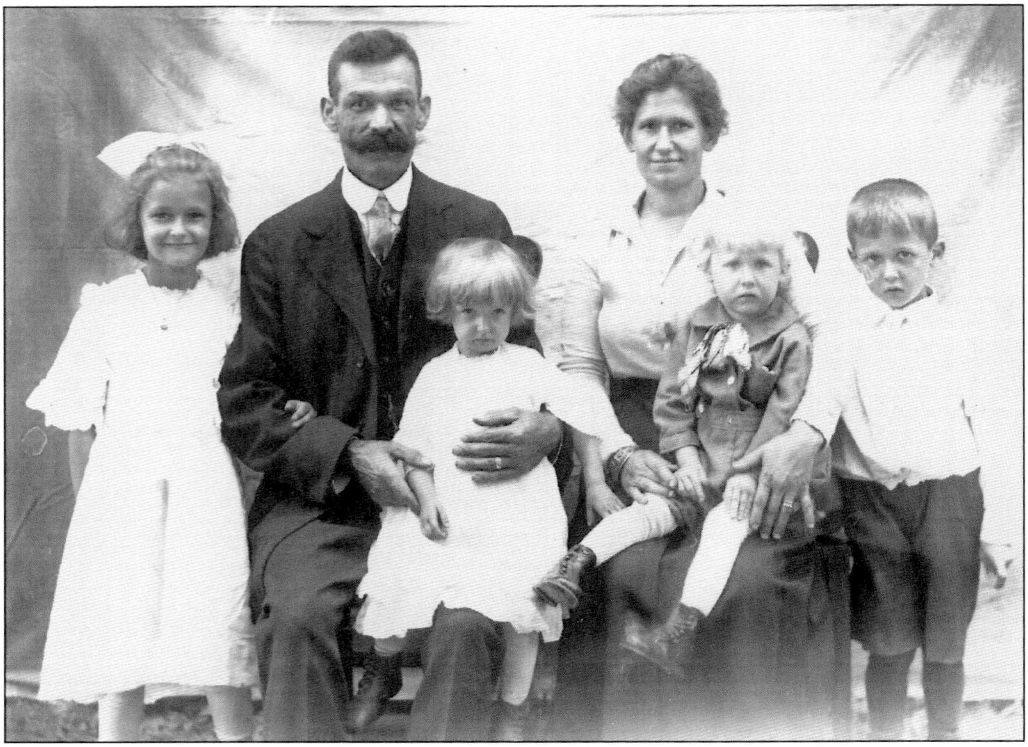

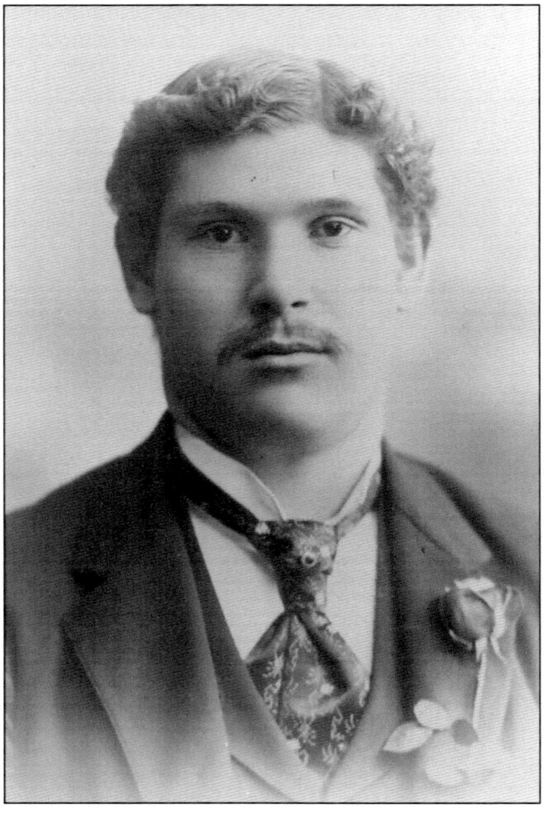

Stanley and Anna (née Ruskevitz) Stellar are pictured with their children in 1919. Family members, from left to right, are Helen, Bernice, Bernard, and Paul. Anna was born in Poland, and Stanley, an educated young man, emigrated from White Russia to seek employment as a horticulturist. The family settled in Morton Grove, and Stanley began working for the Poehlmann Brothers Company—one of the largest floral industries in the world.

Joseph Brooks, shown here in a formal portrait, began working in greenhouses at age 17. He later worked as a foreman at Poehlmann Brothers Company and then opened his own greenhouse and Brooks Floral Shop. He and his wife, Lena (née Gabel) Brooks, were also active in organizations such as the Lion's Club and Women's War Working Circle. (Courtesy of Larry and Judy Brod.)

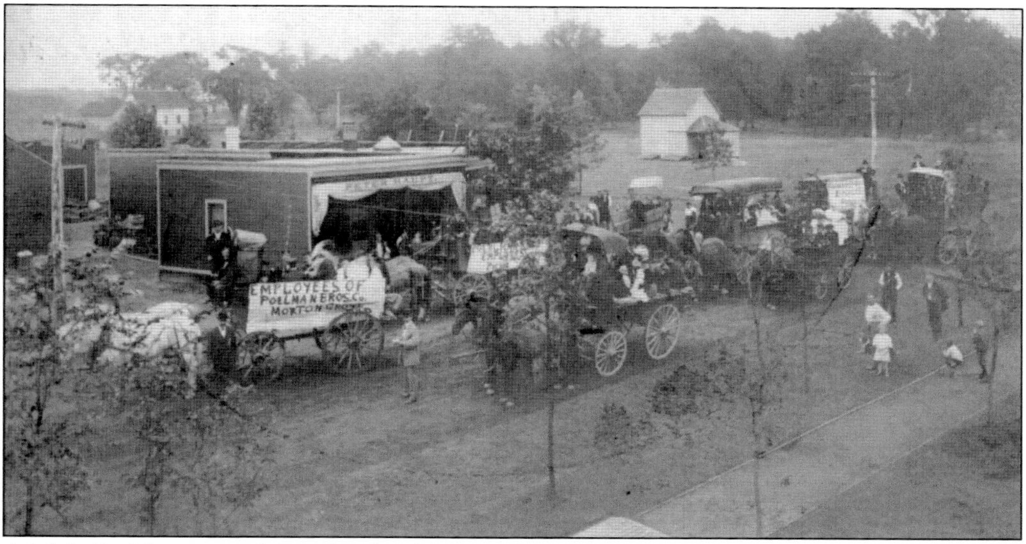

Adolph Poehlmann and Otto Mailander started Morton Grove's floral industry in 1885 with a greenhouse on Oakton Avenue. In 1890, Poehlmann, with his brothers August and John, bought out Mailander and formed the Poehlmann Brothers Company. This wholesale flower business quickly grew into a large-scale operation. Horticultural collectors were sent to tropical areas of the world to gather orchids, palms, and other exotic plants that were grown in greenhouses, as well as traditional European and American flowers. The Poehlmann Rose won first place at the 1904 St. Louis World's Fair, bringing additional notoriety. This 1908 parade of Poehlmann Brothers employees on Lincoln Avenue also shows Peter Haupt's butcher shop, now the Bringer Inn, at Fernald Avenue in the background. The group photograph of Poehlmann employees from approximately 1900 shows only a portion of the staff, which totaled as many as 500 at one time. The company also grew physically, building a second facility north of Dempster Street, which was then the world's largest greenhouse.

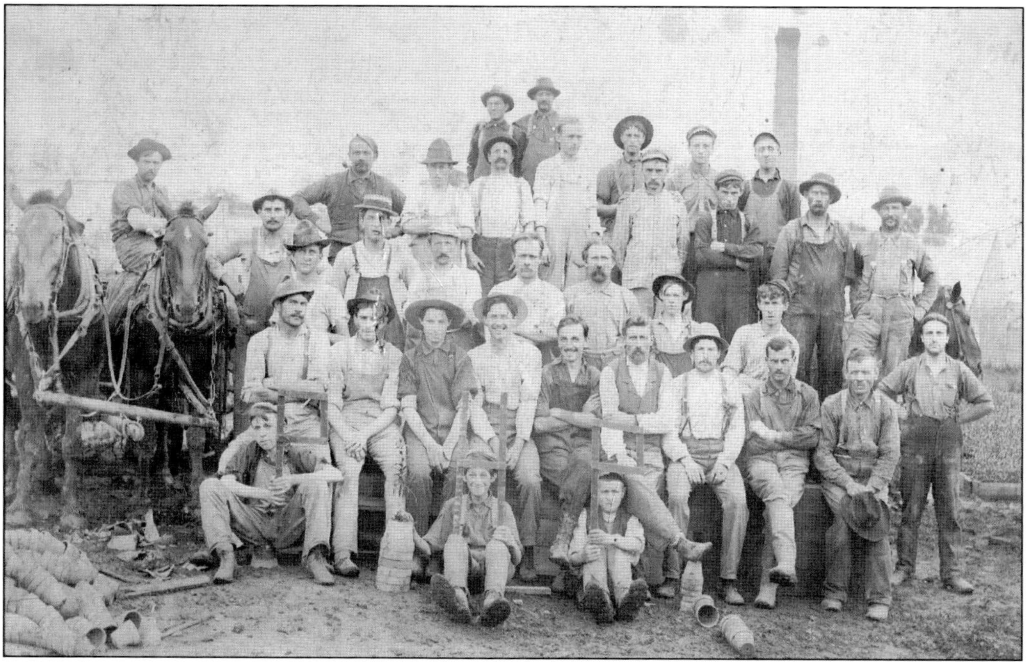

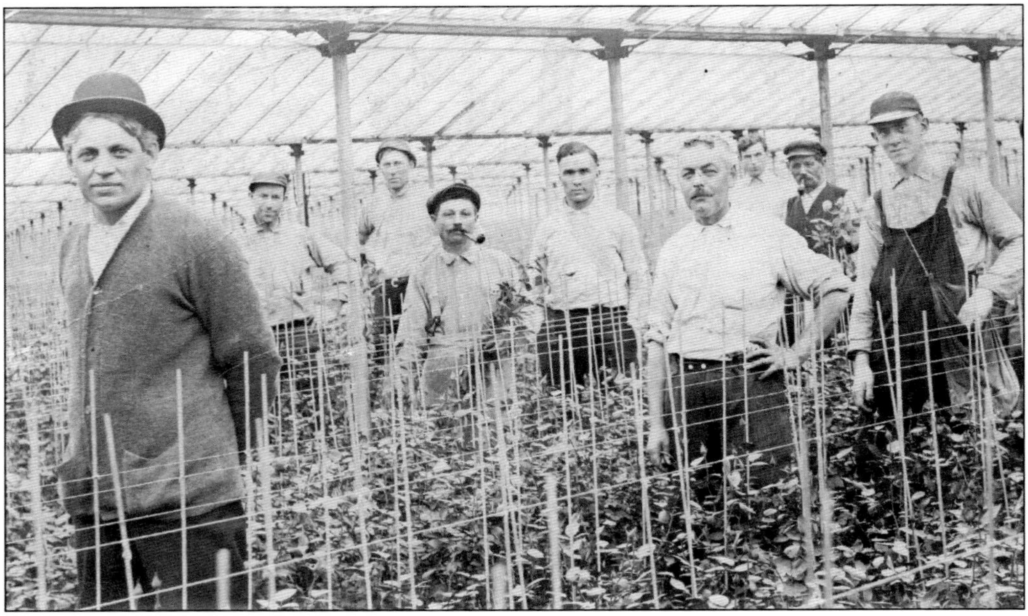

The front row of this photograph includes, from left to right, Mathias Yehl, Tom Berg, and Dick Kruse. The others are unidentified. Yehl worked as a foreman for Poehlmann Brothers Company and lived down the street on Lincoln Avenue. His daughter Dorothy Yehl recalled that the workers were not allowed to listen to the radio, so the Yehl family set up a system using flags to show the status of ongoing Chicago Cubs baseball games. The Poehlmann Brothers Company closed in 1931 as a result of the Great Depression. The greenhouses north of Dempster made way for what would become parts of Harrer Park, Parkview School, and Linne Woods. Remains of cement posts that once supported the flower beds in Poehlmann Brothers Company greenhouses can be seen in Linne Woods. (Above, courtesy of Larry and Judy Brod.)

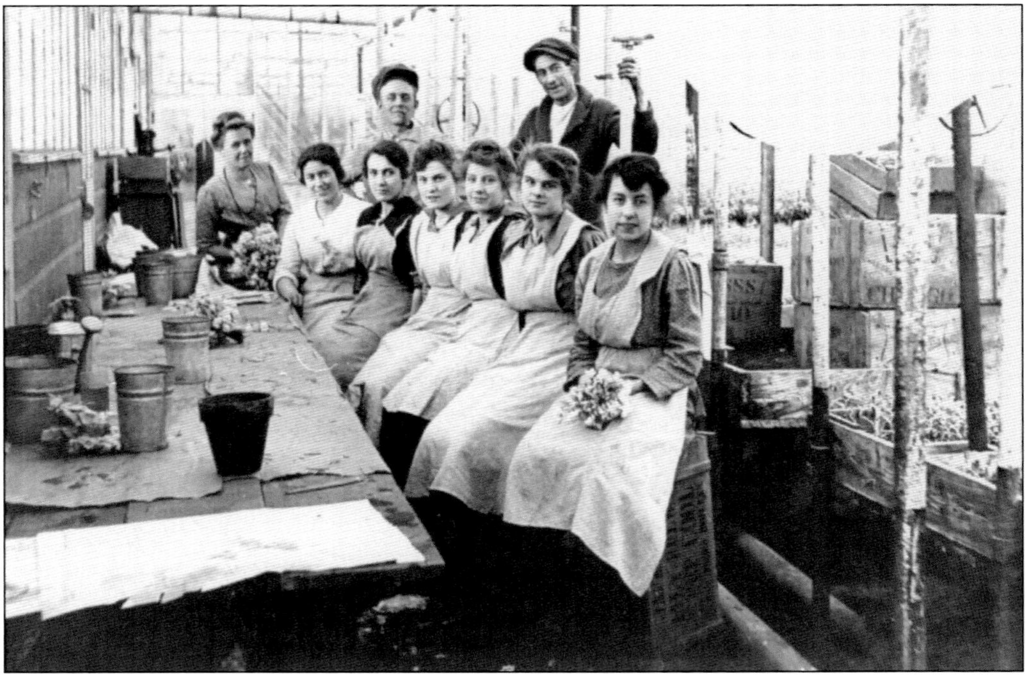

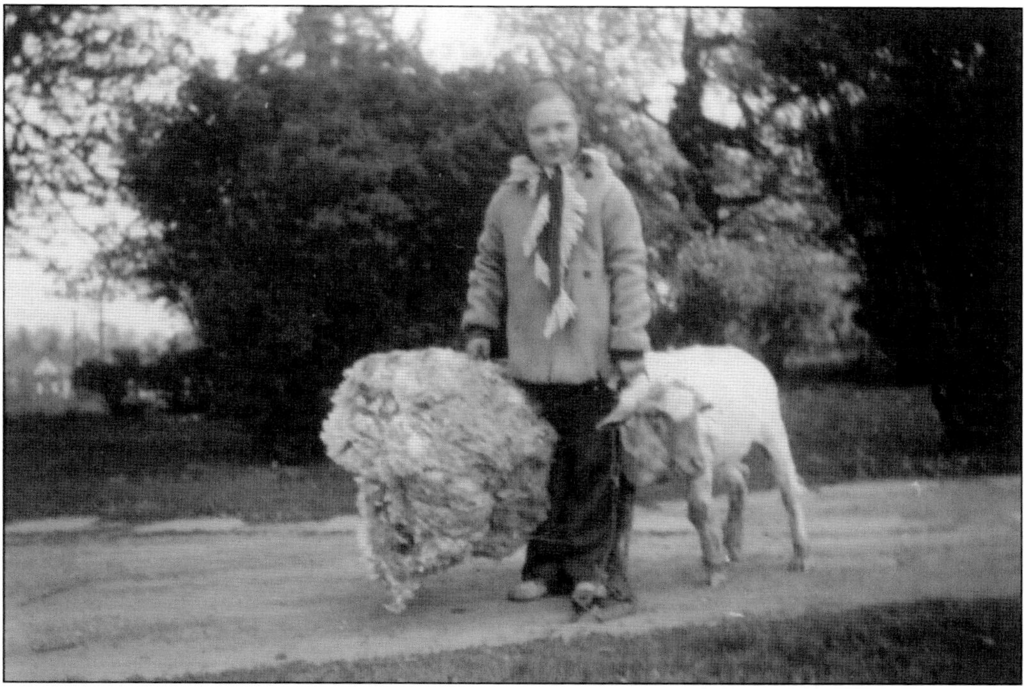

Patty Yehl, granddaughter of Mathias and Elizabeth Yehl, is pictured with their pet lamb Bambi. Elizabeth recalled Bambi being very fond of Matt and having a sense of where he was about town. Bambi would often bang on the door at the barbershop until he came out and would follow him to Grove School, where he worked for a time. Children were delighted when they were allowed to play with Bambi.

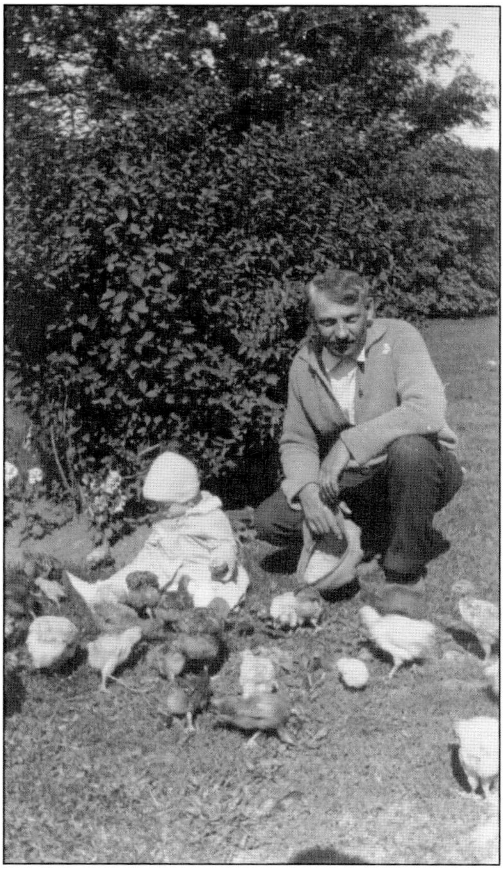

Bernice Brod (left) and her grandfather Mathias Yehl are shown with chicks on Yehl's farm. Nicholas and Magdalena Haupt built the family's farmhouse in 1888, but both died within four years, leaving their eight children alone in the house. Elizabeth Haupt married Mathias Yehl in 1901, raising a family of six in Elizabeth's childhood home. (Courtesy of Larry and Judy Brod.)

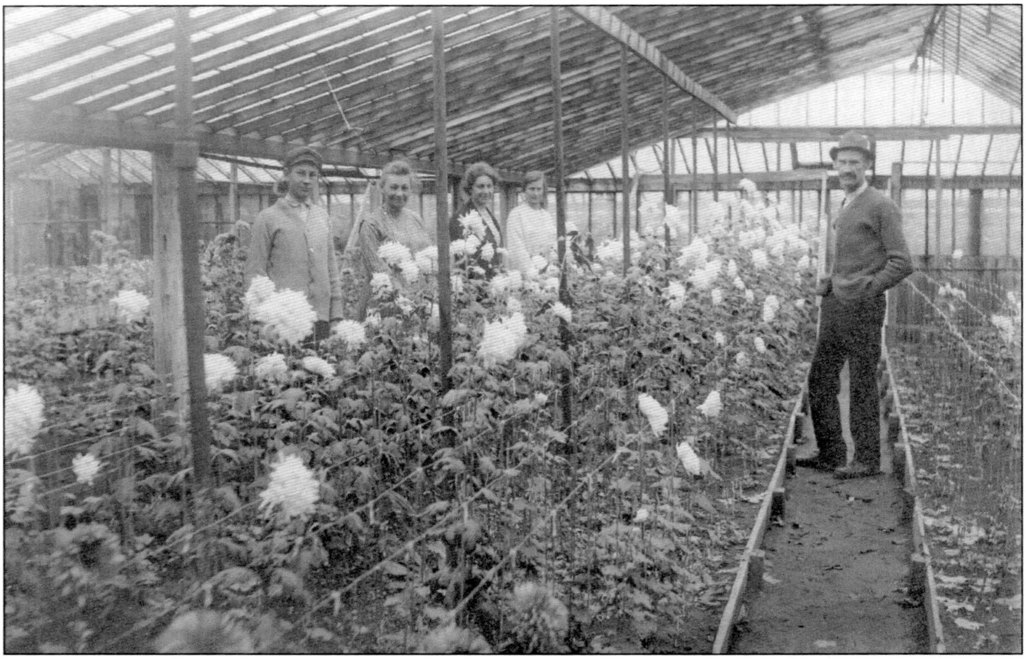

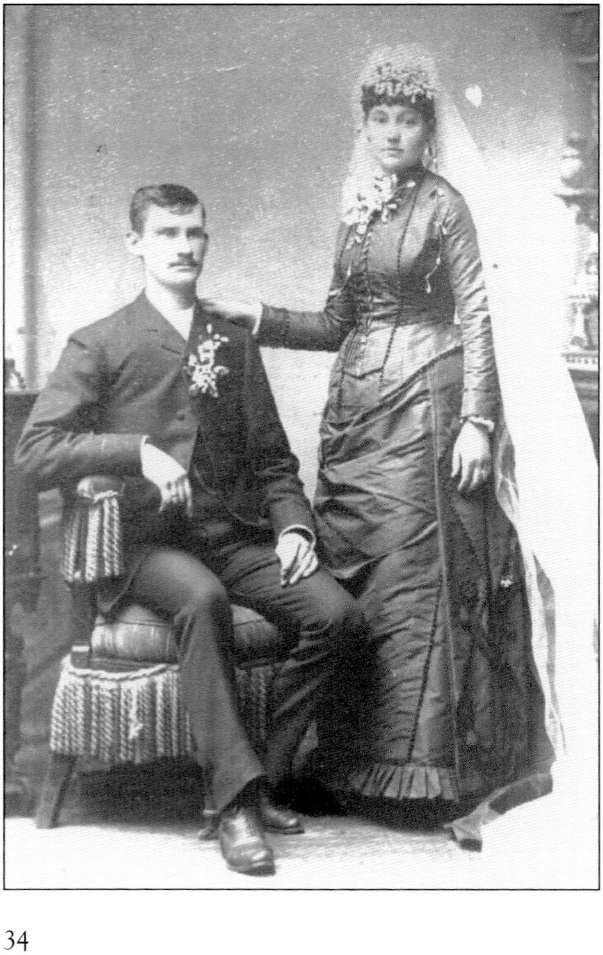

Ray, Mary, Olive, Ernestine, and George Harrer are pictured from left to right in their greenhouse near Theobald Road and Mansfield Avenue. George was the grandson of Wolfgang Harrer, who emigrated from Kaltenbrunn, Bavaria, in 1840, arriving first in New York City, settling for a time in Chicago, and eventually purchasing land in Niles Centre. Henry, one of Wolfgang's sons, owned a grocery store and saloon in what is now Skokie. Henry's two sons, Adam and George, ran the family business before following similar paths in life. George married a Morton Grove girl named Mary Yehl, raising a family of nine together. Pictured at left are George and Mary (née Yehl) Harrer on their wedding day on December 28, 1886, at St. Peters Church in Niles Center. George sold the family business and opened a greenhouse in Morton Grove, serving as the first mayor of Morton Grove upon its incorporation in 1895. George's brother Adam served as the first mayor of Niles Centre, also making a living in the floral industry.

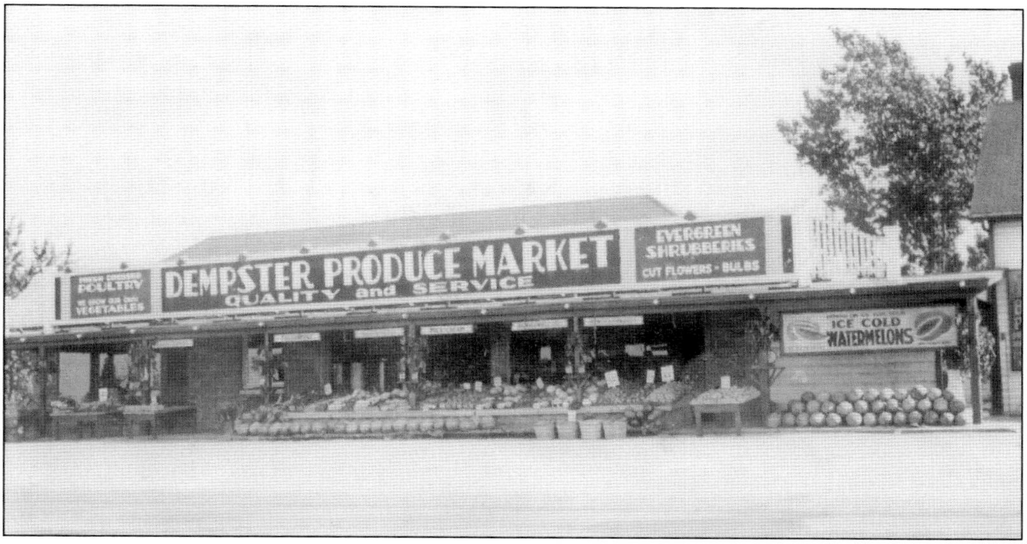

George Boznos Sr. purchased 15 acres southwest of Waukegan Road and Dempster Street in 1926. One of the first businesses the family operated on this spot was the Dempster Produce Market, pictured here in 1935. As the sign on the far left indicates, the family grew vegetables to sell at the market.

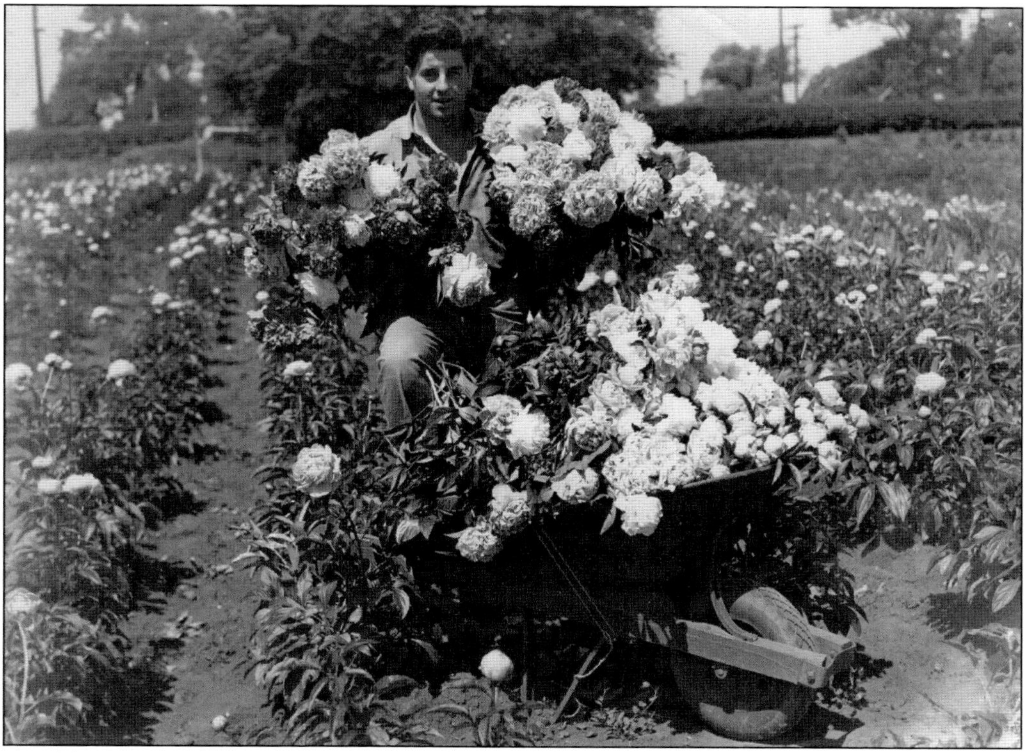

In addition to vegetables, the Boznos family also grew flowers. Nick Boznos, one of George Boznos's sons, is shown gathering peonies as part of the family's flower-growing business. Nick and other Boznos family members ran several businesses and remained active in civic service with organizations, such as the Morton Grove Volunteer Fire Department and the Morton Grove Park District.

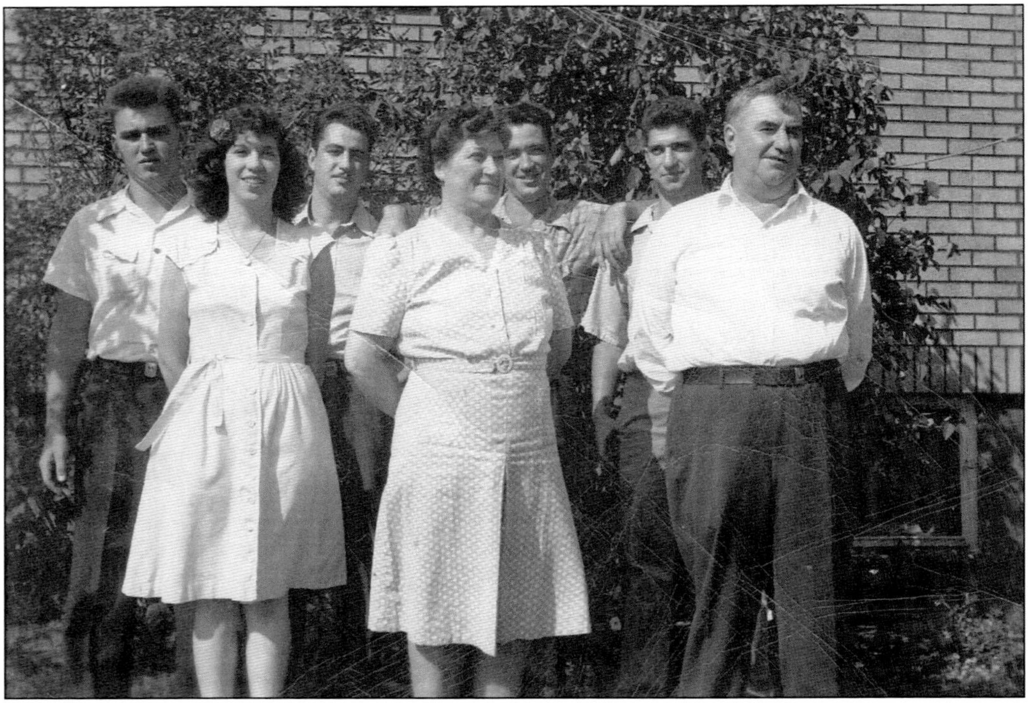

Eugene Koeune was born in 1894 in the village of Harlange, Luxembourg. He was a cowherd and worked his parent's fields until the age of 17 when he traveled to America. He married Barbara Wagner in 1919. Nicholas, Barbara, Henry, Barbara, August, Eugene Jr., and Eugene Koeune Sr. are pictured from left to right at 5509 Lincoln Avenue, where they rented greenhouses from the Platz family in 1939. They were able to purchase the greenhouses shortly after they went into business, which were in operation until 1974. After Eugene Sr. retired in 1950, the Koeune brothers took over the family business, and it became known as K-B Garden Center. (Courtesy of Paul Minx.)

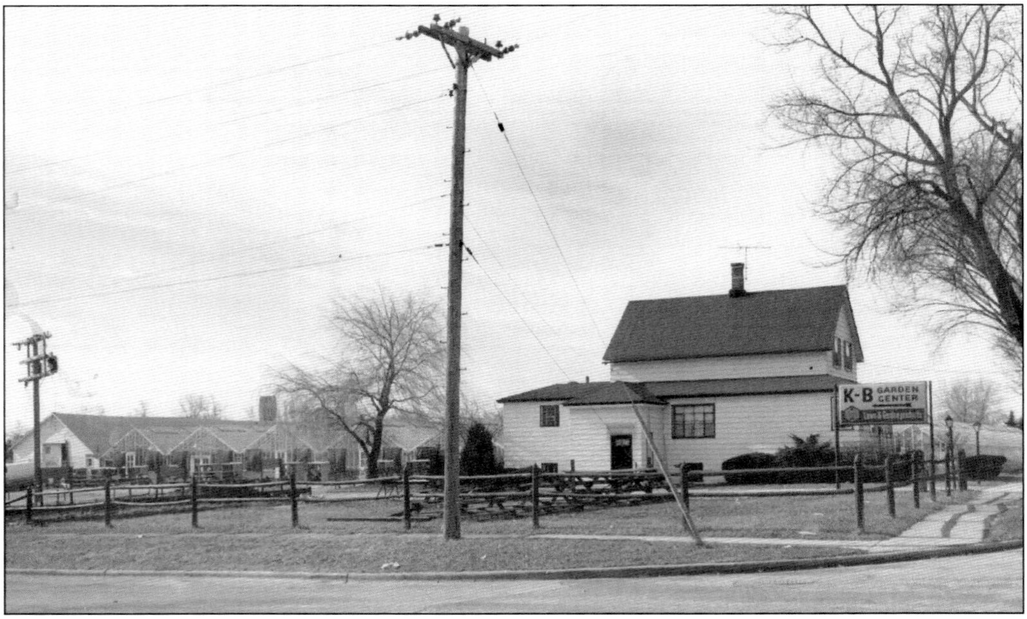

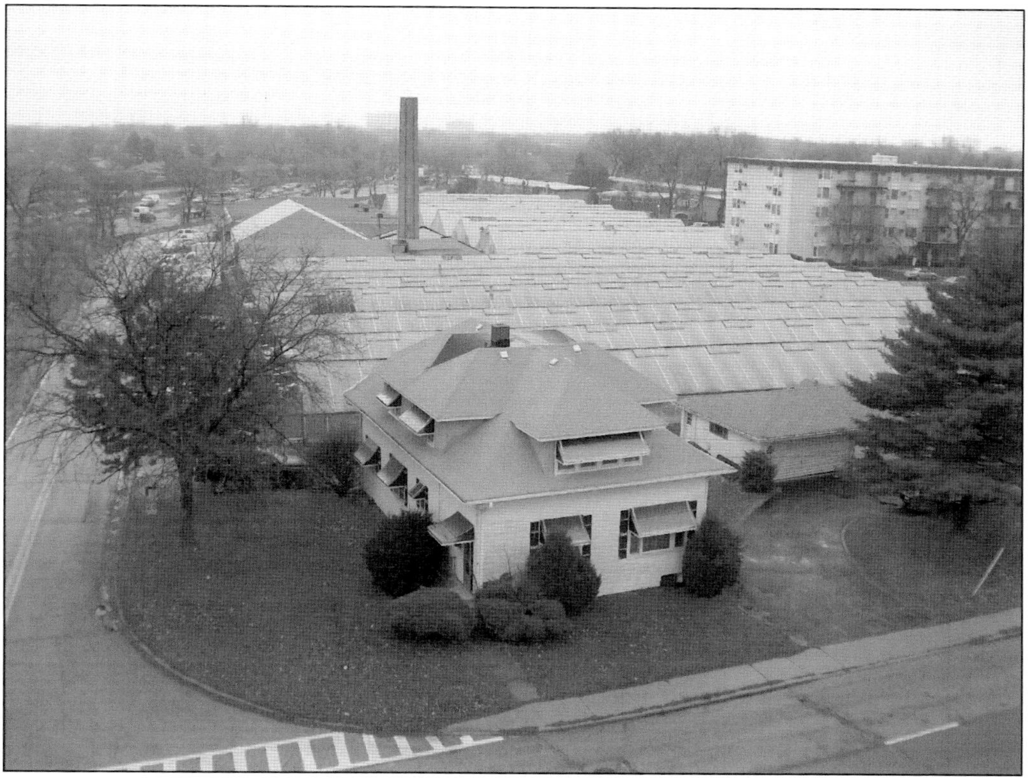

The Platz homestead and greenhouses are pictured north of Lincoln Avenue, east of the Eden's Expressway. Emigrating from Esch, Luxembourg, Nicholas Platz preceded his wife and six children, who followed in 1892. They farmed for a living, but when a flu epidemic hit, a demand for funeral flowers developed, and they began growing and selling roses at the South Wabash flower market. Nicholas and Marie both succumbed to the flu in 1923, dying within 24 hours of each other. Their sons Paul and Victor carried on the business, responding to the demand of the times by going back to produce during the Great Depression. Inspired by a Jamaican worker named Clarene Brown, they went into tropical flowers in the 1970s. Platz Wholesale and Jamaican Gardens closed their doors in 2009, being the last of the family-operated greenhouses in Morton Grove.

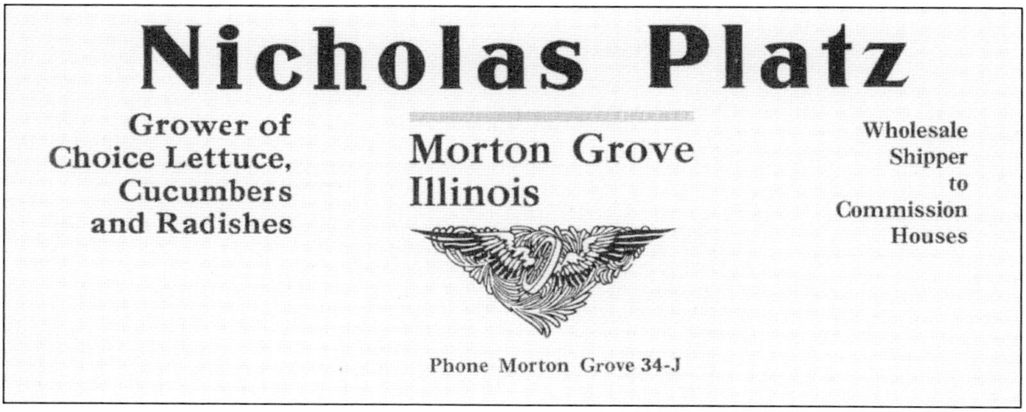

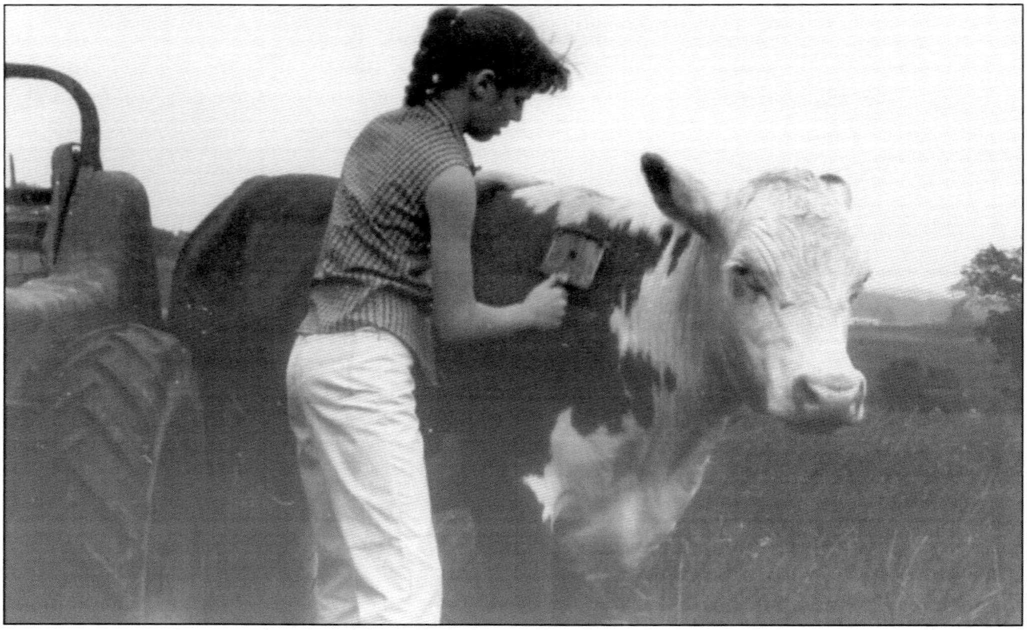

Carl Friedrich Ahrens was born in Germany in 1869. His wife, Elise Dunfriendt, was also born in Germany in 1872. They traveled to America with their parents and later married at St. Paul's Lutheran Church in Skokie in 1882. Along with their 12 children, they farmed the land and ran a vegetable stand at 9342 Harms Road (Cemetery Road). Two of their sons, Edward and Louis, along with their daughter Minnie continued to farm the land for a time after their parents died in the 1940s, selling off land for development and holding on to the home, barns, and pasture for the cows. Carl and Elise's great granddaughter Penny Kruger is pictured grooming the last cow in Morton Grove in 1970.

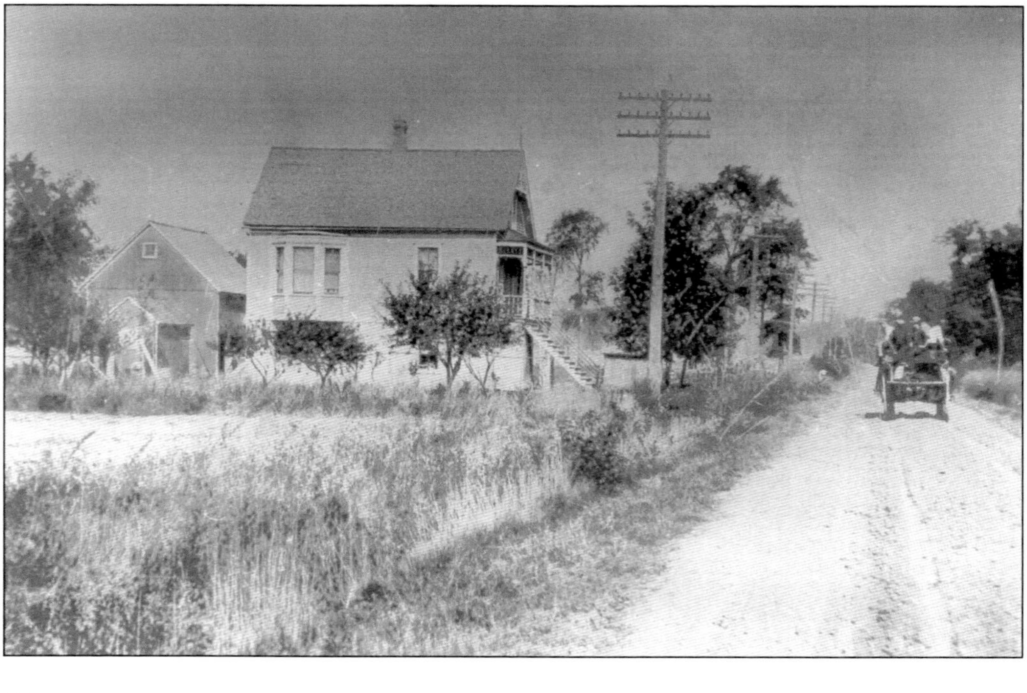

Three

VILLAGE OF VOLUNTEERS

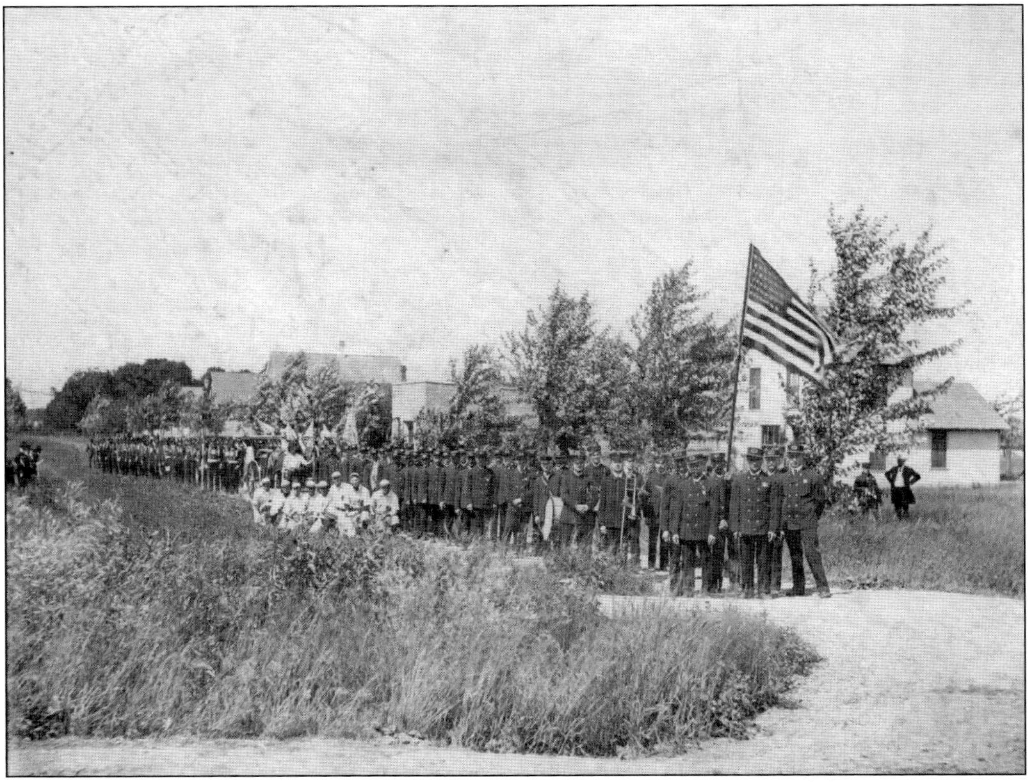

This parade at Callie Avenue and Lincoln Avenue is led by members of the Morton Grove Volunteer Fire Department. The early firemen often owned farmland or small businesses in the village, although some worked in the larger floral or food industry. It was very common for men and women in the early history of Morton Grove to hold several positions in business, fraternal or volunteer organizations, and government.

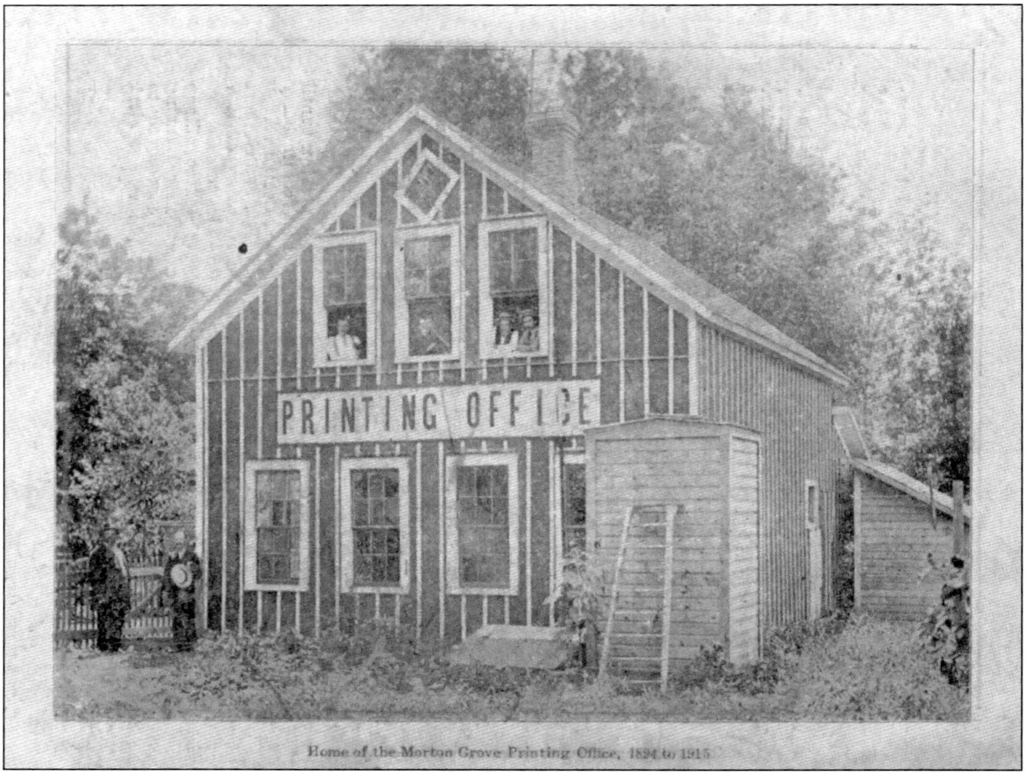

Home of the Morton Grove Printing Office, 1894 to 1915

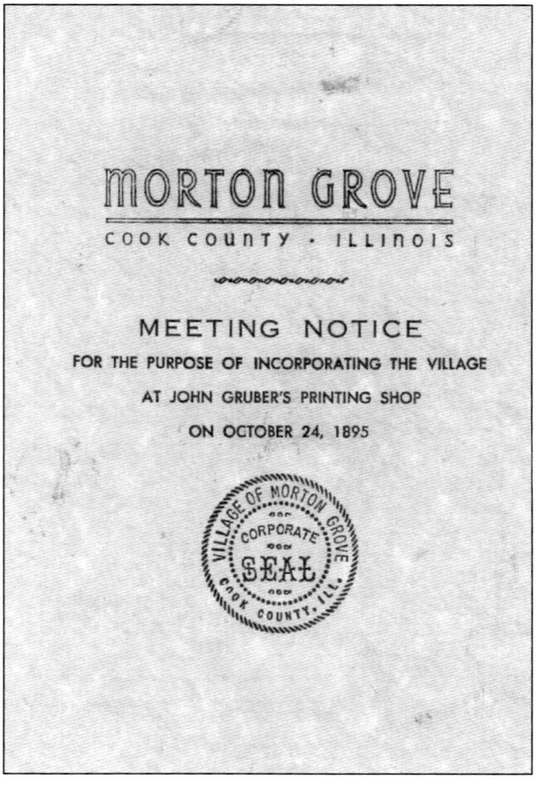

MORTON GROVE

COOK COUNTY · ILLINOIS

MEETING NOTICE

FOR THE PURPOSE OF INCORPORATING THE VILLAGE

AT JOHN GRUBER'S PRINTING SHOP

ON OCTOBER 24, 1895

VILLAGE OF MORTON GROVE CORPORATE SEAL COOK COUNTY, ILL.

A small group of men representing a population of 300 gathered at the Bethesda Brothers Industrial Society printing office to create the village government of Morton Grove, legally incorporated on December 24, 1895. Frank Henning headed this society and founded the convalescence home associated with the German American Hospital of Chicago at this site. A printing plant was installed for creating the society's monthly magazine, as well as engaging in commercial printing. Henning's shop manager, John Gruber, later purchased this facility. On October 24, 1895, members of this community met to elect Morton Grove's first village board. George Harrer became the first mayor of Morton Grove in 1895 and served for 14 years. August Poehlmann, William Mueller, Jacob Hoffman, Charles Guenther, David Fielweber, and Fred Dilg were trustees. Frank Henning served as village clerk, and Medard Lochner became treasurer. Adolph Poehlmann was police magistrate, with John Koller as police marshal.

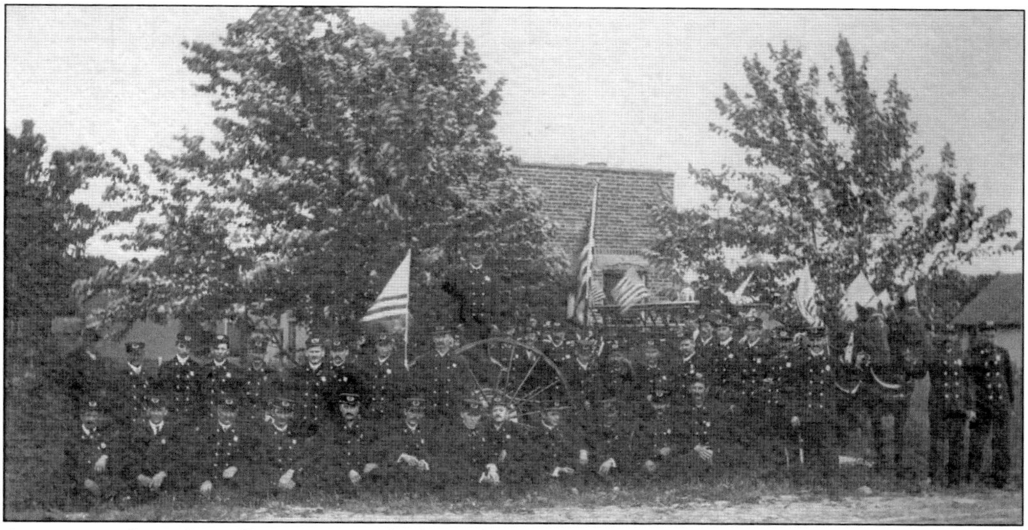

At a time when the village consisted of wooden buildings and sidewalks, kerosene lamps, wood-burning stoves, and the hot cinders flying from locomotives could prove disastrous, a group of 18 men joined together to fight fires, forming the first Morton Grove Volunteer Fire Company in 1904. The company is pictured in 1905 around the horse-drawn hand pumper.

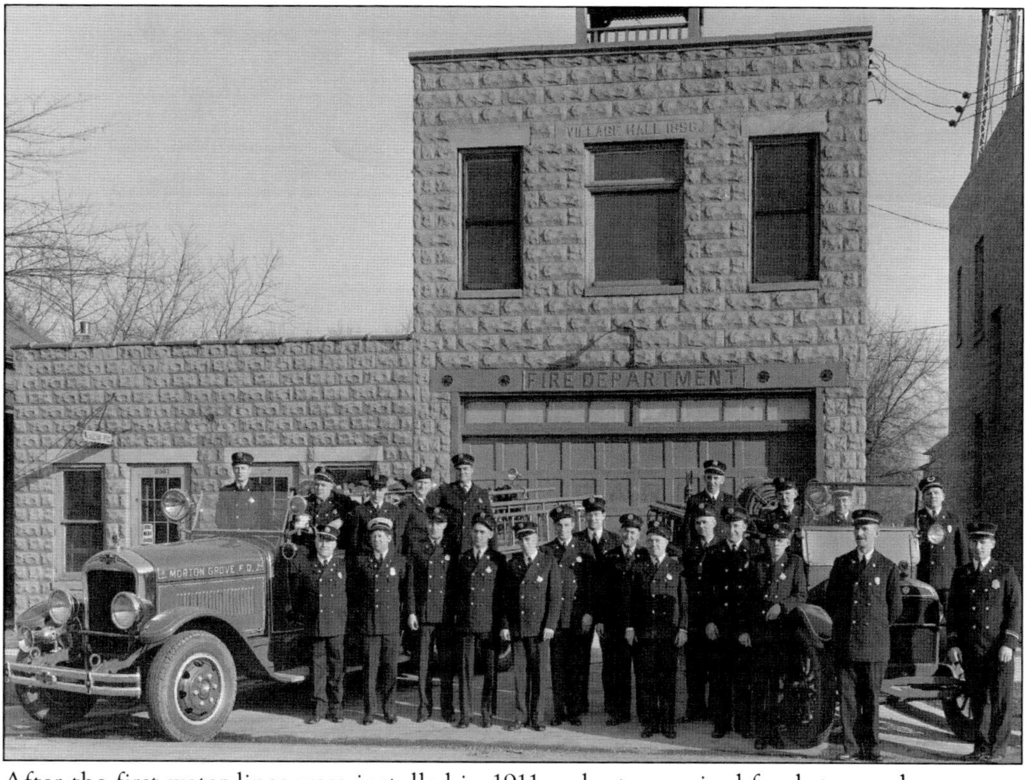

After the first water lines were installed in 1911, volunteers raised funds to purchase a new Howe gasoline engine pumper. In 1917, a Studebaker chemical and ladder truck was purchased, followed by the 1924 Reo pumper. Morton Grove's volunteer fire company is pictured in front of the Village Hall and fire department in 1939 with the 1936 American LaFrance, purchased with $6,000 donated by the Morton Grove Days Committee.

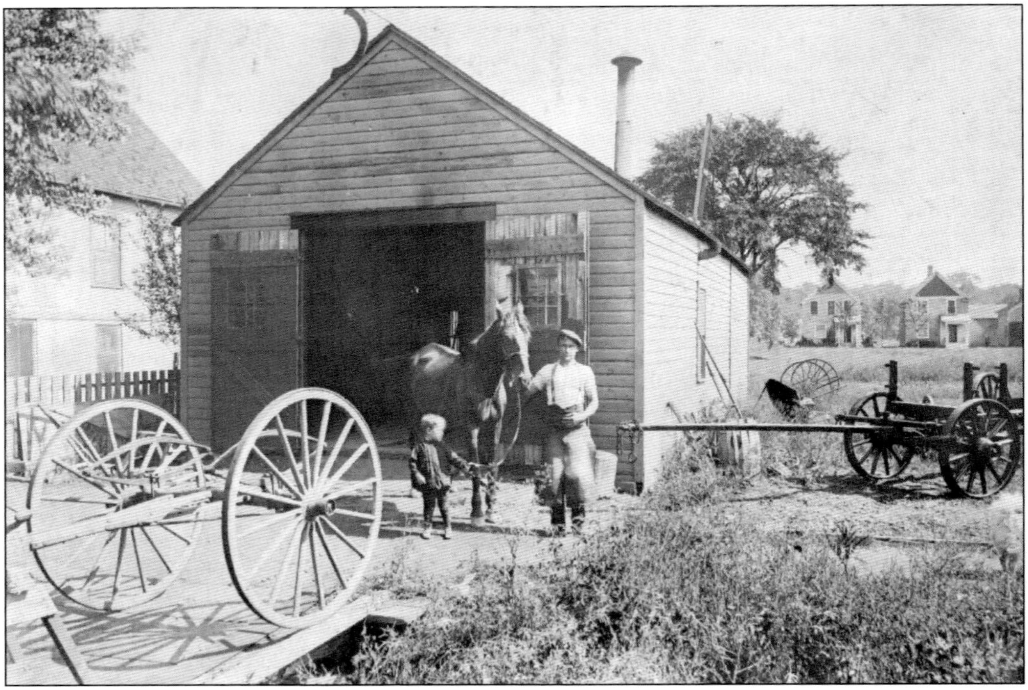

This photograph of Charles Peschke, with his son George Peschke, was taken at his blacksmith shop at 8541 Ferris Avenue. Houses on Callie Avenue are visible in the background. The early blacksmith provided essential services to local farmers and industry by crafting specialized tools and repairing anything made of metal. Horseshoeing was only one part of his work. Charles Peschke also served as one of Morton Grove's first police marshals. He is shown here in the marshal's carriage. Like many other leaders in the early aspects of village life, Peschke was involved in other areas of civic life, including being among the men to organize the Morton Grove Volunteer Fire Department.

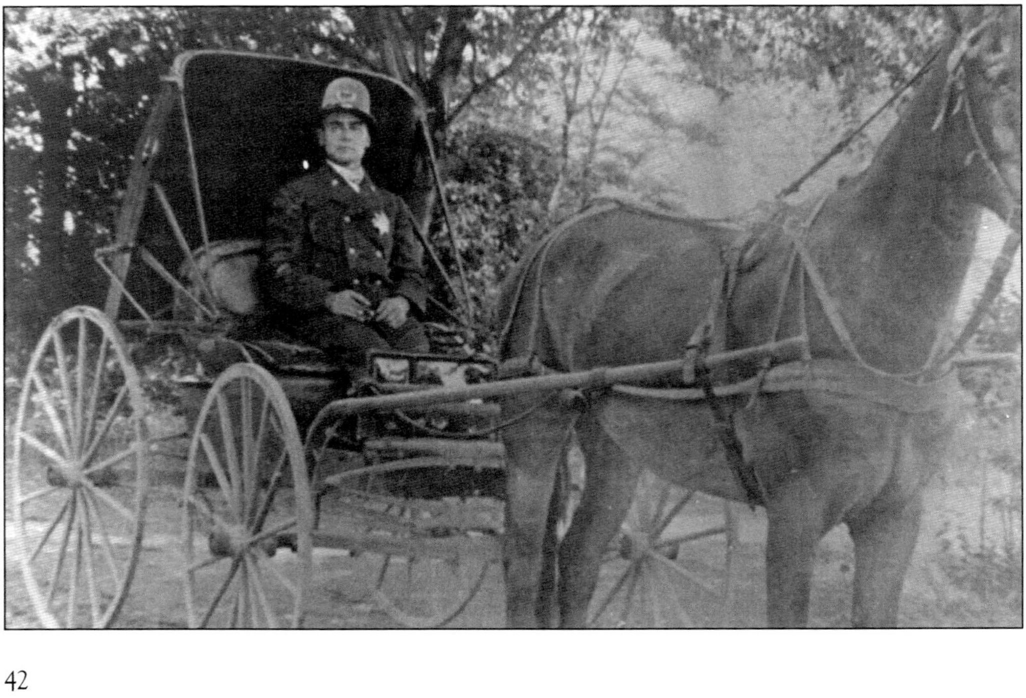

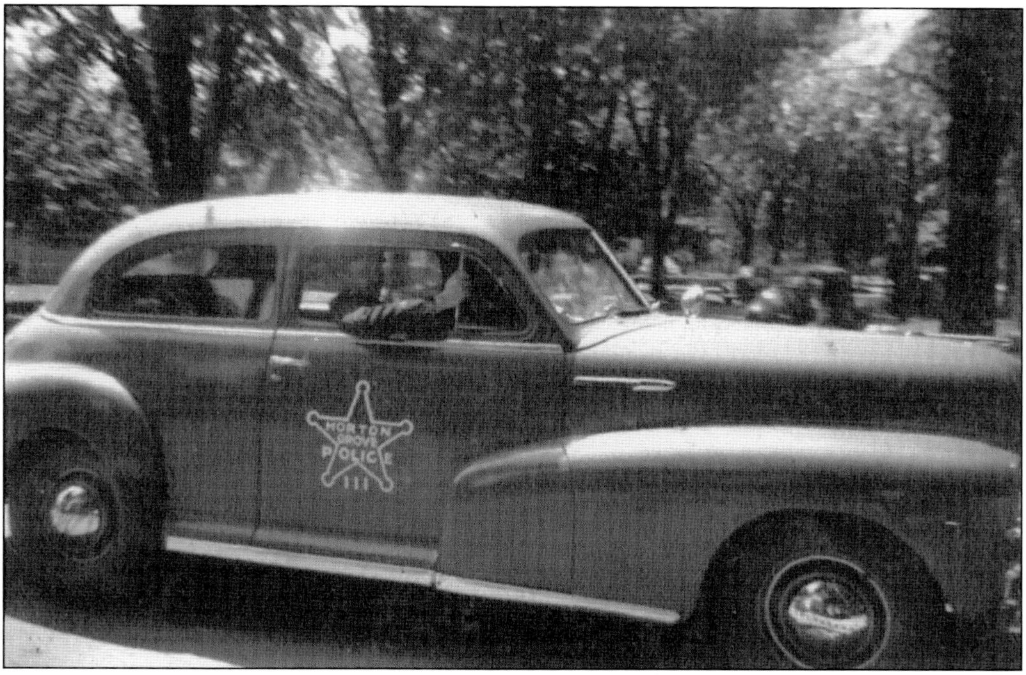

Morton Grove police chief Milton Scanlon is pictured on the passenger side of this early squad car in 1957. Scanlon had been made chief in 1955 and is known for his efforts to make the department more modern and professional. He acquired funding for four new squad cars to replace this one in 1957 and a referendum to bring the police department in line with Illinois training requirements in 1958.

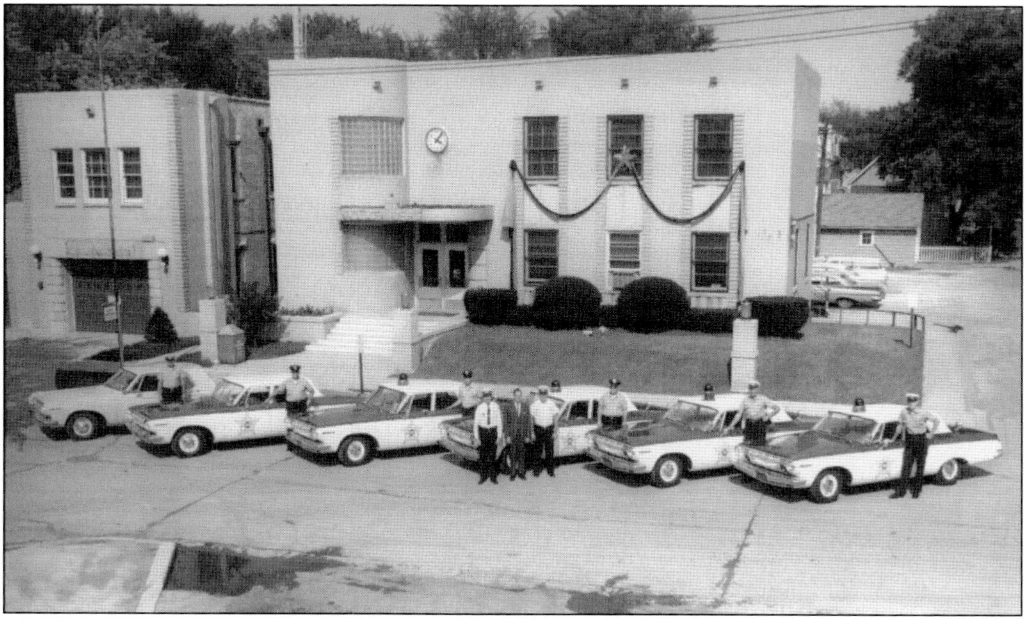

Members of the Morton Grove Police Department gather in front of their headquarters on Callie Avenue in 1963. This building originally operated as Village Hall, which moved into the bank building on the corner of Callie and Lincoln Avenues in 1965. The funeral bunting has been placed in respect for Sgt. William Krueger.

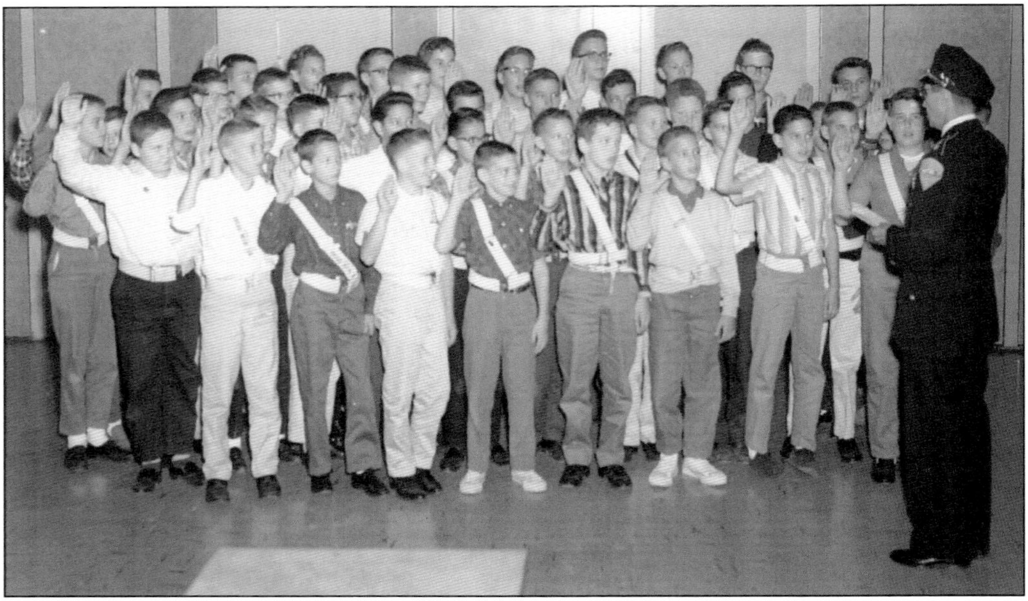

Chief Milton Scanlon served on the Morton Grove police force from 1947 until his retirement in 1970. Patrol boys completing the crossing guard safety training are being sworn in by Chief Scanlon in the early 1960s. The Morton Grove Police Department was also involved in motorcycle and bicycle safety programs during this time period.

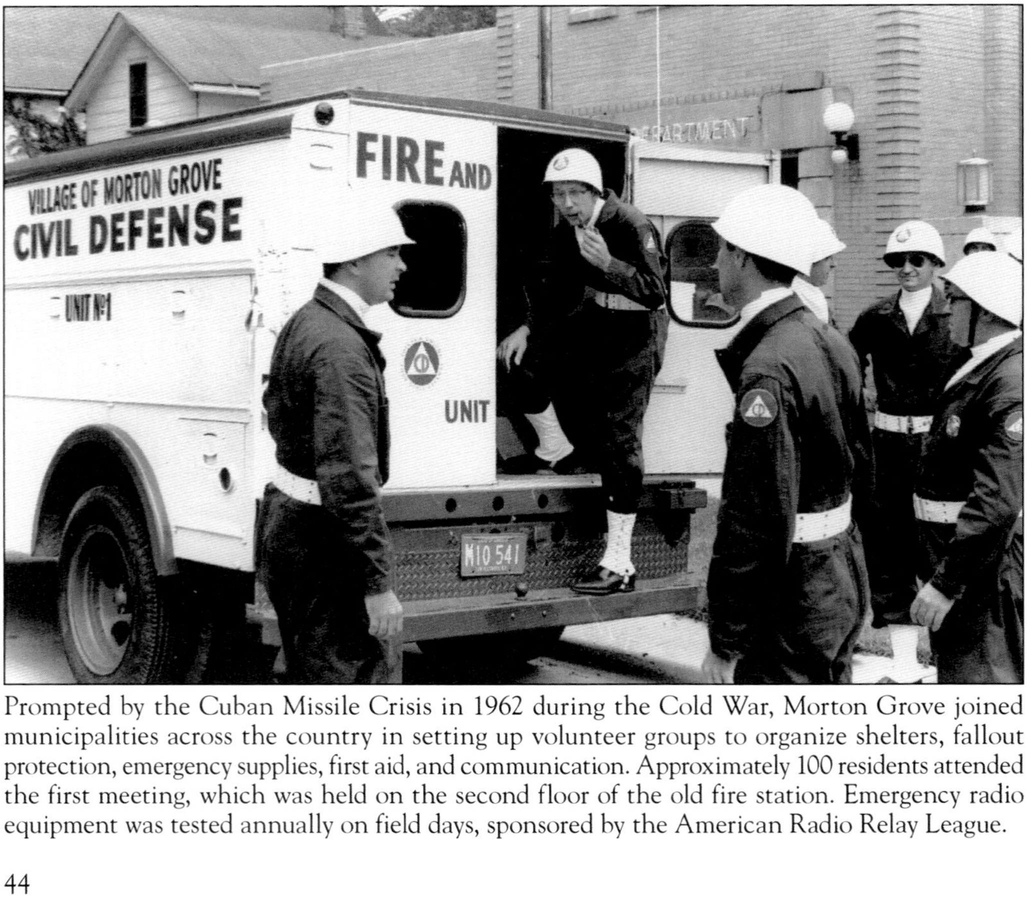

Prompted by the Cuban Missile Crisis in 1962 during the Cold War, Morton Grove joined municipalities across the country in setting up volunteer groups to organize shelters, fallout protection, emergency supplies, first aid, and communication. Approximately 100 residents attended the first meeting, which was held on the second floor of the old fire station. Emergency radio equipment was tested annually on field days, sponsored by the American Radio Relay League.

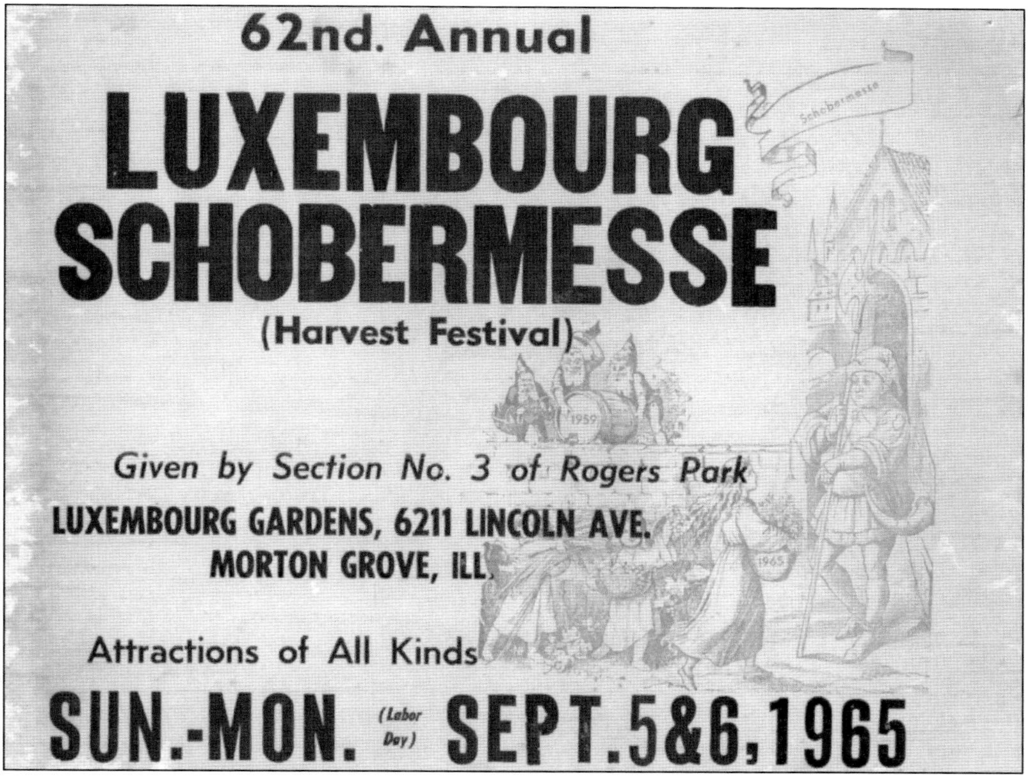

Eugene Koeune, pictured in the Koeune greenhouses in Morton Grove in 1965, became a member of the Luxembourg Brotherhood, Section No. 3, in Rogers Park shortly after his arrival to America in 1911. The Luxembourg Brotherhood, which was founded as a fraternal insurance agency on the south side of Chicago in 1887, is the oldest Luxembourg-American organization in the United States. Koeune held the offices of marshal, president, and vice president during his membership and served as a trustee and Schobermesse Committee Chair in 1955. He was highly regarded by his fellow members. His grandson Paul Minx recalls attending his funeral luncheon in the Luxembourg Garden's restaurant on Lincoln Avenue in 1966 and wandering through the picnic groves out back, where the property had just been sold and the picnic shelters and concessions were beginning to be torn down. (Below, courtesy of Paul Minx.)

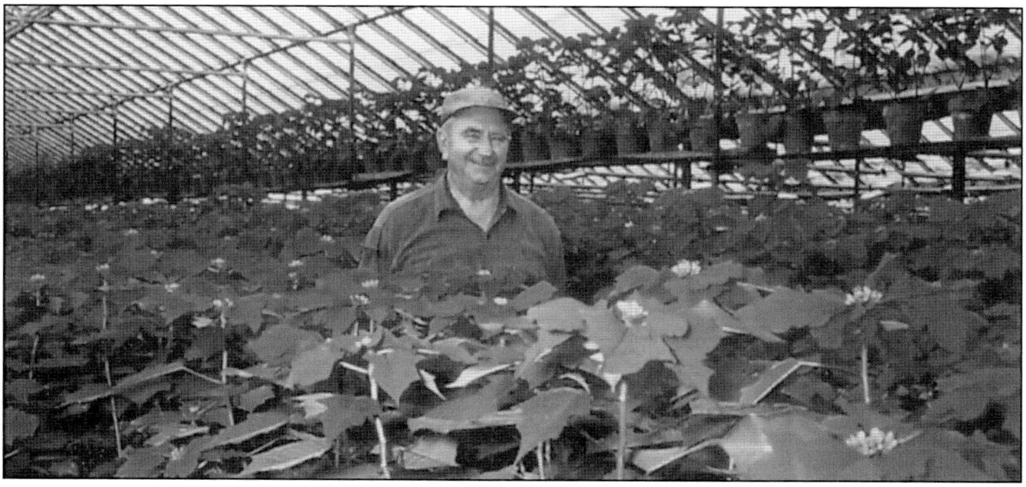

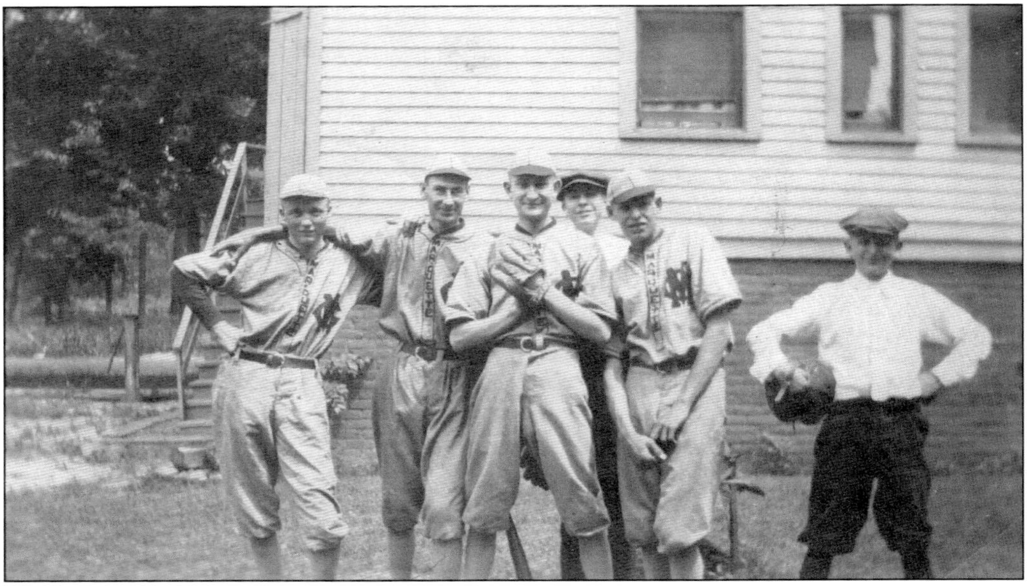

As with much of America, baseball has been a significant pastime in Morton Grove throughout its history. This 1920 photograph shows young men in Morton Grove Baseball Club uniforms. Pictured above from left to right are Edward Schiller, Raymond Harrer, John Loutsch, Rudolph Winckler, Ralph Gabel, and Arthur Loutsch. Other members of the team included Jacob Baumhardt, George Baumhardt, Frank Boemmel, Emile Bringer, Charles Brunke, George Loutsch, Harry Loutsch, Louis Sickinger, Raymond Schwarz, and Arthur Wachlin. The team played at a field west of Lehigh and Lincoln Avenues. Morton Grove's early baseball team played against those from other local towns. The banquet photograph below shows local teams at the Ferris Inn celebrating the 1922 season.

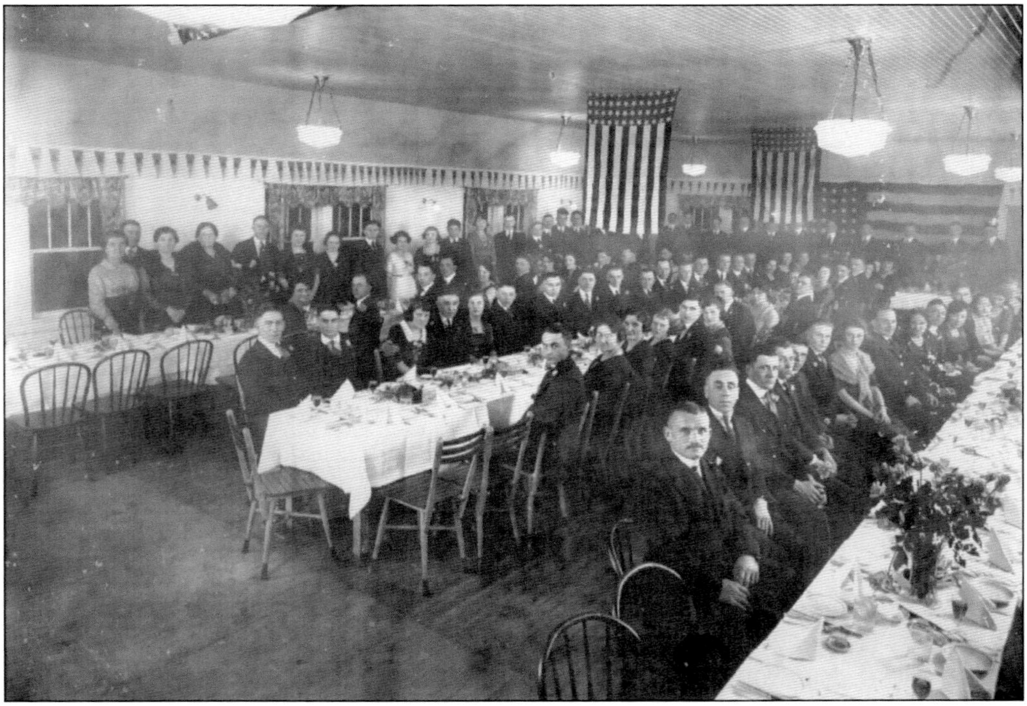

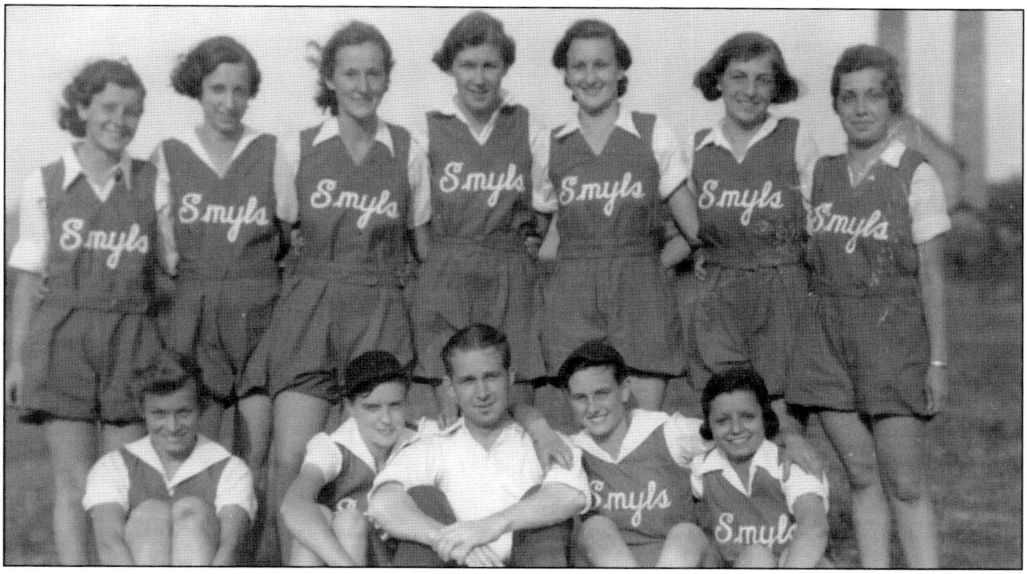

St. Martha's Young Ladies Society organized a softball team in 1933 under the guidance of Rev. Lawrence Wand, coached by Walter Rahling, and assisted by Lambert Harrer and Bernard Stellar. Visiting teams labeled them the "hicks." Boys' teams played on choice fields, but the girls mowed a vacant lot on Lincoln Avenue, skinned the diamond, marked the baselines, and put up a makeshift backstop. Pictured from left to right are (first row) Marion Haupt, Eleanor Winandy, Walter Rawling, and Florence Huscher; (second row) Margaret Sesterhenn, Agnes Theobald, Jeannette Platz, Ruth Riha, Virginia Sabel, Catherine Mueller, and Theresa Meier. Joining the Catholic Youth Organization League in 1935, they won division championships in 1935, 1937, and 1938.

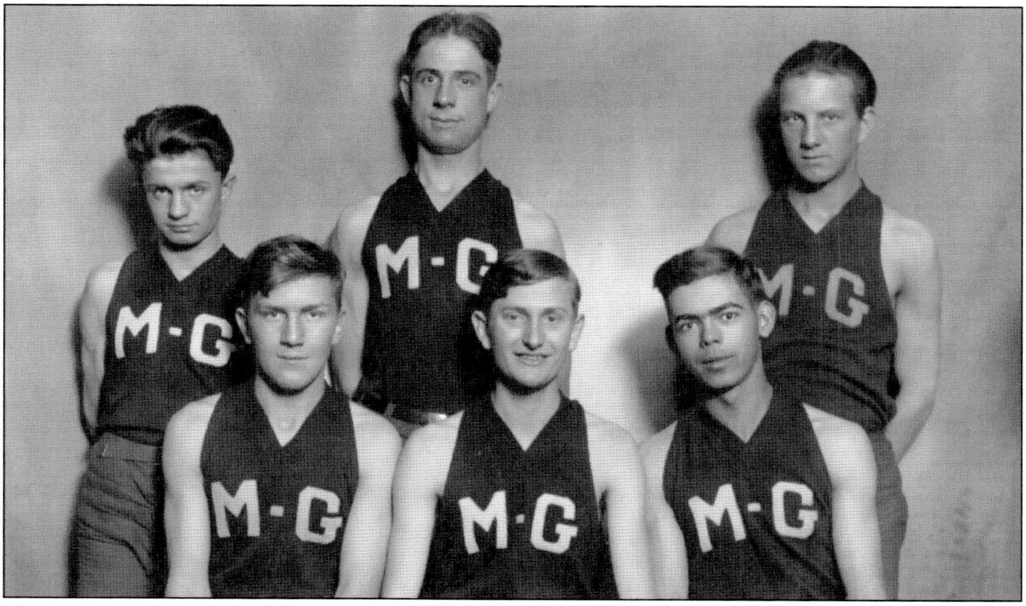

This image of the 1924 Morton Grove basketball team includes, from left to right, (first row) Art Ketz, Art Loutsch, and Fred Heidemann; (second row) Norm Sickinger, Willard Hand, and Lawrence Wedel. Like other youth sports teams, they played teams from nearby towns such as Des Plaines, Palatine, Northbrook, Arlington Heights, Deerfield, and Lake Zurich.

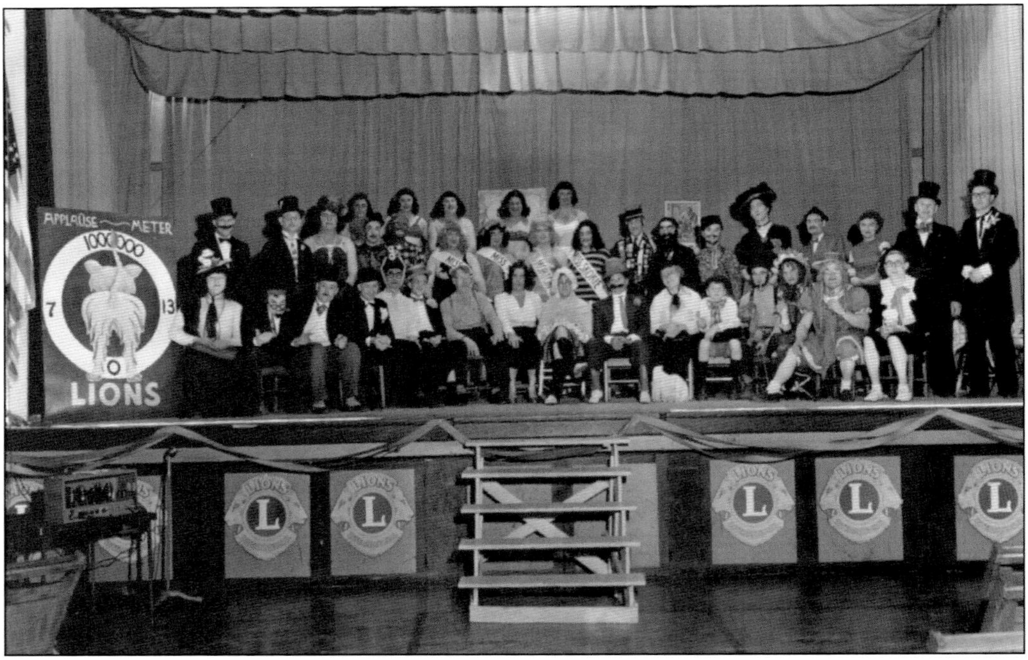

The Morton Grove Lion's Club was formed in 1940 with Herbert Dilg as the first president. The club focuses on charitable and social events, as well as civic involvement, with a goal of community improvement. This group photograph of a Lion's Club fundraising performance shows members in costume after a Peter Perkins Party performance.

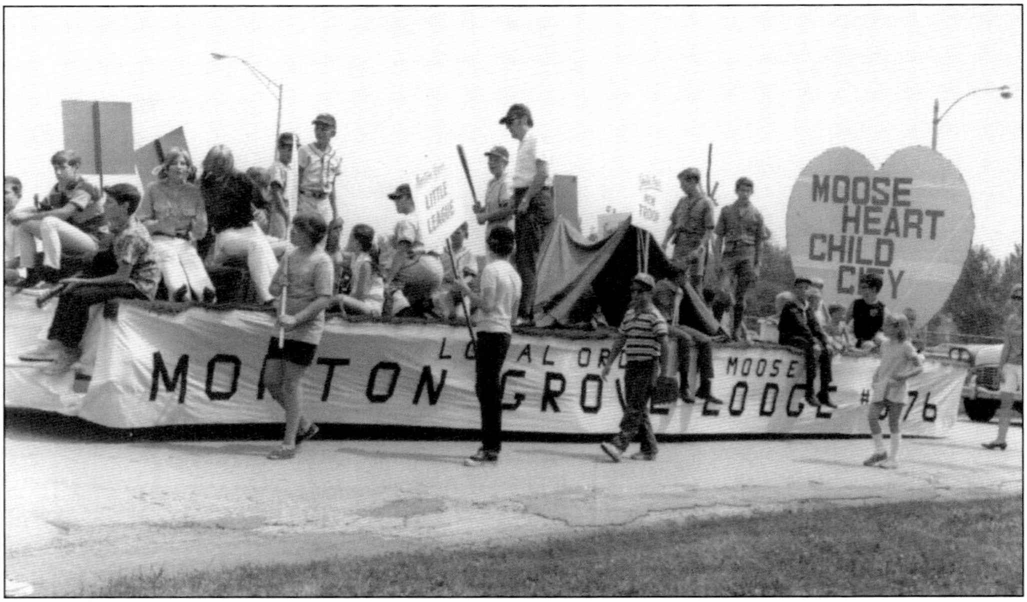

The Loyal Order of the Moose Lodge No. 376, founded in Morton Grove in 1951, raised funds to erect the fraternal organization's headquarters at 6419 Chestnut Street by 1961. The Women of the Moose auxiliary is connected to this lodge. Together, the men and women of this family fraternity support many community programs along with Mooseheart Child City & School and Moosehaven, City of Contentment. Members of Morton Grove Little League and local Boy Scout troops are represented on the Moose parade float during a Morton Grove Days celebration.

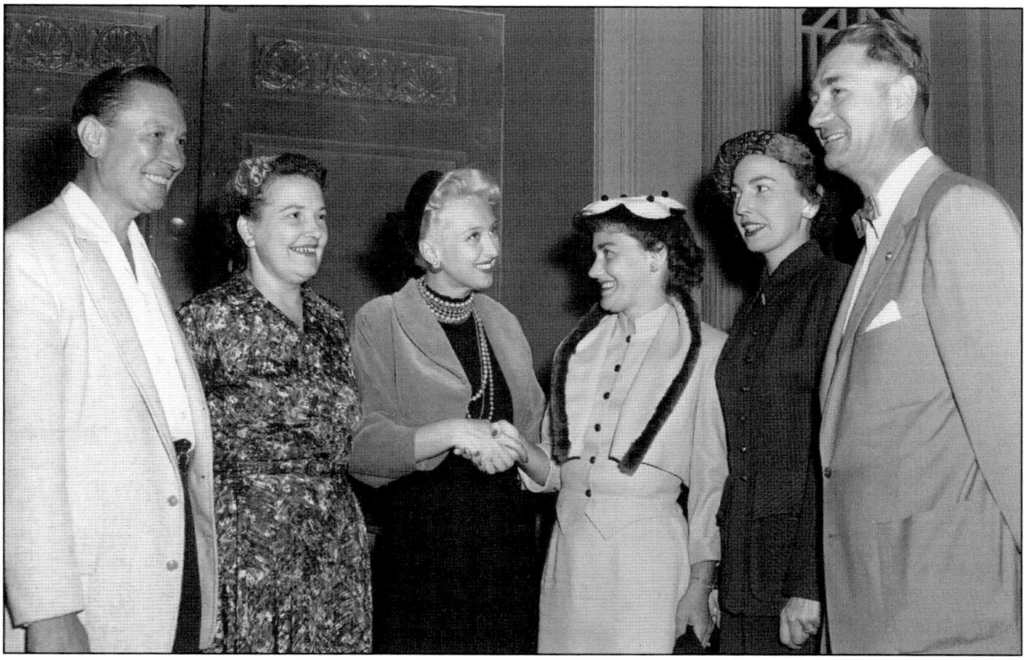

Local officials from the Mother's March of Dimes are shown receiving visiting celebrity Celeste Holm in 1953. From left to right are Niles mayor Frank Stanke, Sally Stanke, Celeste Holm, philanthropy committee member ? Johnson, Morton Grove Women's Club president Elizabeth Orphan, and Morton Grove postmaster Robert Lutz.

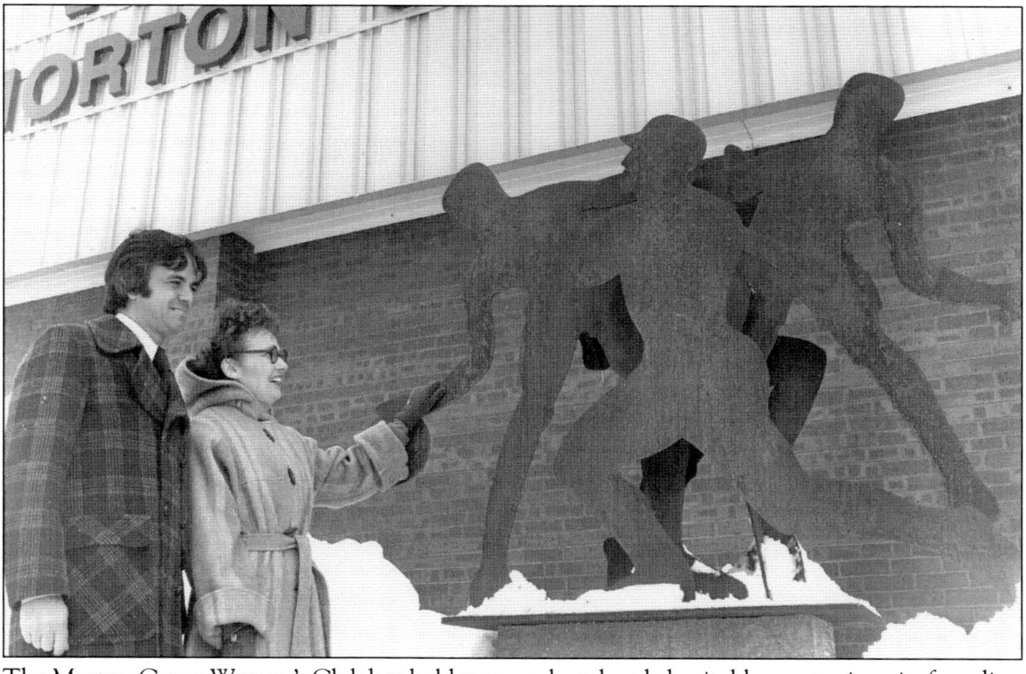

The Morton Grove Woman's Club has held many cultural and charitable events since its founding in 1953. The woman's club commissioned artist Joseph Burlini to create a sculpture for Prairie View Park and Community Center. Burlini and Morton Grove Woman's Club president Mary Jane Meyers are shown at the sculpture's dedication on January 28, 1979.

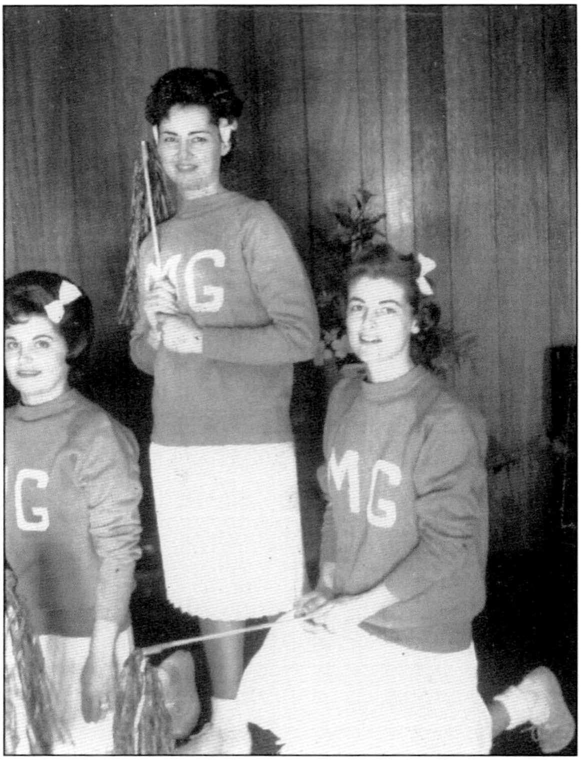

Members of the Morton Grove Woman's Club, in the *Our Fair Ladies* review during a regular meeting held at the Ed Roberts' Colonial Restaurant and Hotel in 1964, include (from left to right) Irehne Bencivenga, Rita Frese, and Dolores Wilander

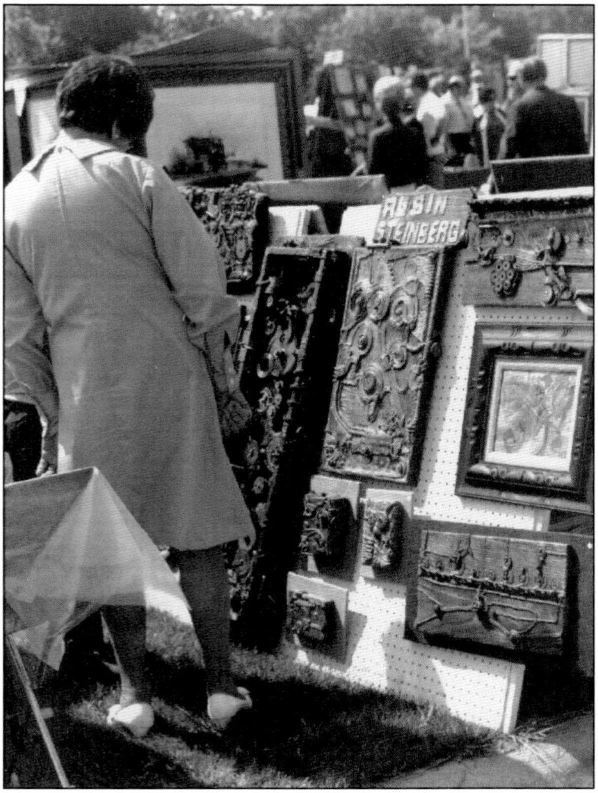

This photograph from the Morton Grove 75th Diamond Jubilee celebration on July 26, 1970, shows an art exhibit held by the Morton Grove Art Guild. The guild was formed in 1963 and held classes and guest lecturers through the Morton Grove Park District. The guild held many similar fairs, as well as exhibits in local businesses.

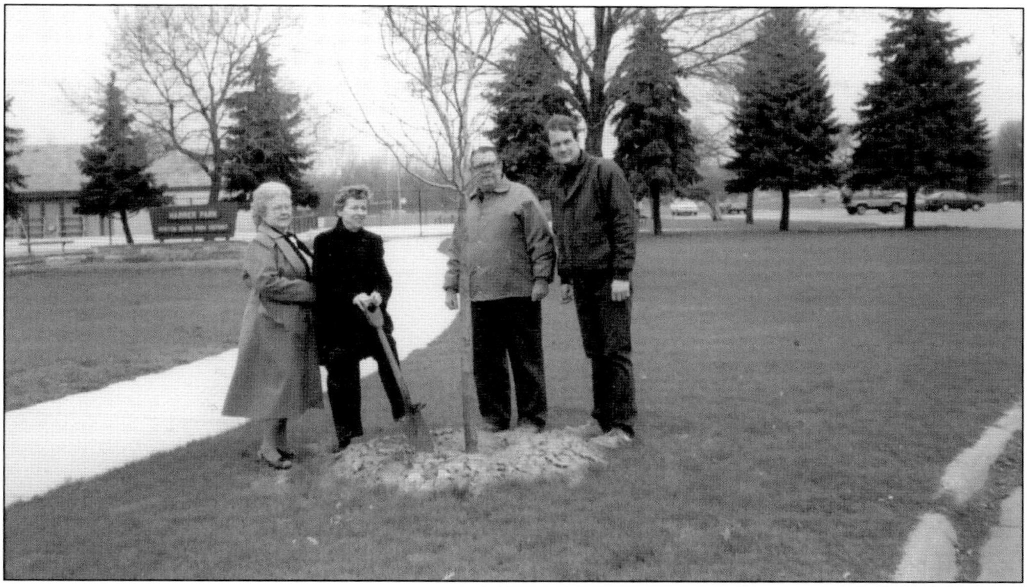

The Morton Grove Garden Club was organized in 1953. Here, officials celebrate the 20th anniversary of Earth Day by planting a tree in Harrer Park on April 19, 1990. From left to right are Myrna Taylor (Morton Grove Garden Club president), Hilde Sue Braske (Morton Grove Woman's Club president), Dan Scanlon (Morton Grove village trustee and later mayor), and Dan Staackmann (Morton Grove Park District president and future Morton Grove mayor).

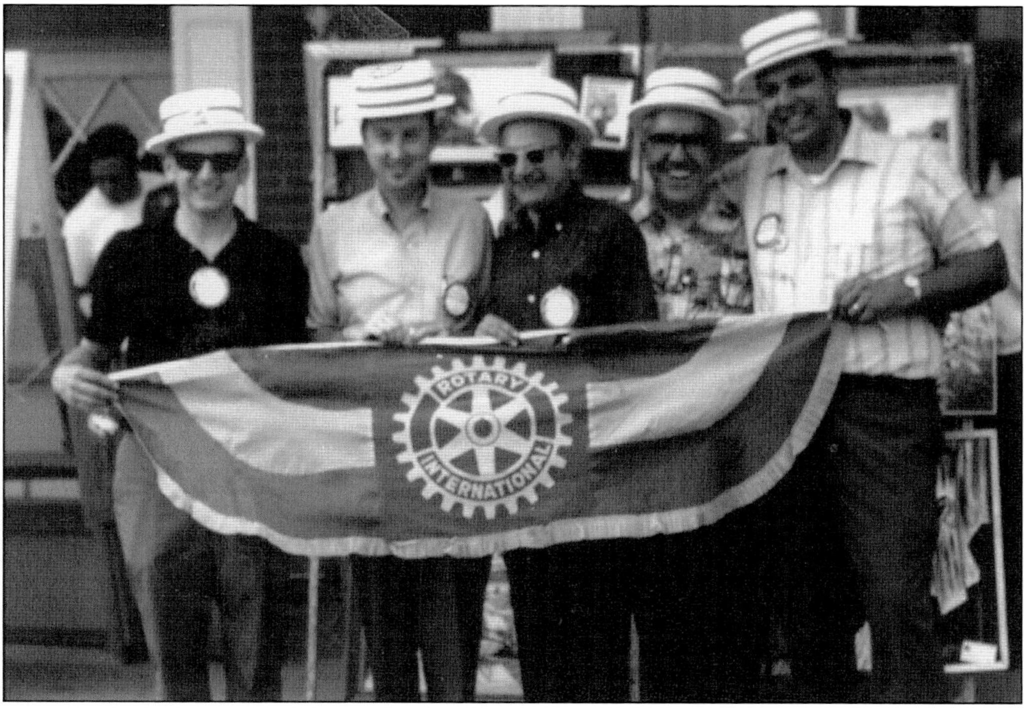

The Morton Grove Rotary Club was chartered in 1966 and sponsored by the Park Ridge unit. Members are pictured at the Rotary Club Art Fair at Golf View Plaza displaying a Rotary International banner, which stands for the four ideals to which members subscribe. Is it the truth? Is it fair to all concerned? Will it build goodwill and better friendships? Will it benefit all concerned?

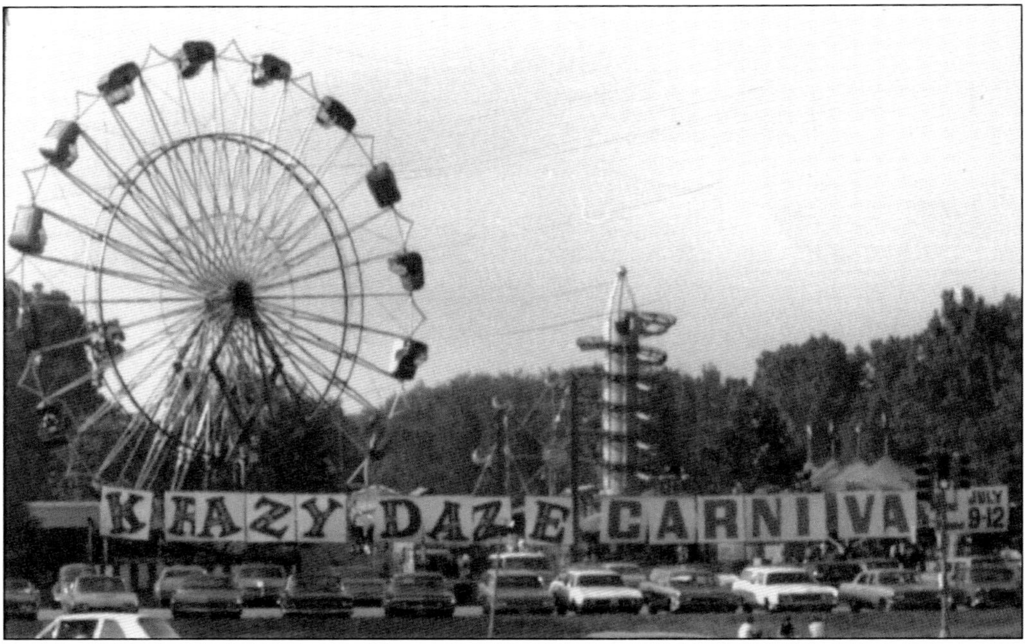

In 1947, the first annual carnival sponsored by American Legion Post No. 134 was held adjacent to their meeting location at Deckert's Picnic Grove on Lincoln Avenue. Beginning in 1950 and continuing through 1972, the annual Krazy Daze Carnival sponsored by the American Legion was held in Linne Woods. Other locations were utilized until 1979 when it was relocated to the post grounds at 6140 Dempster Street.

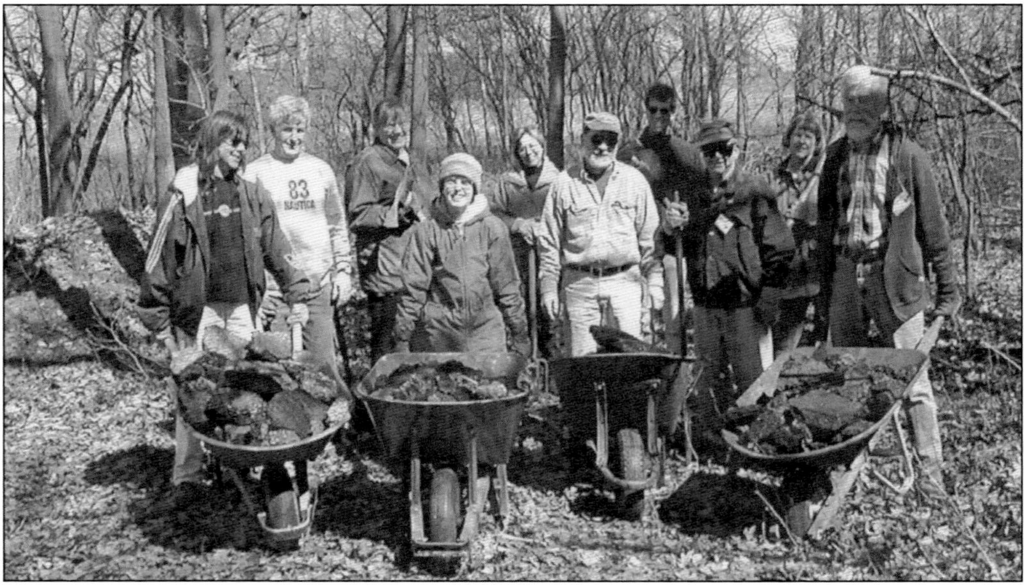

Friends of the Morton Grove Forest Preserve members, organized in 1997, are pictured removing asphalt dumped in Linne Woods. Together, with members of the North Branch Restoration Project, (pictured from left to right) Mary Busch, Rett Donnelly, Rebecca Parker, Marian Thill, Donna Clesen, John Thill, Eric Parker, Raymond Solal, Linda Masters, and Kent Fuller serve as advocates and stewards for the conservation and ecological restoration of local natural areas and waterways.

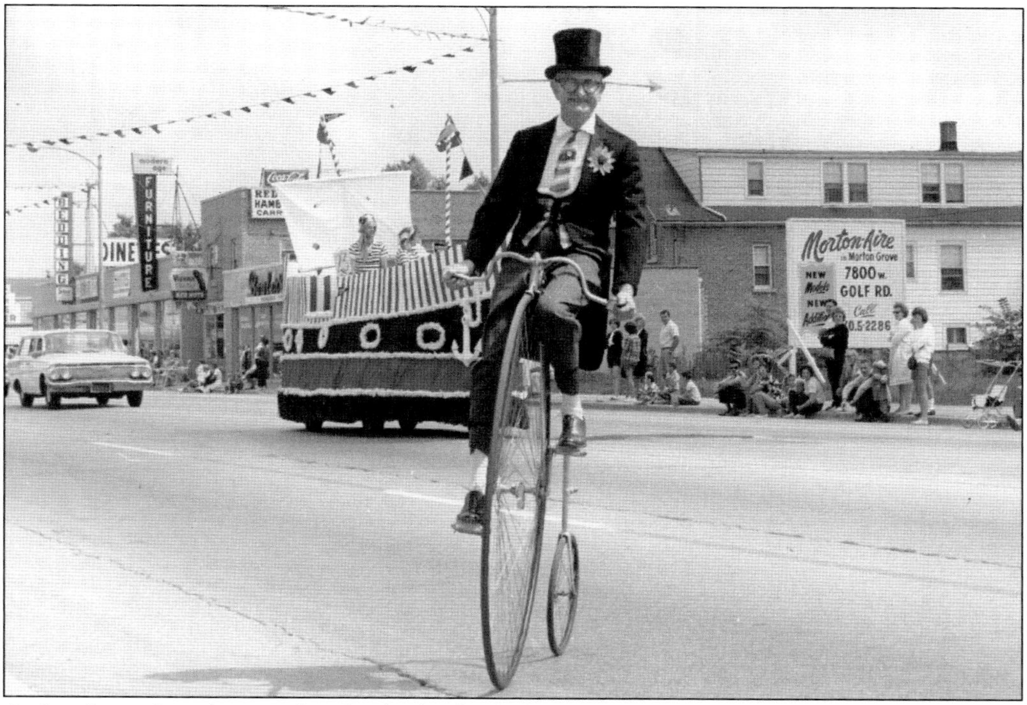

Arthur Loutsch is shown riding his high-wheeler bicycle at Mango Avenue and Dempster Street in a 1960s Morton Grove Days parade. Loutsch, a son of early Morton Grove butcher and civic leader Henry Loutsch, had an insurance office at 6120 Lincoln Avenue. He was active as a local historian and participated in civic organizations.

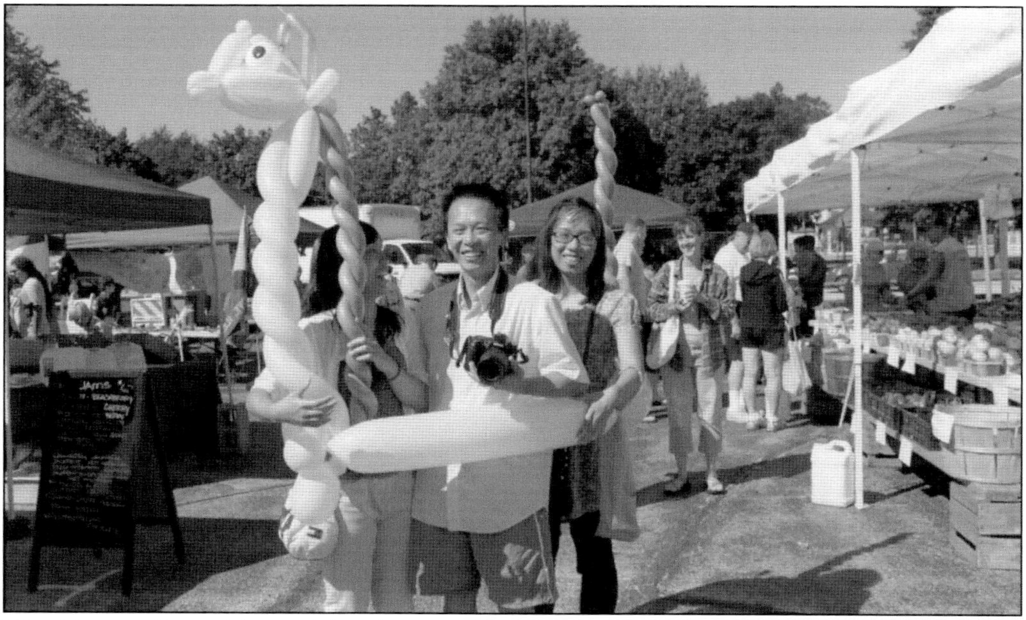

The Morton Grove Farmers' Market was formed in 2009 by a group of local residents. The volunteer-run market hosts many vendors and offers live music, community groups, and children's activities each week. A division of the chamber of commerce, the market serves as a popular place for locals to shop, eat, mingle, and build community.

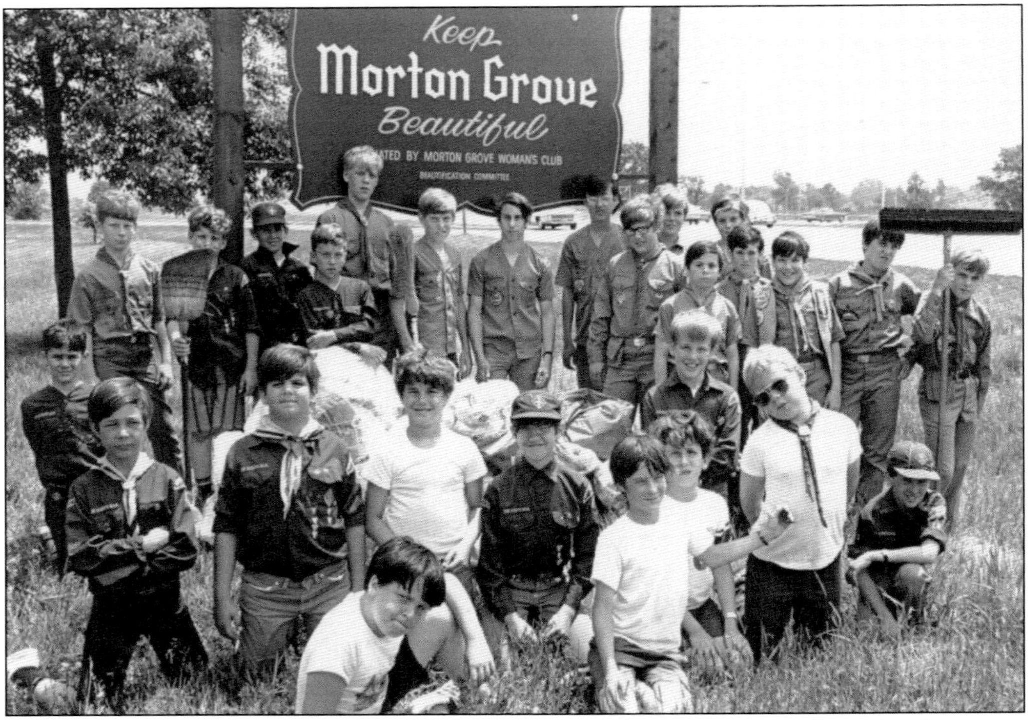

The Morton Grove Beautification Committee organized representatives from the American Legion, Woman's Club, Garden Club, Boy Scouts, and Girl Scouts to remove litter and care for plants in green spaces ranging from forest preserves, waterways and parks, to roadsides. In the 1970s, the committee held a litter cleanup day at the end of April each year. Boy Scouts are shown posing at Dempster Street near the entryway to Edens Expressway (I-94) with bags of trash they collected. Girl Scouts are pictured cleaning and planting flowers in a sidewalk planting space. They are near the Prairie Schooner along Waukegan Avenue north of Dempster Street.

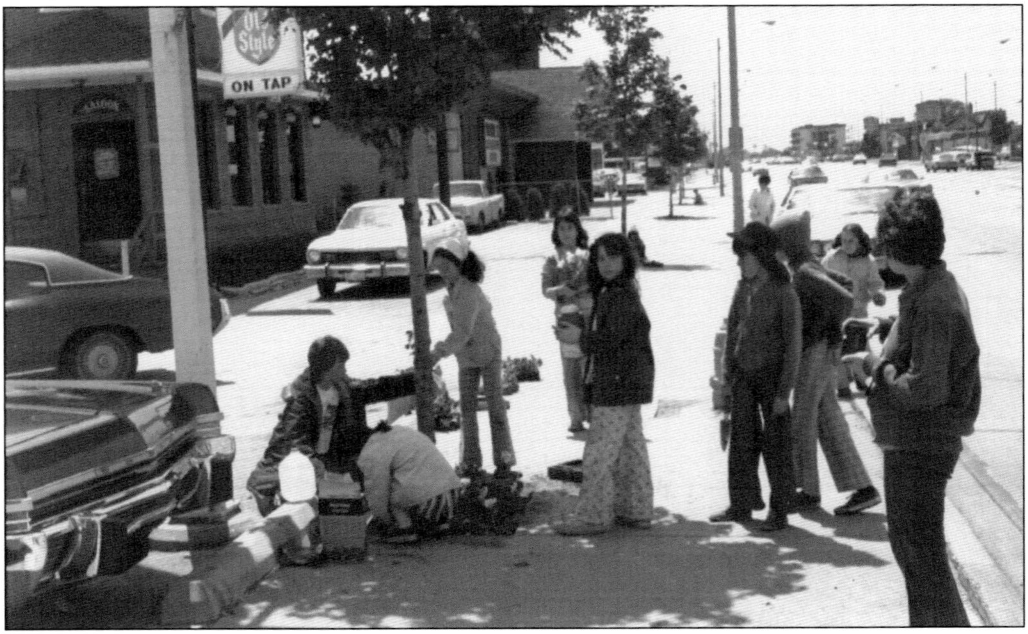

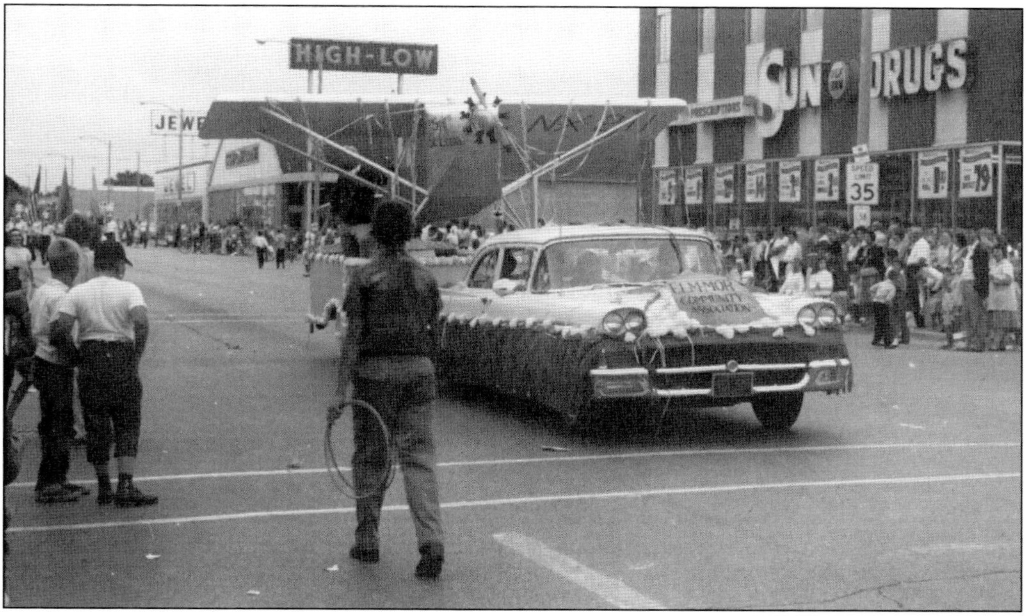

The Elm-Mor Community Association was founded in 1957. This homeowners association actively participated in many community events and hosted dances, holiday parties, and square dancing on Elm Street. Individual members served on village and park district boards, the junior chamber of commerce, civil defense, and local parent-teacher associations. Members decorated this parade float to honor the *Spirit of St. Louis* flight in 1927.

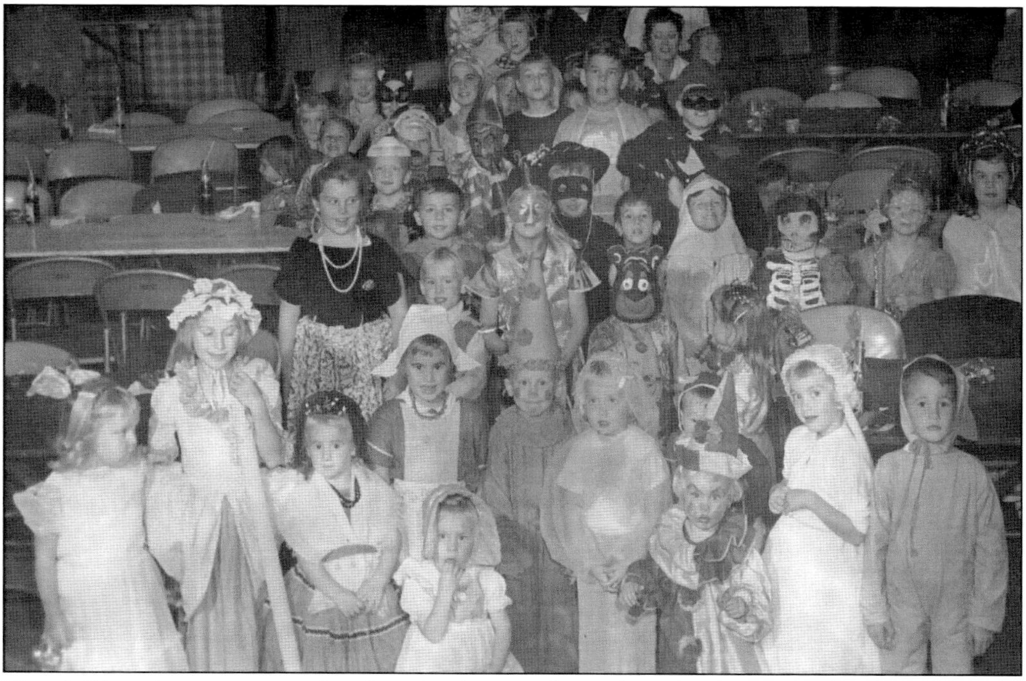

The children in costume are lined up for the grand march at the first annual Halloween party of the Elm-Mor Community Association, held at the Luxembourg Gardens on Lincoln Avenue in the 1960s. This photograph was taken by their publicity chair, Clyde W. White. Thirty-six homes make up this subdivision, located at Elm Street and Morton Avenue.

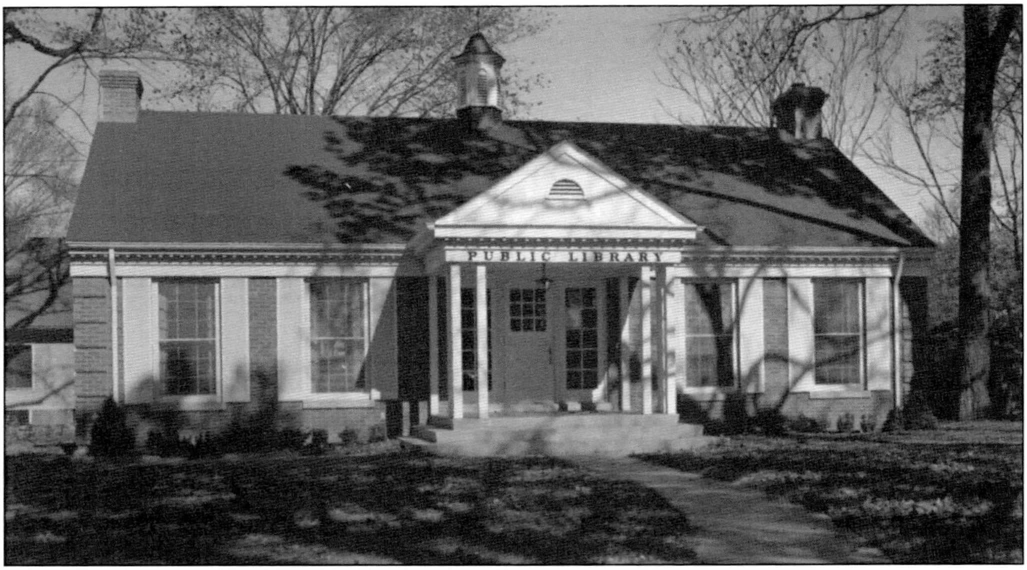

The Morton Grove Public Library was established in 1938 with Works Progress Administration (WPA) financial assistance. The library began as an all-volunteer organization, with 300 book donations collected in a barrel at Village Hall. Opening at 6100 Lincoln Avenue, a location that later became Tad's TV Service, the library moved to a storefront at 6244 Lincoln Avenue and once again to the second floor of the Village Hall on Callie Avenue before making its home at 6140 Lincoln Avenue in 1952 (pictured above).

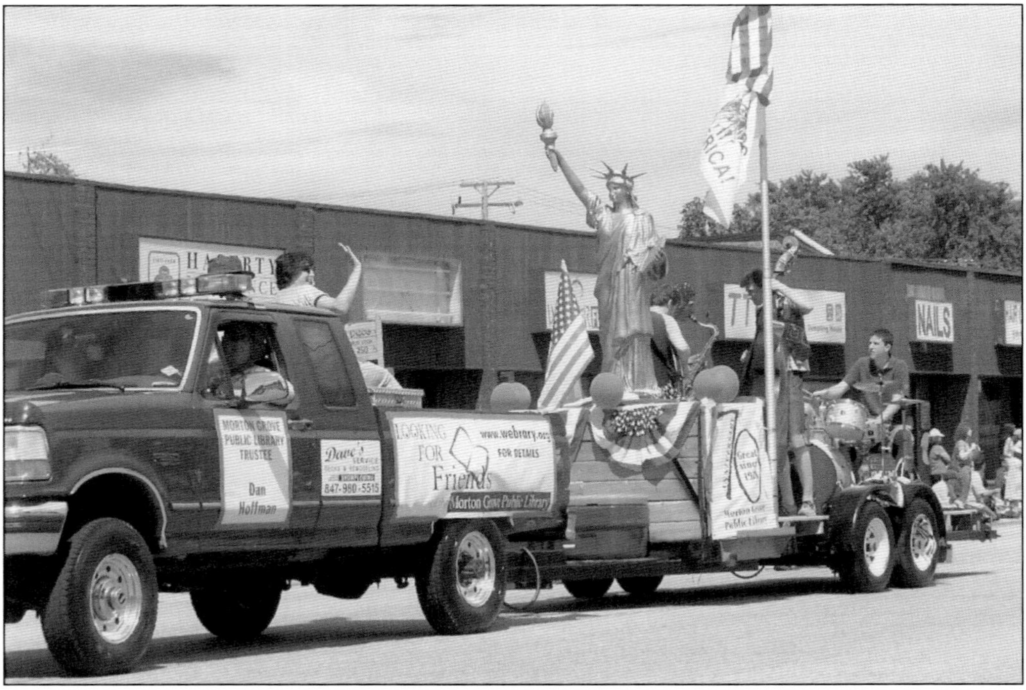

The Morton Grove Public Library float proceeding down Dempster Street celebrates its 70th anniversary with the motto, "Great since 1938," along with a banner for the Friends of the Morton Grove Public Library. Musicians entertain the crowds lined up along the parade route. (Courtesy of Brian Kabat Photography.)

Four

MAIN STREET MORTON GROVE

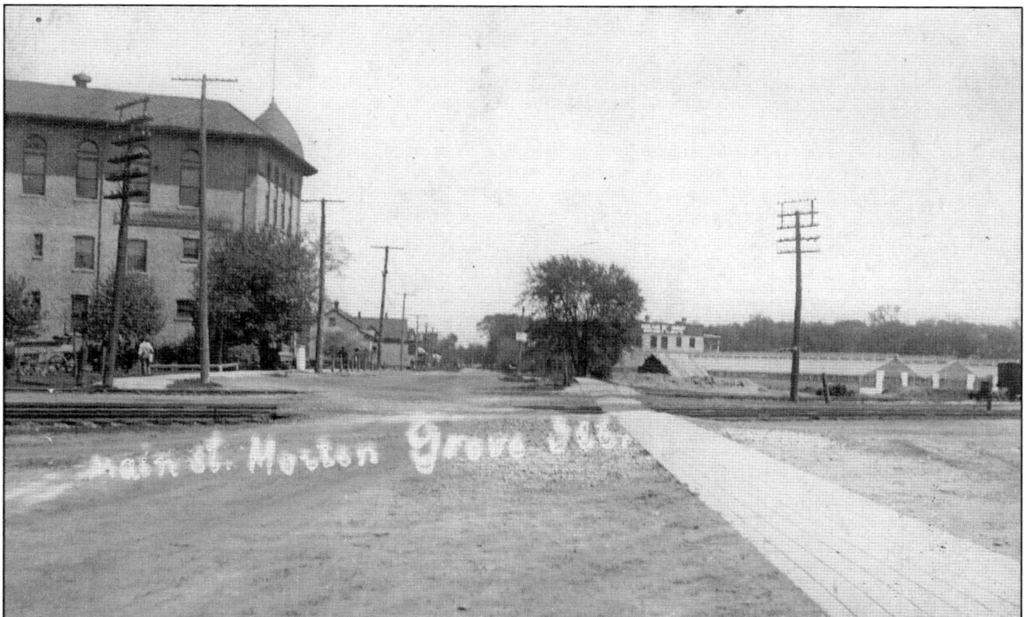

The dirt road with wooden sidewalks shown in this 1917 postcard was originally a Native American trail. It was called Miller's Mill Road, after the sawmill nearby on the North Branch of the Chicago River, during the time of the area's early European settlement. Called Main Street around the time of Morton Grove's founding as a village, it was later renamed Lincoln Avenue and remains so today.

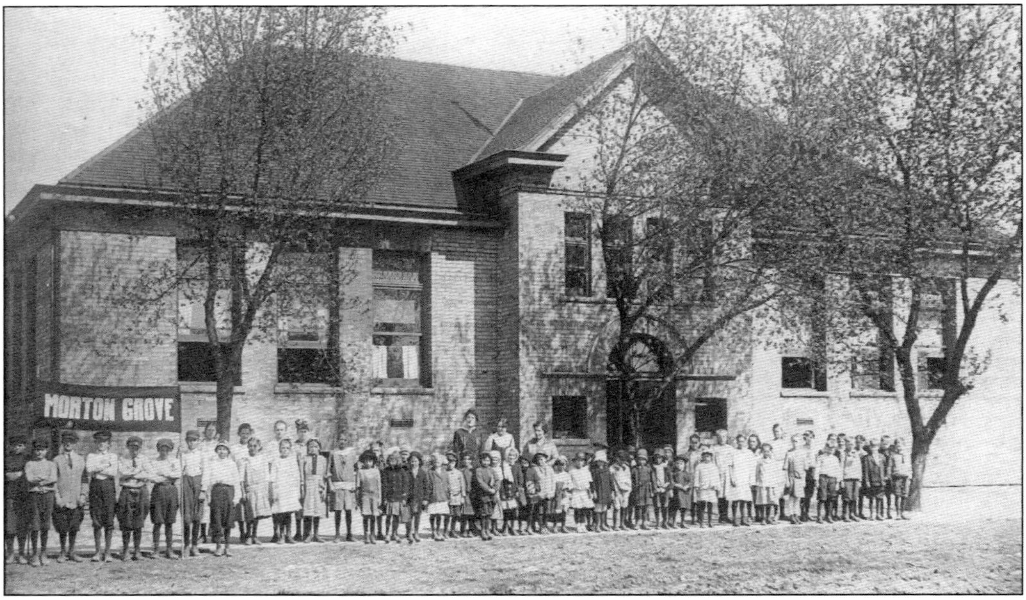

In 1897, a school board was elected, and one acre was purchased at School Street and Capulina Avenue to build Morton Grove School, later called Grove School. Only one room in the building was used as a classroom at that time. The facilities were altered and expanded in 1901, with more classrooms and indoor plumbing being added in 1923. A gymnasium was added in 1927, and specialized classrooms were created in 1936. A final expansion of the building happened in 1951. Park View School was built in 1953 as a response to Morton Grove's rapid growth. Grove School became Morton Grove Village Hall in 1978.

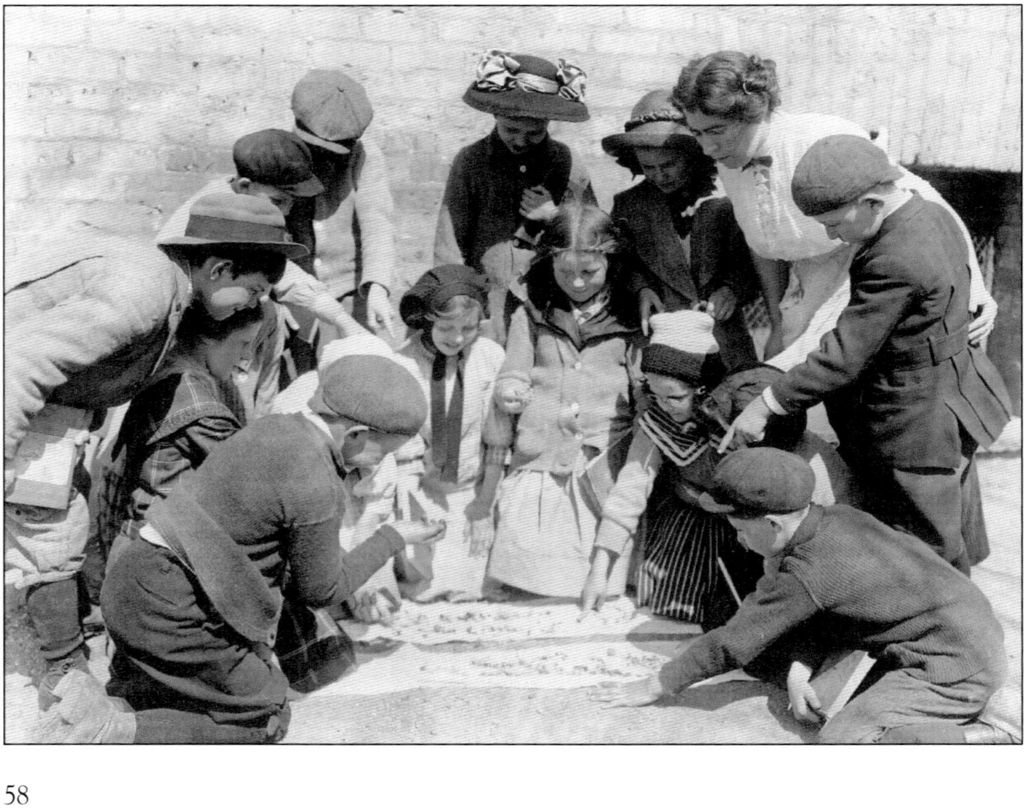

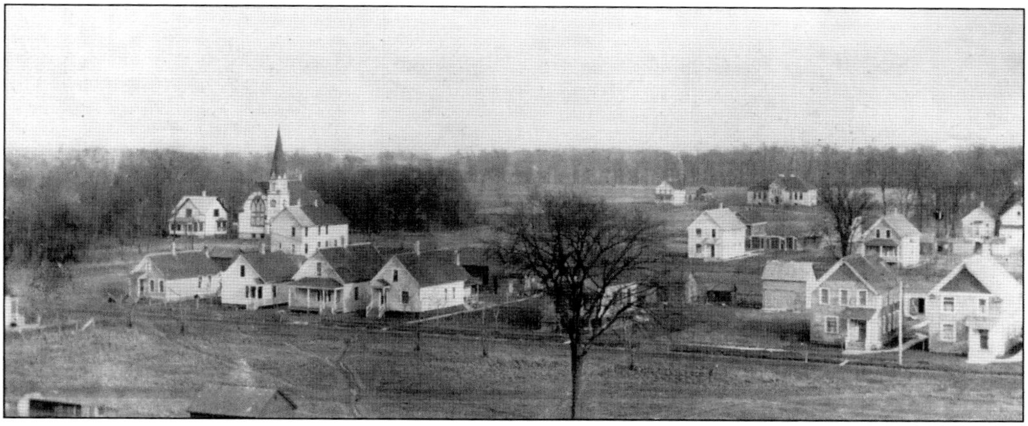

This view over Morton Grove was photographed by early resident William Washington Sonne in 1905 from the top of the three-story Dilg Building at the northwest corner of Lincoln and Ferris Avenues. Jerusalem Evangelical Lutheran Church can be seen on the far left, with houses along Callie Avenue in the foreground. Morton Grove School (now Village Hall) is in the background.

Jerusalem Evangelical Lutheran Church is Morton Grove's first church, organized as Die Evangelische Lutherische Jerusalem Gemeinde on July 5, 1902, and incorporated on December 21, 1903. The church building shown here was constructed in 1904 on land donated by real estate developer John C. Ahrensfeld. This building was clad in brick after a fire in 1929. The brick building stood until it was replaced in 1963.

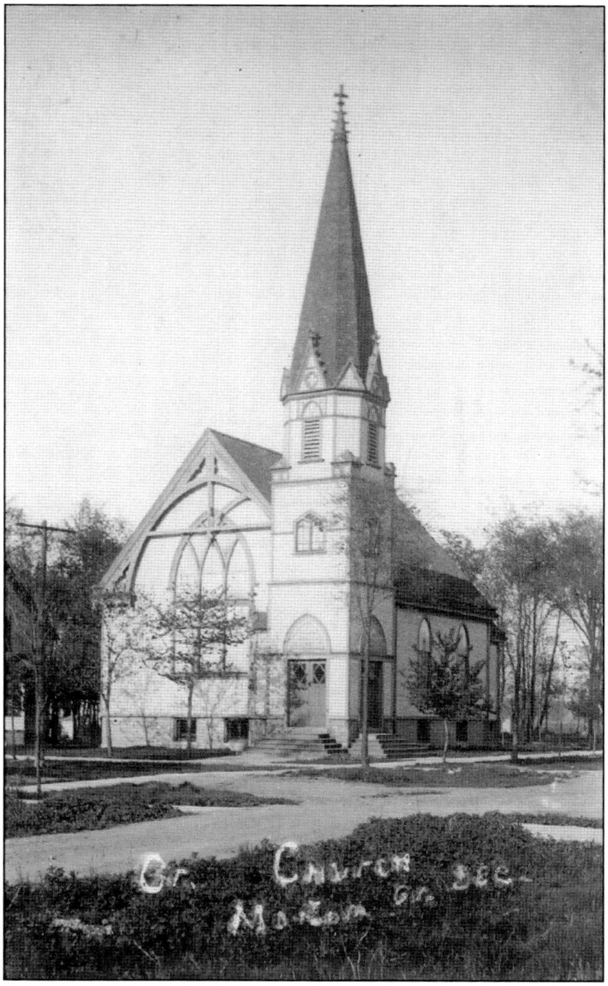

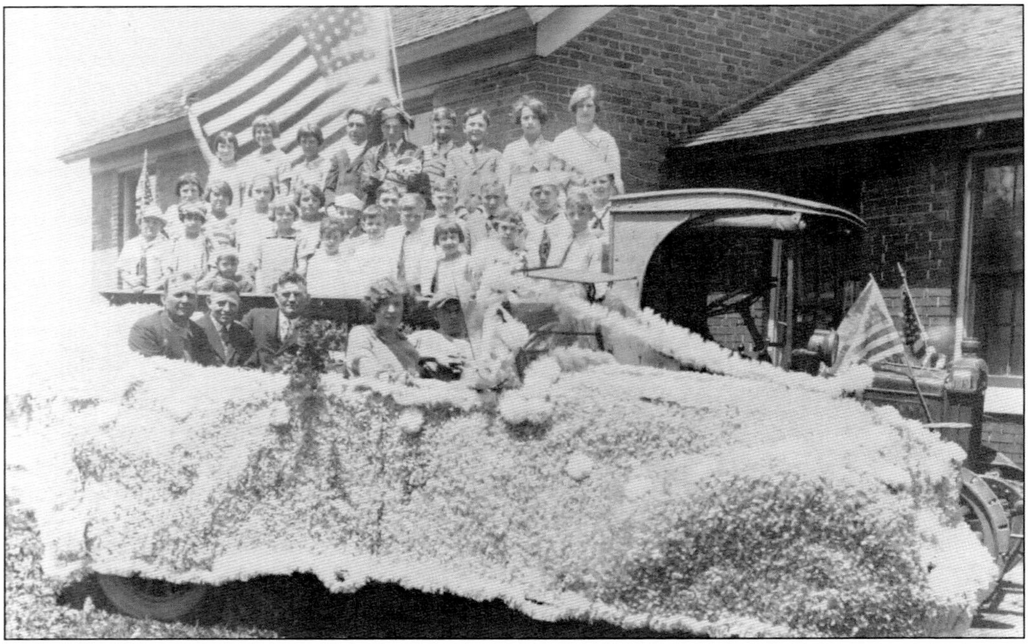

Golf Elementary school was constructed in 1927 on property located at 9401 Waukegan Road as a four-room school. It was expanded four times before being supplemented by Hynes Elementary School in 1957, and Golf Junior High School was added on the property in 1961. Here, students from Golf Elementary School surround a parade car with school board members.

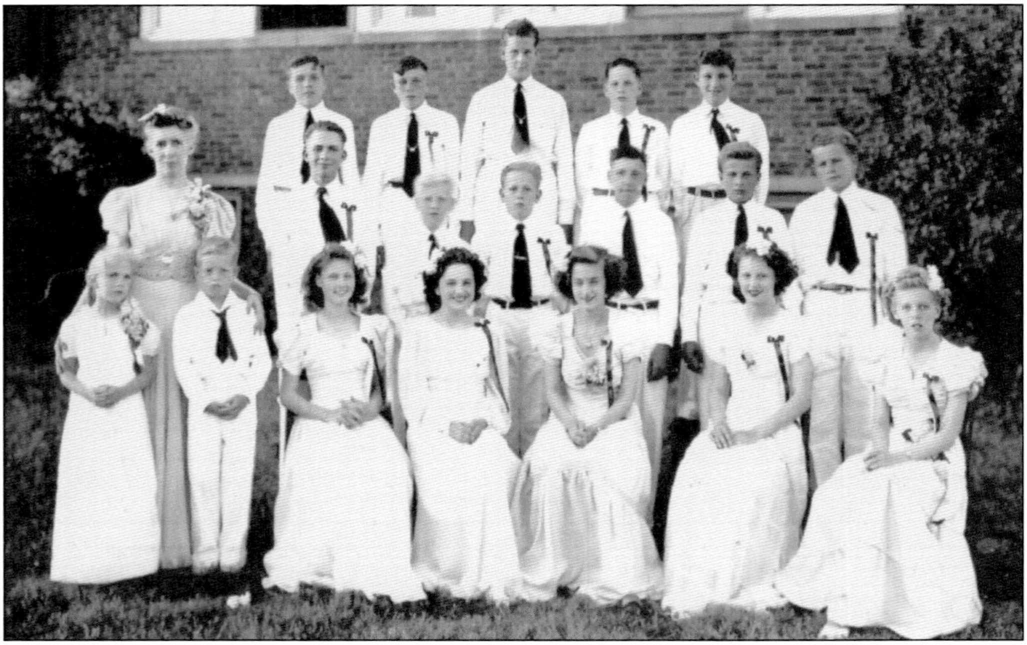

Irene Hynes Elementary School was built at 9000 Belleforte Avenue in 1957 as a result of population growth in Morton Grove. This school is named for former Golf School teacher and superintendent Irene Hynes. Hynes is pictured (left) with the 1943 eighth-grade graduating class. George Hoffman, the son of Urban and Helen (née Lochner) Hoffman, both of early settling families, is pictured in the third row on the right.

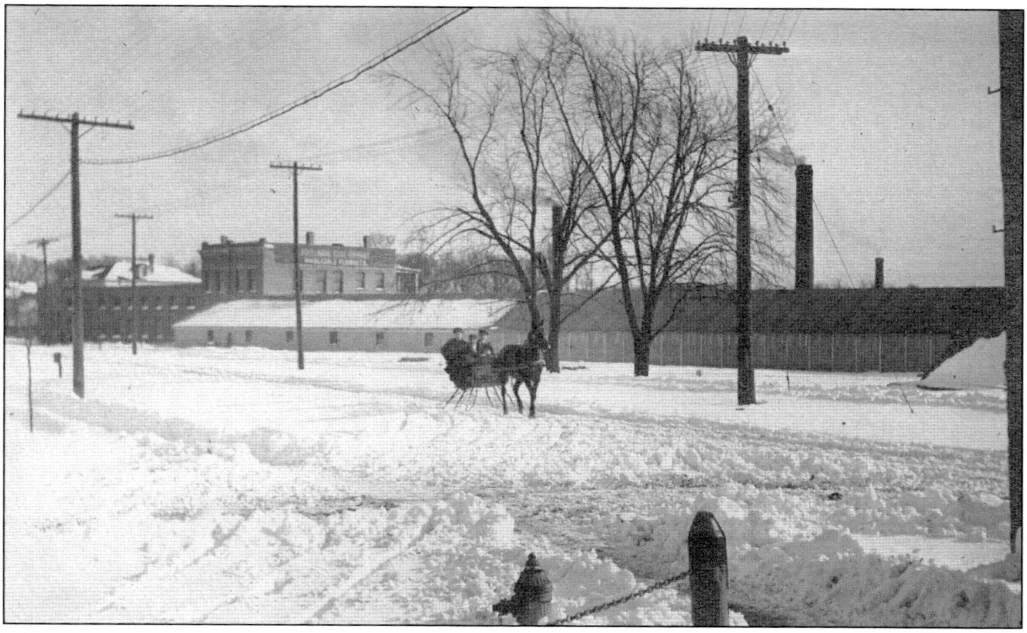

This postcard of four riders in a horse-drawn sleigh was sent to Arthur Loutsch in Tampa, Florida, from his brother Harry, postmarked on January 15, 1917. The "Poehlmann Brothers Company Wholesale Florists" sign can be seen in the background. This winter scene was photographed from the Dilg Building, located on the northwest corner of Ferris and Lincoln Avenues.

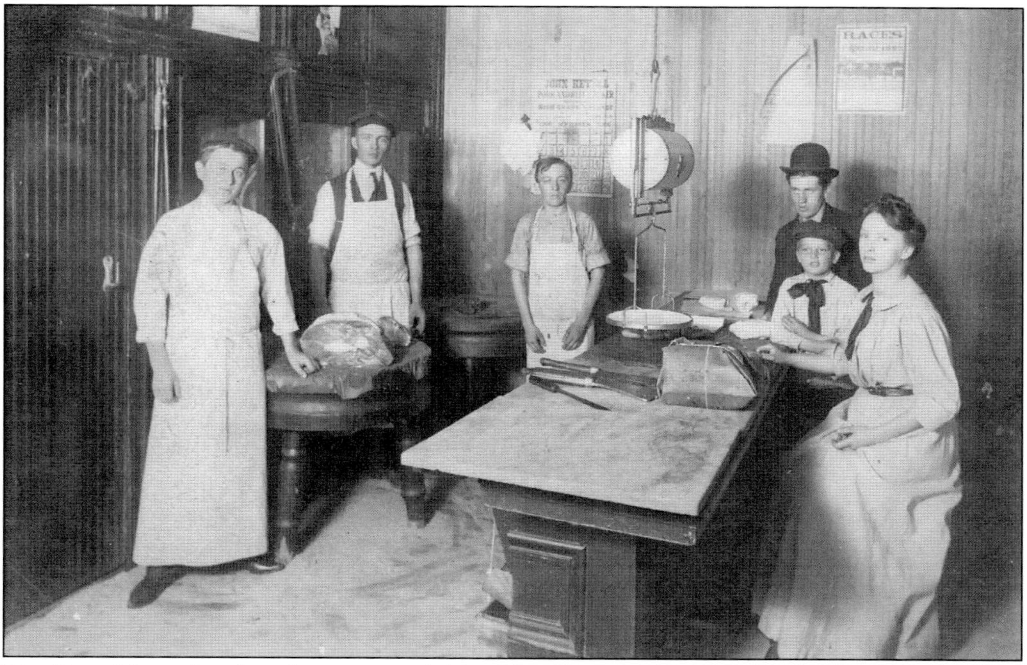

The Peter Haupt butcher shop is one of the earliest businesses along Lincoln Avenue. Pictured in 1906 from left to right are unidentified, Peter Haupt, Leo Haupt, two unidentified persons, and Clara Haupt. The eight orphaned Haupt children remained very close throughout their lives following the passing of their mother, Magdelena, from a flu epidemic in 1888, closely followed by their father, Nicholas, four years later.

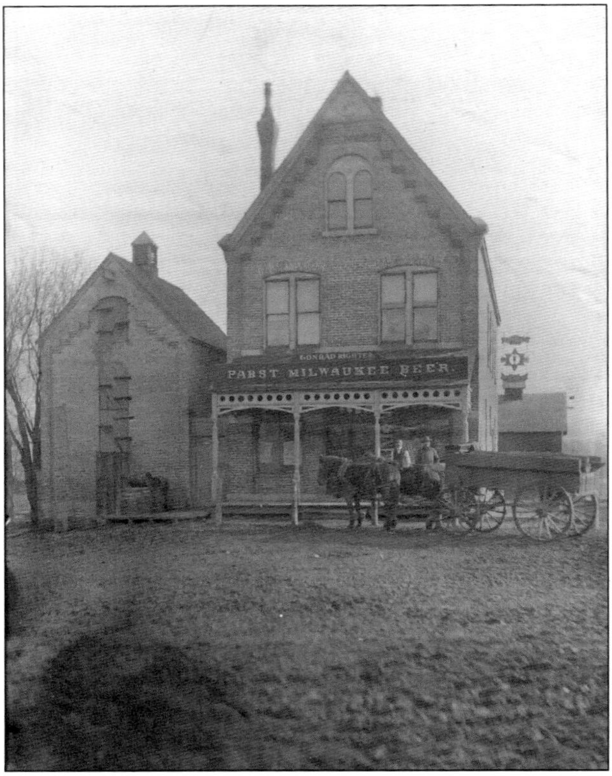

At left, local men are pictured with a horse and wagon in front of Conrad Richter's Bridge Inn in the late 1800s. Medard Lochner, a retired Civil War veteran, became the first postmaster at this site in 1874. Before the establishment of the Chicago, Milwaukee & St. Paul Railway in 1872, mail was delivered by stagecoach to Dutchman's Point along the old Northwestern plank road in what is Niles today. As in many similar establishments, the Bridge Inn sold supplies, food, and drinks. The icehouse to the left of the main building served as cold storage for various goods and also contained a supply of ice to be distributed to individual homes throughout the warm months. Below, men and a boy are shown on the steps of this building that was located at the southeast corner of Dempster Street and Lincoln Avenue.

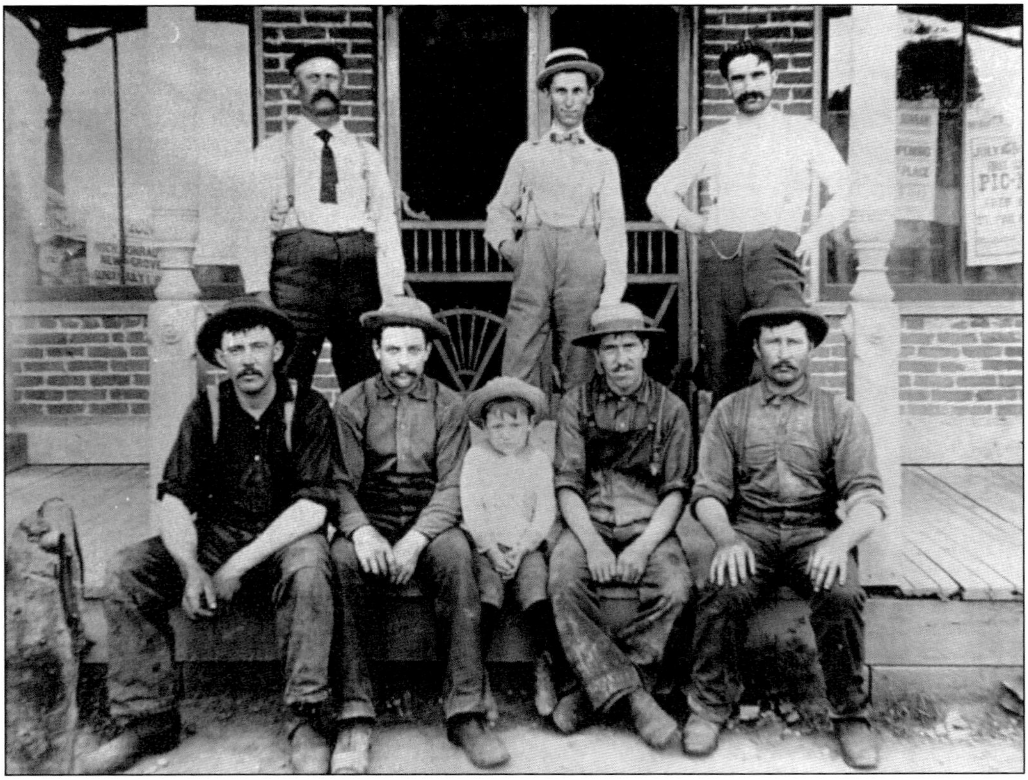

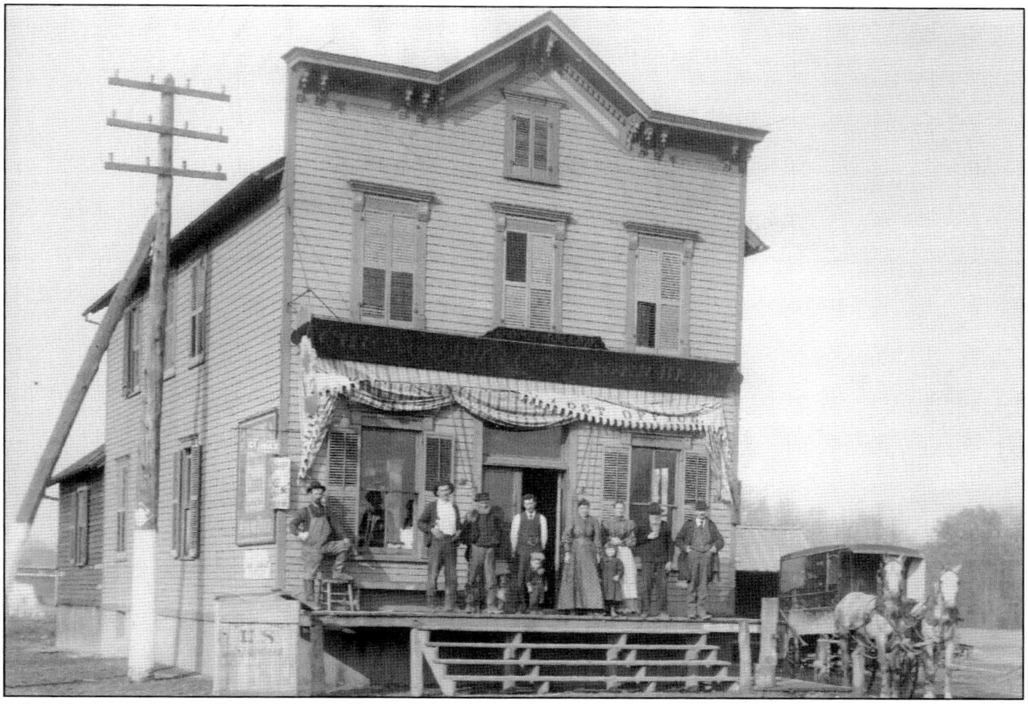

John Koller operated the Morton Grove Exchange at the northwest corner of Lincoln and Ferris Avenues. Koller married Dorothy Dilg and later sold the exchange to her brother Fred Dilg. The building was later moved and stands today at the corner of Ferris and Capulina Avenues.

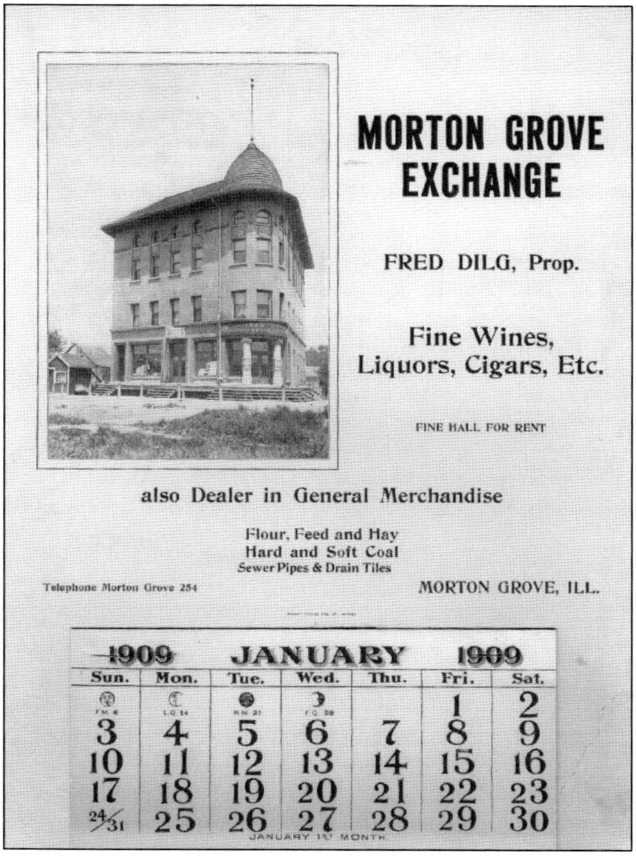

Despite objections from family members who operated a tavern and general store nearby, Fred Dilg expanded his Morton Grove Exchange to include a general store, tavern, and post office. In 1904, he constructed a new three-story brick building at Lincoln and Ferris Avenues. Dilg died in 1909 at the age of 46. Some blamed his death on the stress caused by rapidly expanding his business.

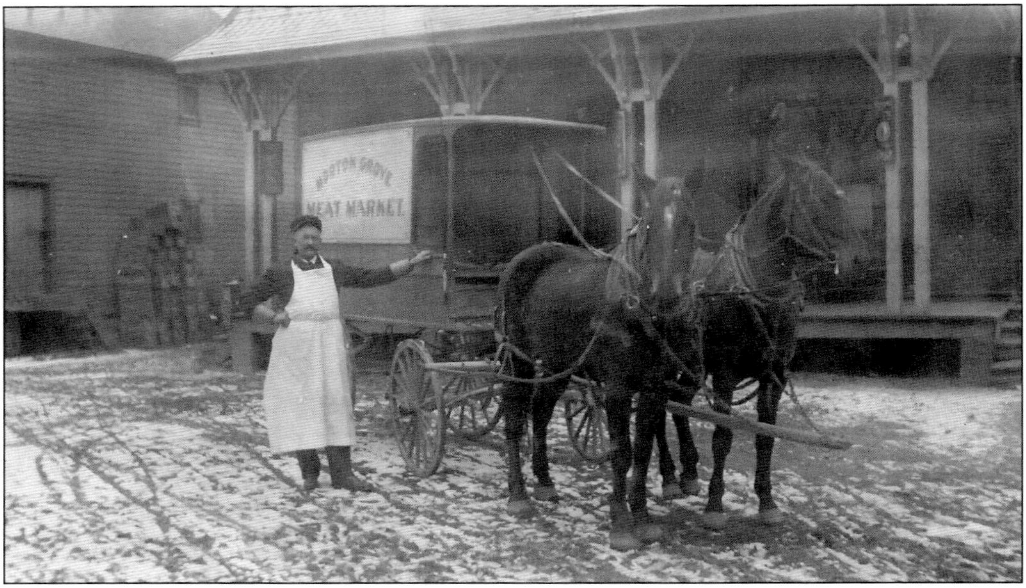

Henry and Catherine Loutsch moved to Morton Grove from Niles Center in 1907 with their four sons. The four Loutsch brothers—Harry, John, Arthur and George—worked with their father during the 55 years the Loutsch family ran the meat market and general store. Here, Henry Loutsch is pictured in 1915 with his meat wagon in front of the Dilg General Store on Waukegan Road.

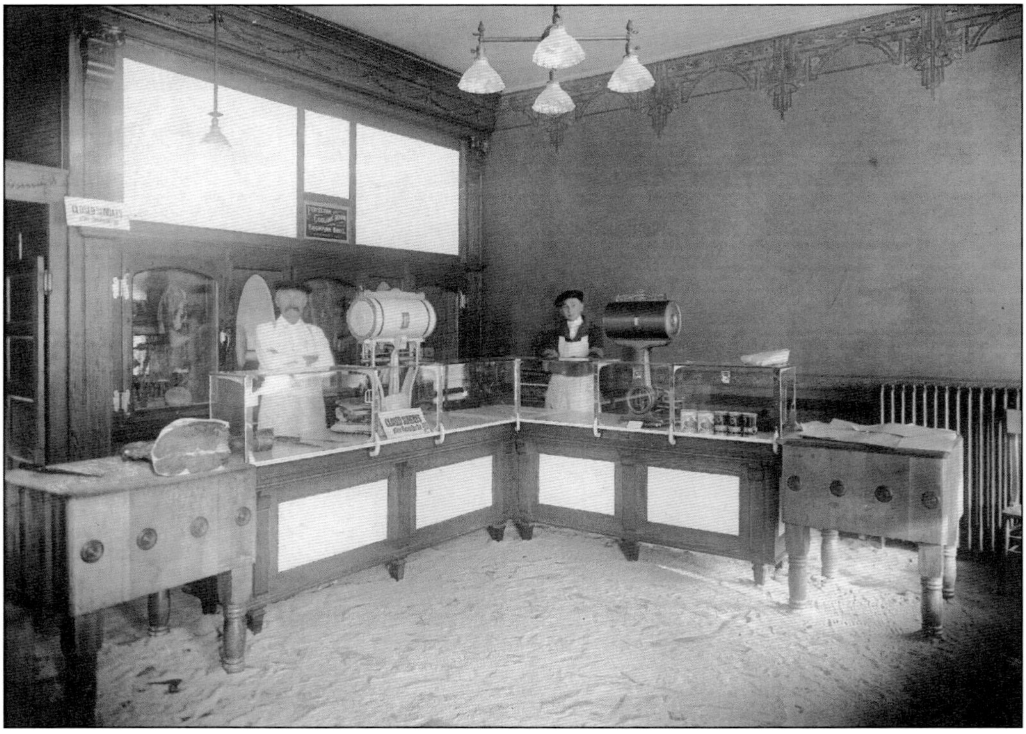

Henry Loutsch (left) and his son George Loutsch are pictured inside the Loutsch butcher shop. The walk-in cooler, with windows to display and offer access to products, as well as sawdust-covered floors, show the technology used by butchers in the early 1910s. George Loutsch was later mayor of Morton Grove in 1927, but he died in office the following year.

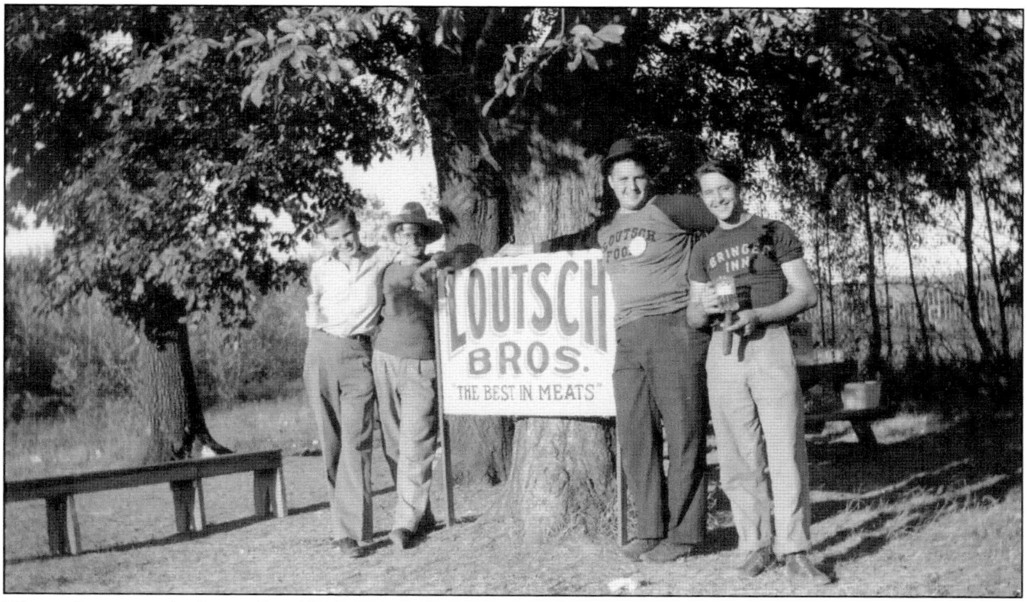

This photograph from the 1939 Loutsch Bros. Foods picnic shows some of the employees who took part in competitions such as tug-of-war, egg carry, races, throwing, and softball. About 30 employees and former employees participated. The strong sense of community involvement among Main Street businesses in Morton Grove has always been important to the village's identity.

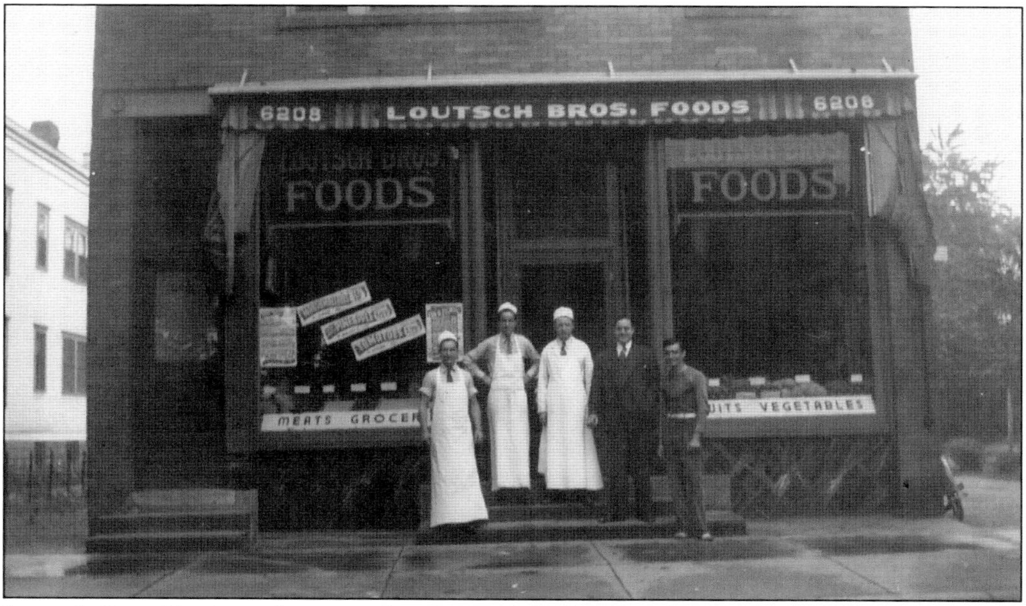

Loutsch Bros. Foods workers stand in front of the butcher shop at 6208 Lincoln Avenue in 1939. Pictured from left to right are Robert Haupt, Peter Gebel, Ed Schiller, Harry Loutsch, and Arthur Loutsch. This building still stands, although somewhat modified, and is now used as office space.

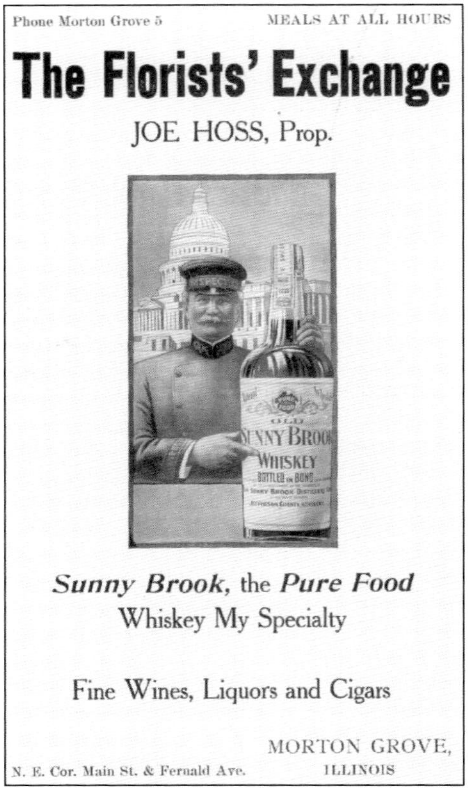

Jacob Hoss settled in Niles Centre after coming to America in 1870 from Nilder Kor, Luxembourgh. His son Joseph purchased property on the northeast and northwest corners of Lincoln and Fernald Avenues. The Florists' Exchange, operated by Joseph, was originally the Peter Haupt butcher shop. The Hoss family also ran a livery service, restaurant, and boardinghouse on these sites. Richard P. Hohs, a local historian and the village president from 1988 to 1996, is a descendant of the Hoss family, though the spelling of the family name deviated through time.

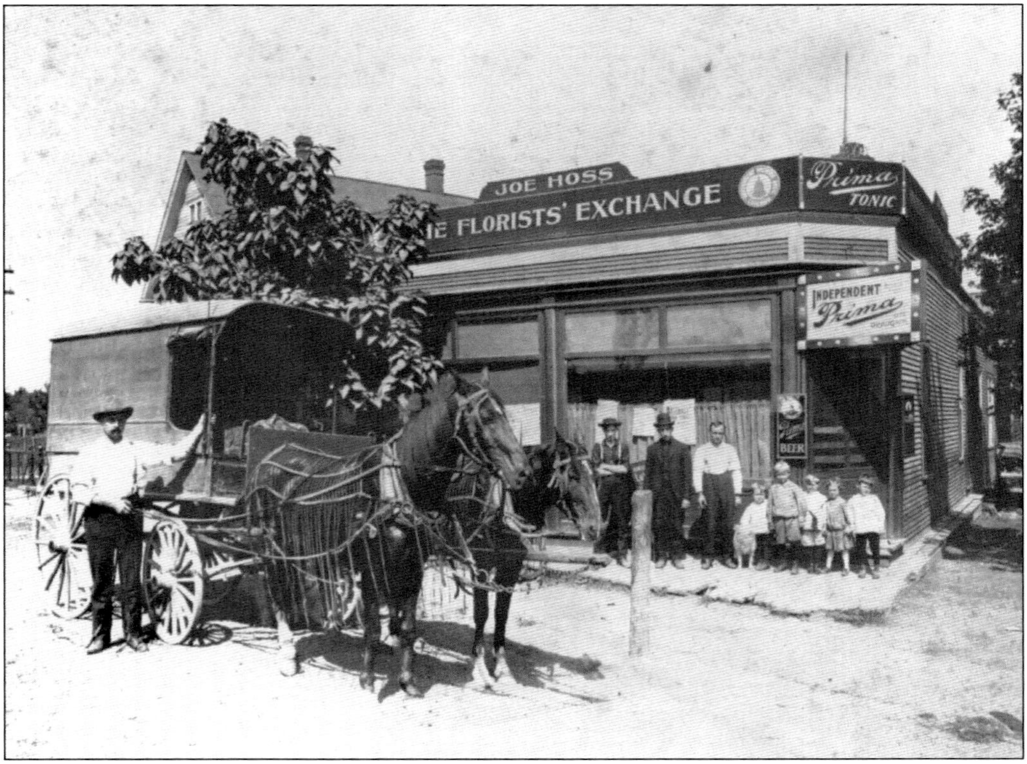

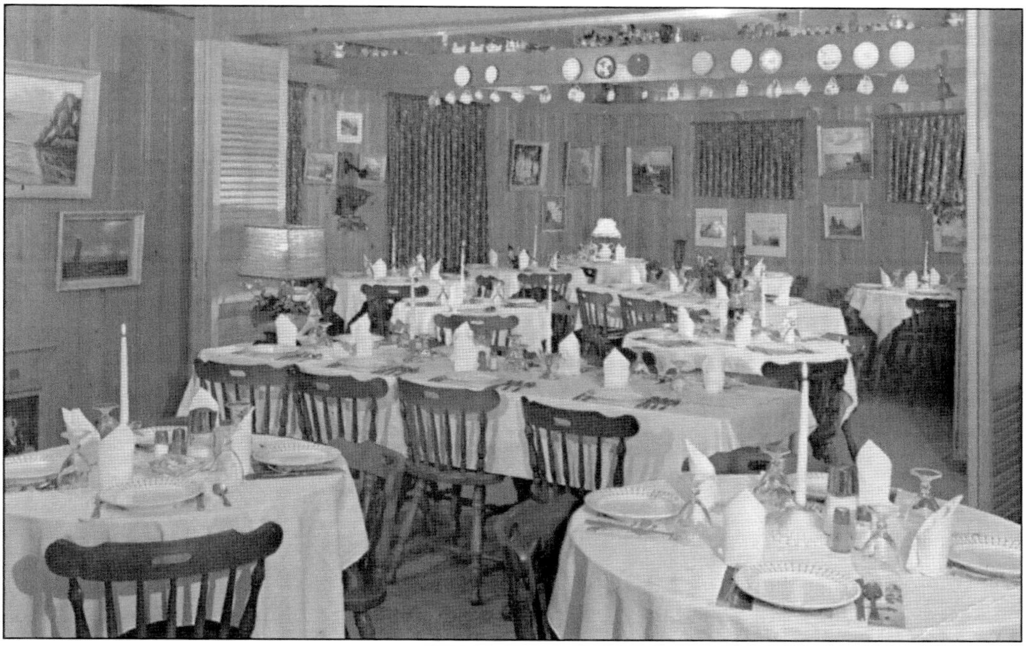

This is a historical postcard of the Golden Dinner Bell, located at 8520 Fernald Avenue. Many businesses have occupied this small wood-framed building. Phillipy's Chocolate Shop is documented in 1929. Kurt Burger's Chocolate Shoppe operated here in 1939, and Scott's Coffee Shoppe opened in 1946, doing business for 11 years. The Golden Dinner Bell restaurant served the community following Scott's with Pequod's Pizza currently operating at this location for over three decades.

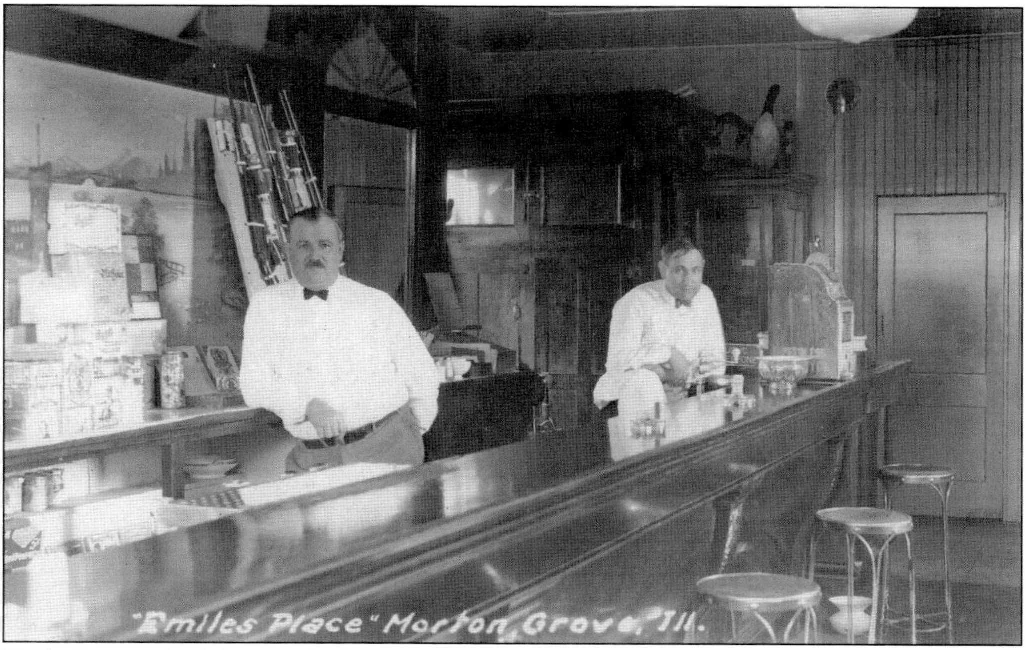

Emile Bringer (right) turned a former blacksmith's shop into his tavern, Emile's Place, at 8541 Ferris Avenue. This same business was later called the Bringer Inn, both before and after a move to the corner of Lincoln and Fernald Avenues. The Bringer Inn remains at that location. The Ferris Avenue location is now Burt's Place Pizza.

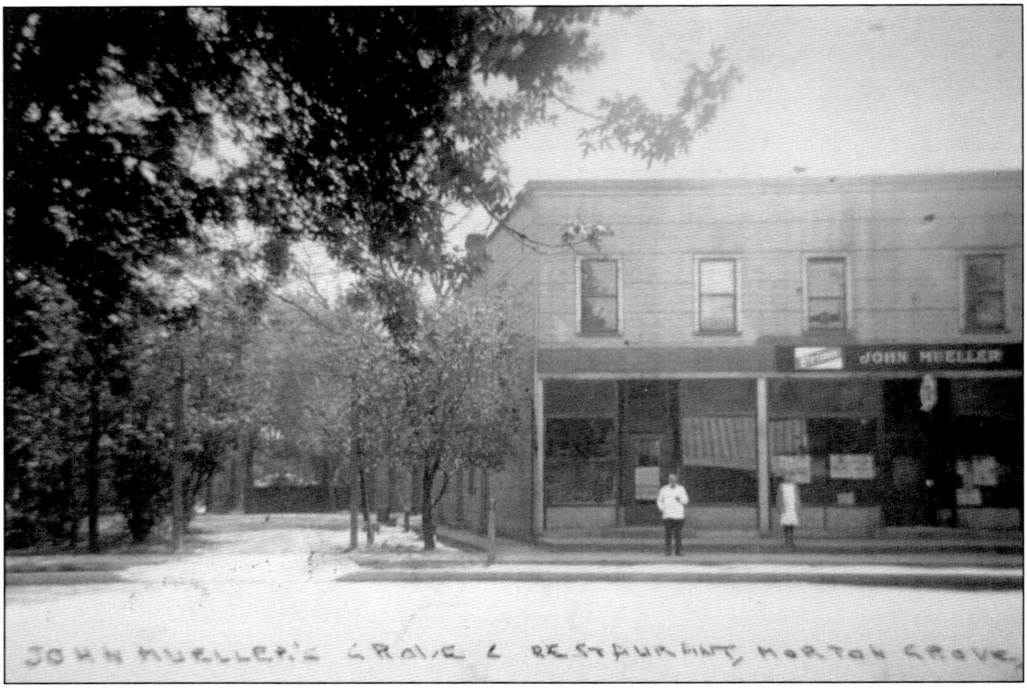

This photograph of the John Mueller picnic grove and dance hall taken in the 1920s shows the entrance to the expansive grounds used for picnics and festivals through the years at 6209 Lincoln Avenue. The group below is pictured inside John Mueller's hall during the holiday season. This land was owned by the Lochner family and sold to A. Frank Henning for the Bethesda German American Convalescence Home in 1894. John Gruber's printing office operated at this location in 1900 for 14 years. In 1914, Herman Ketz became the proprietor of the Edelweiss Buffet, hotel, and picnic grove. After Mueller's, Otto Deckert is known to have operated Deckert's Hall in the 1940s through the early 1950s, with the Luxembourg Gardens becoming a popular spot for food and festivals from the mid-1950s throughout the 1960s.

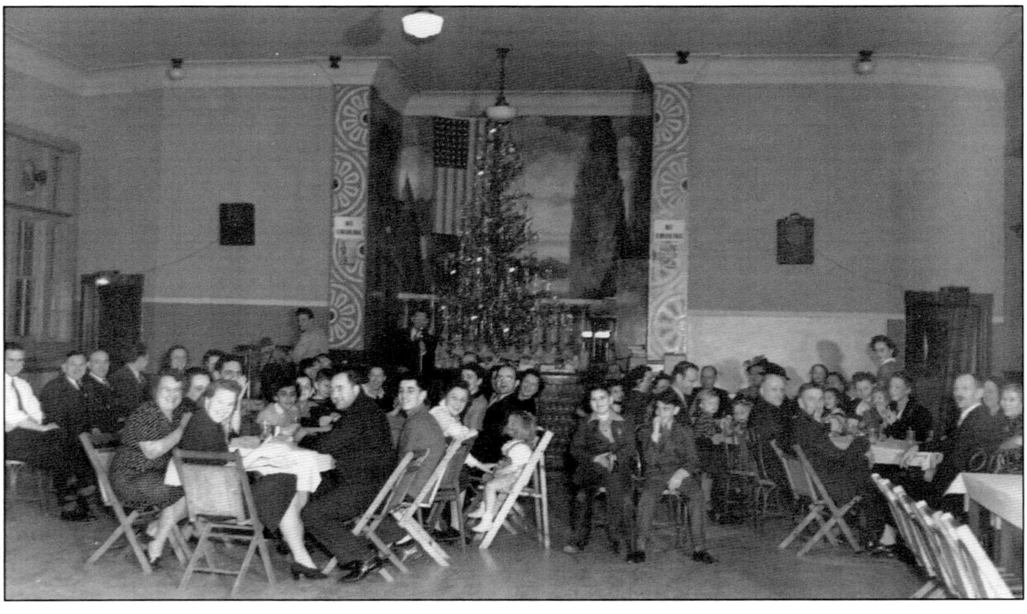

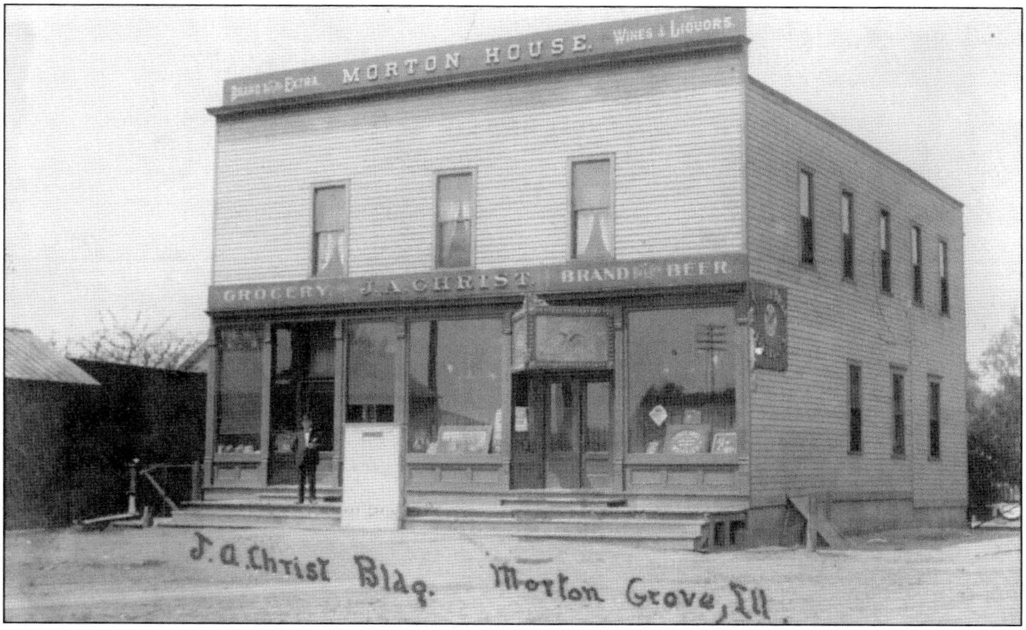

The Morton House has been a landmark from early settlement until the demolition of Hoffman's Morton House in 1999. Many proprietors have run general stores, taverns, restaurants, halls, and boardinghouses at this site. Frank Navroth and Daniel Lumpp preceded J.A. Christ, who ran the grocery and tavern pictured in this 1907 postcard. Ed Niemann, Robert Lotz, Emil Dohl, and Ken and Howard Hoffman were among the business owners who continued to provide services at this location on the southwest corner of Lehigh and Lincoln Avenues under the Morton House name. Fires and renovations changed the face of this business many times, as seen in the photograph of the Stromberg construction workers in front of the newly remodeled Dohl's Morton House in 1955 following a fire.

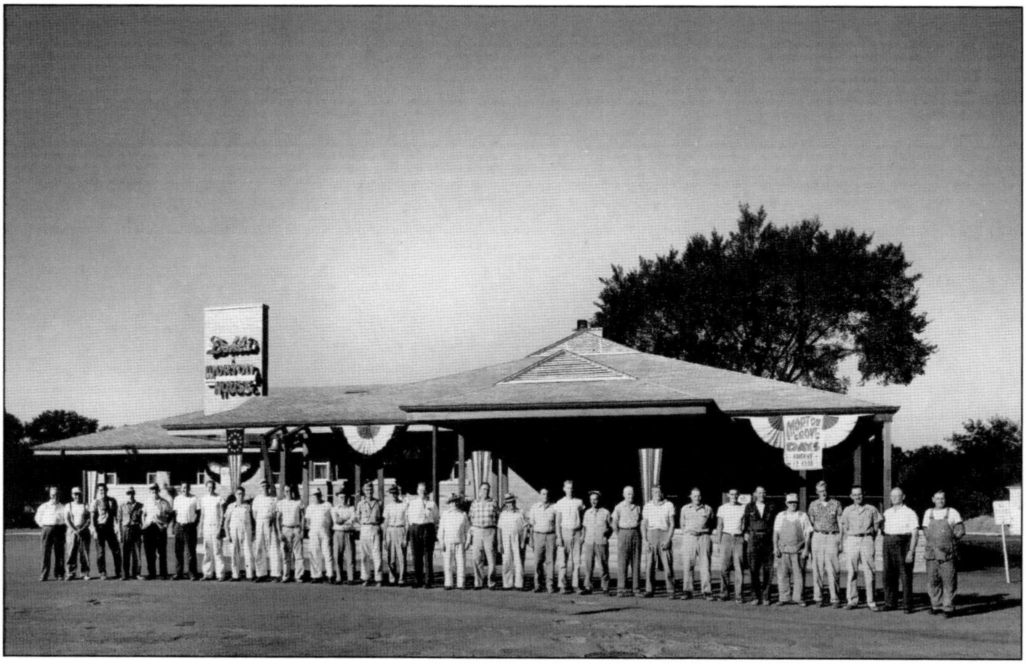

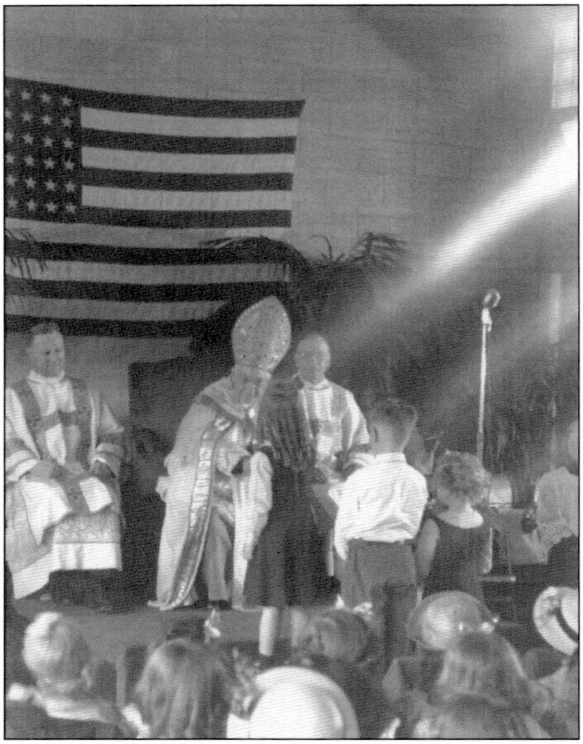

Morton Grove's Catholic community first held its own services in a former saloon at Lincoln and Georgiana Avenues in 1919. Fr. Martin Schmidt, who was also pastor at Our Lady of Perpetual Help in Glenview at the time, organized the new St. Martha Catholic Church. Later, they constructed their own building. This photograph shows Cardinal Stritch (center) during the 1951 dedication of St. Martha School, with Father Wilhelmi (far right).

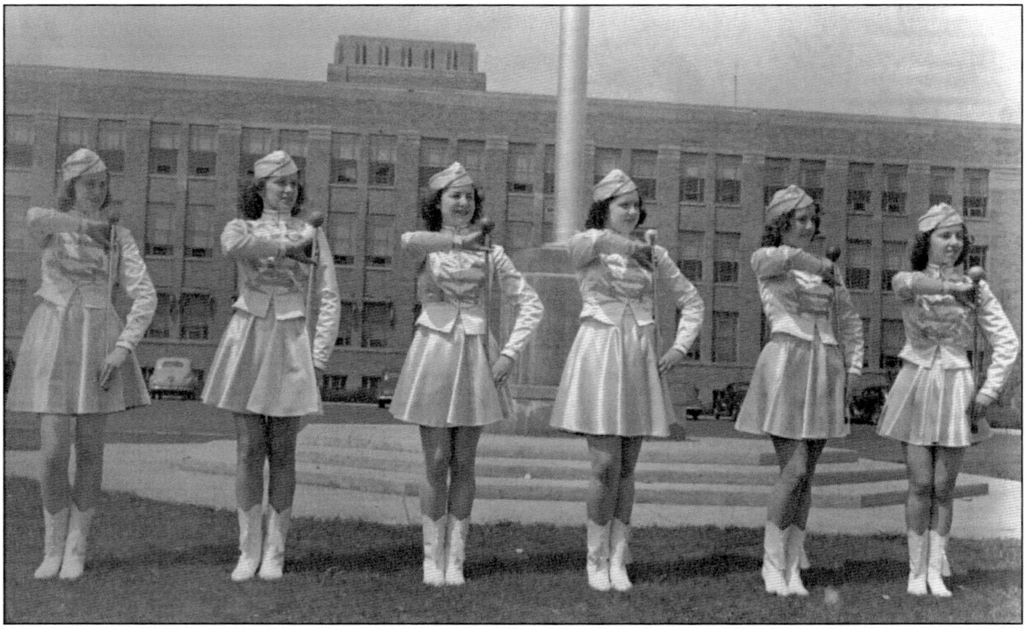

Interest in a township high school came about in 1914 and failed to gain support again in 1928. The creation of Lincoln High School, renamed Niles Centre High School in 1932, had an enrollment of 49. By 1936, the Niles Township High School District was created, serving Morton Grove, Niles Centre, Lincolnwood, Golf, and Niles. Annaliese Nachbauer, attending from 1941 to 1944, is pictured second from the left with the "Nilehi" corps of baton twirling majorettes. (Courtesy of the Neumann and Anzelone family.)

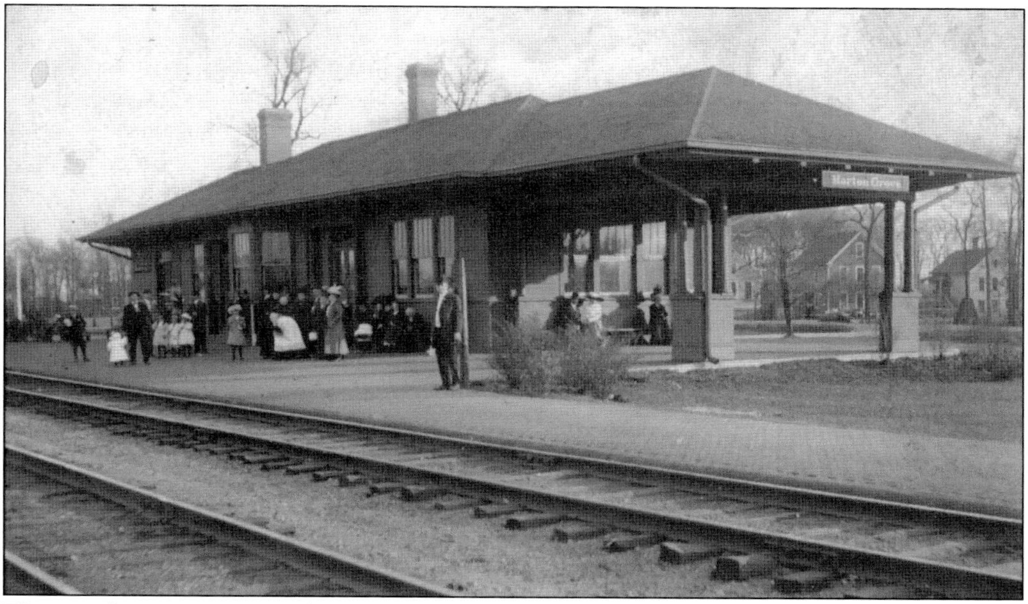

The wooden train station shown here was built in 1922 on the west side of the train tracks, south of Lincoln Avenue. It stood until 1974. This station replaced a wooden structure on the east side of the tracks. Houses on Elm Street are visible in the background. That area, closer to the North Branch of the Chicago River than most homes in Morton Grove, was nicknamed "Duck Town."

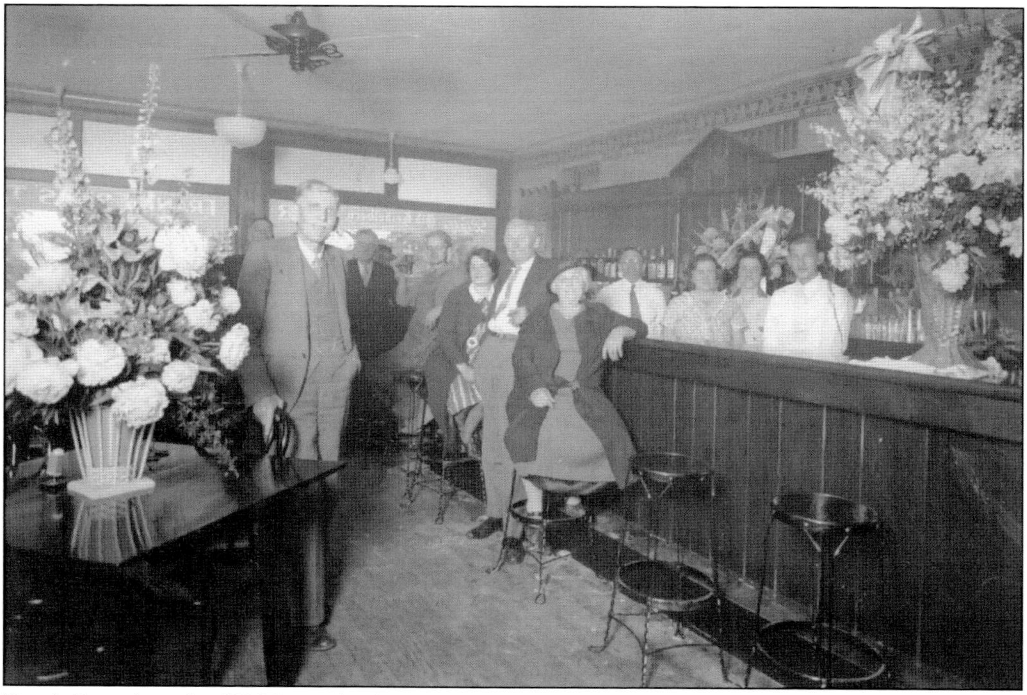

Frank Frees bought 6230 Lincoln Avenue in 1924 and used it for a restaurant, ice cream parlor, and relief station during the Great Depression. The space was also used for other businesses or rented until it was sold to the Platz family in the early 1940s. The interior of Frank Frees' Place is shown on the day of its grand opening. This location is now the Bringer Inn.

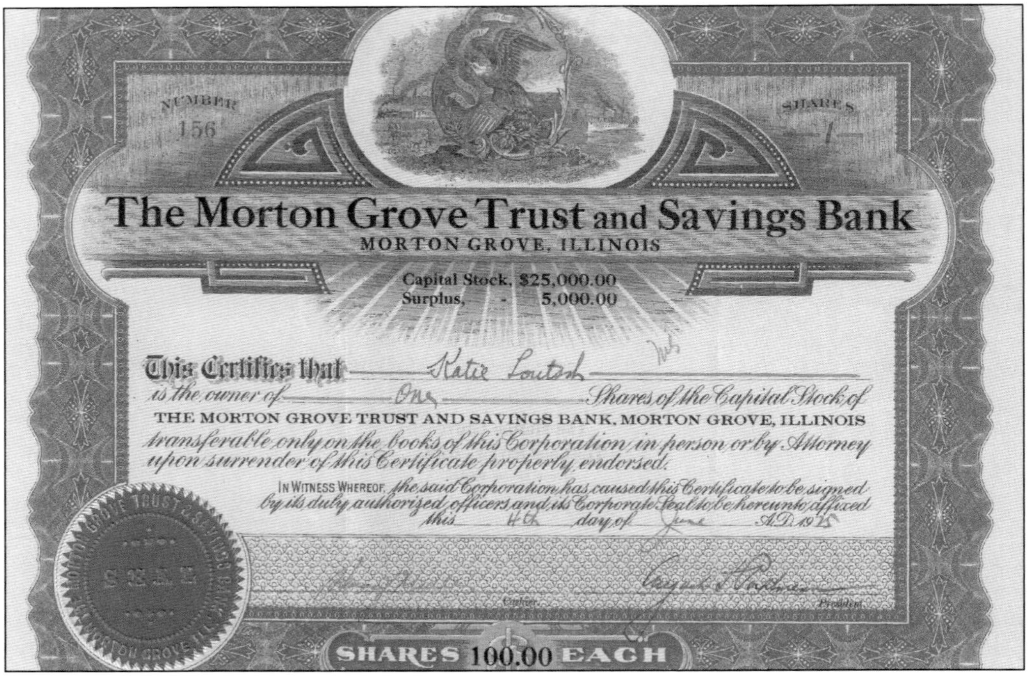

NUMBER 156

SHARES 1

The Morton Grove Trust and Savings Bank

MORTON GROVE, ILLINOIS

Capital Stock, $25,000.00
Surplus, - 5,000.00

This Certifies that Katie Loutsch is the owner of One Shares of the Capital Stock of THE MORTON GROVE TRUST AND SAVINGS BANK, MORTON GROVE, ILLINOIS transferable only on the books of this Corporation in person or by Attorney upon surrender of this Certificate properly endorsed.

In Witness Whereof, the said Corporation has caused this Certificate to be signed by its duly authorized officers and its Corporate Seal to be hereunto affixed this 4th day of June A.D. 1915

Cashier

President

SEAL

SHARES 100.00 EACH

Morton Grove Trust and Savings Bank, located at Lincoln and Callie Avenues, issued similar stock certificates to many local residents who placed their savings in the bank. The president at the time this certificate was issued in 1915 was August Poehlmann. He was also part owner of Poehlmann Brothers Company and the mayor of Morton Grove.

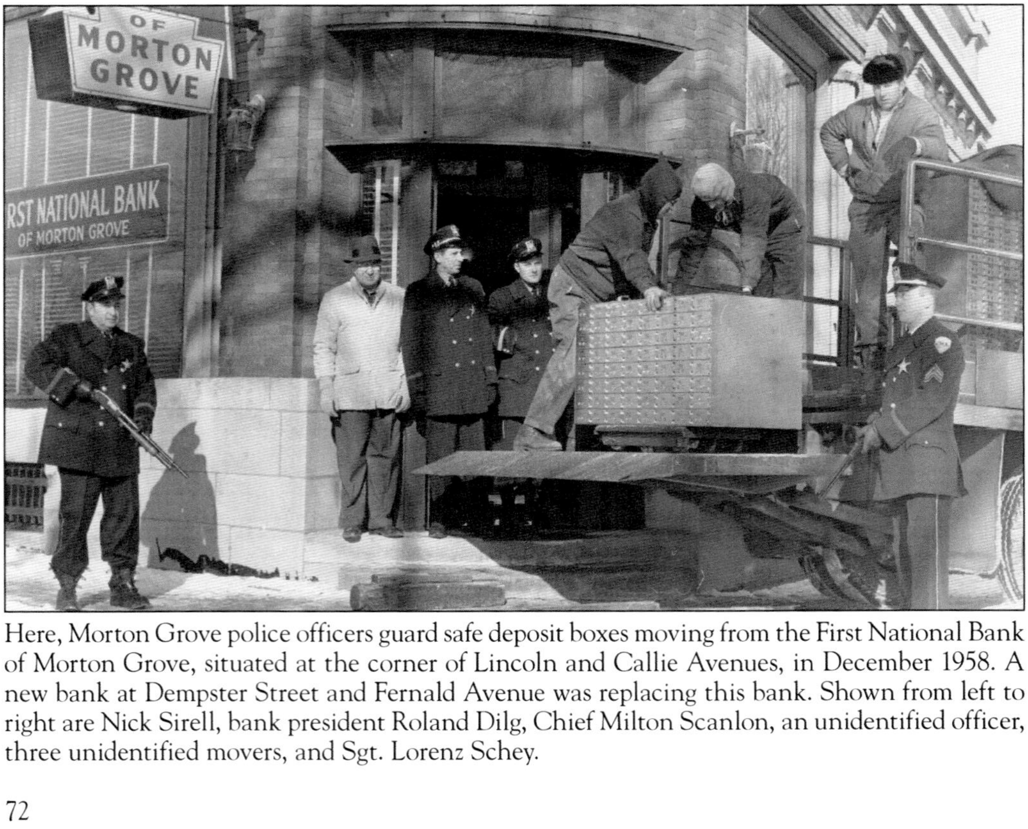

Here, Morton Grove police officers guard safe deposit boxes moving from the First National Bank of Morton Grove, situated at the corner of Lincoln and Callie Avenues, in December 1958. A new bank at Dempster Street and Fernald Avenue was replacing this bank. Shown from left to right are Nick Sirell, bank president Roland Dilg, Chief Milton Scanlon, an unidentified officer, three unidentified movers, and Sgt. Lorenz Schey.

Five

Nightclubs and Prohibition

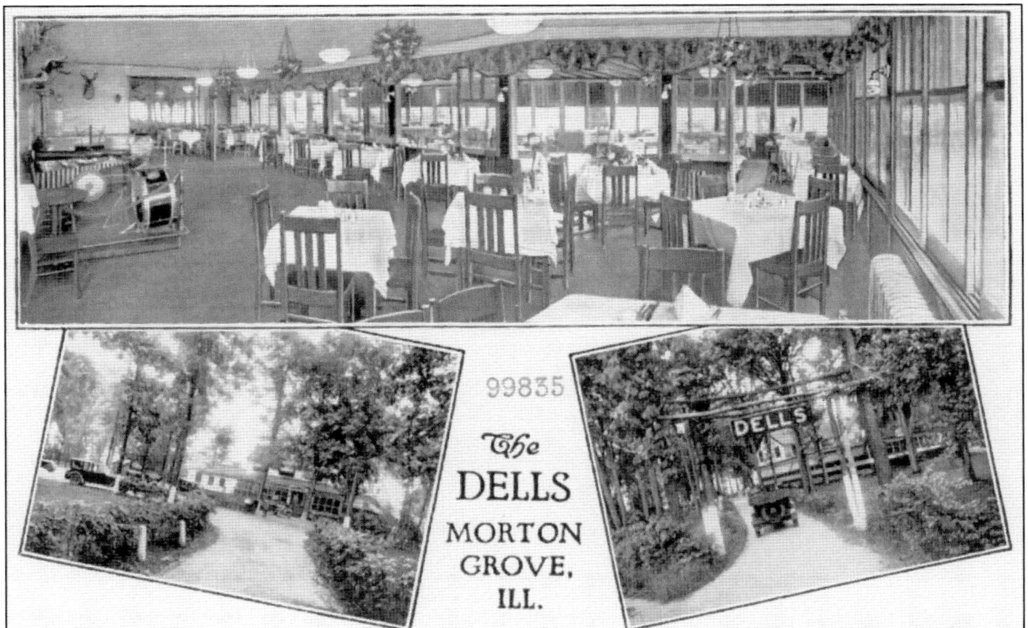

In the 1920s, Morton Grove was particularly well known for its nightclubs and roadhouses, especially the Dells (shown here) and the Lincoln Tavern. These venues provided extravagant surroundings and fine dining to accompany performances from extremely popular vaudeville and musical acts. However, many of Morton Grove's residents at the time recall that these settings also attracted some interest from Chicago's gangland personalities. (Courtesy of Lake County, Illinois, Discovery Museum, Curt Teich Postcard Archives.)

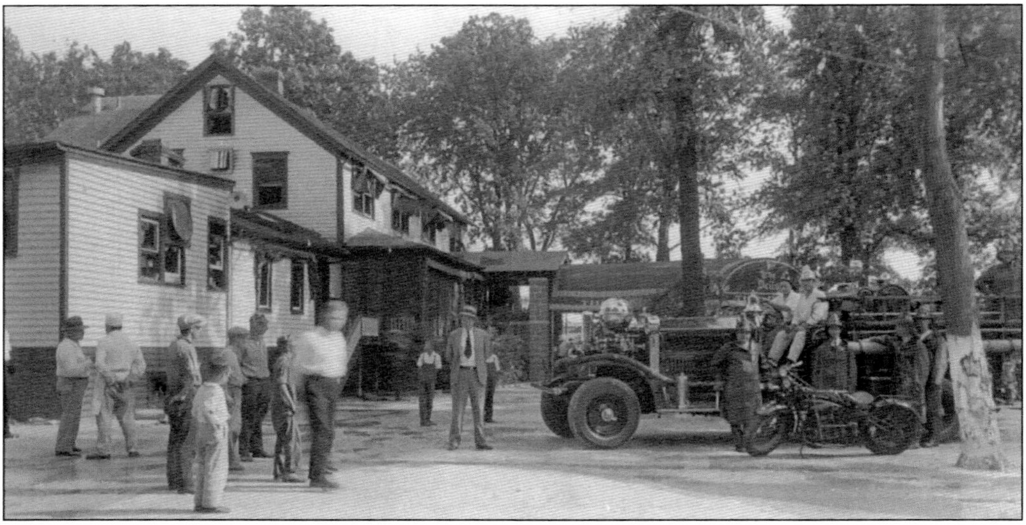

During the 1920s and 1930s, Morton Grove was on the border between Al Capone's gang (which controlled Chicago) and that of Roger Touhy (who controlled territory to the north and west). In July 1933, Jake Factor was leaving the Dells when his kidnapping was staged. Factor remained in hiding for a time until a ransom was supposedly paid. The kidnapping was a hoax later credited to Capone. Touhy was blamed and jailed after a controversial trial. This led to the dissolution of Touhy's gang and Capone's expansion. Touhy was eventually released in 1959 but killed soon after. The Dells is pictured above in 1934, following a witness report that armed men set fire to the nightclub. The blaze is credited to gang conflicts. Below, Ted Lewis (front) is shown in front of the Dells. Directly behind Lewis, appearing slightly to the right is Morton Grove trustee William Kirscht. Lewis was one of many traveling performers featured at the venue. (Below, courtesy of Gayle Kenney Dompke.)

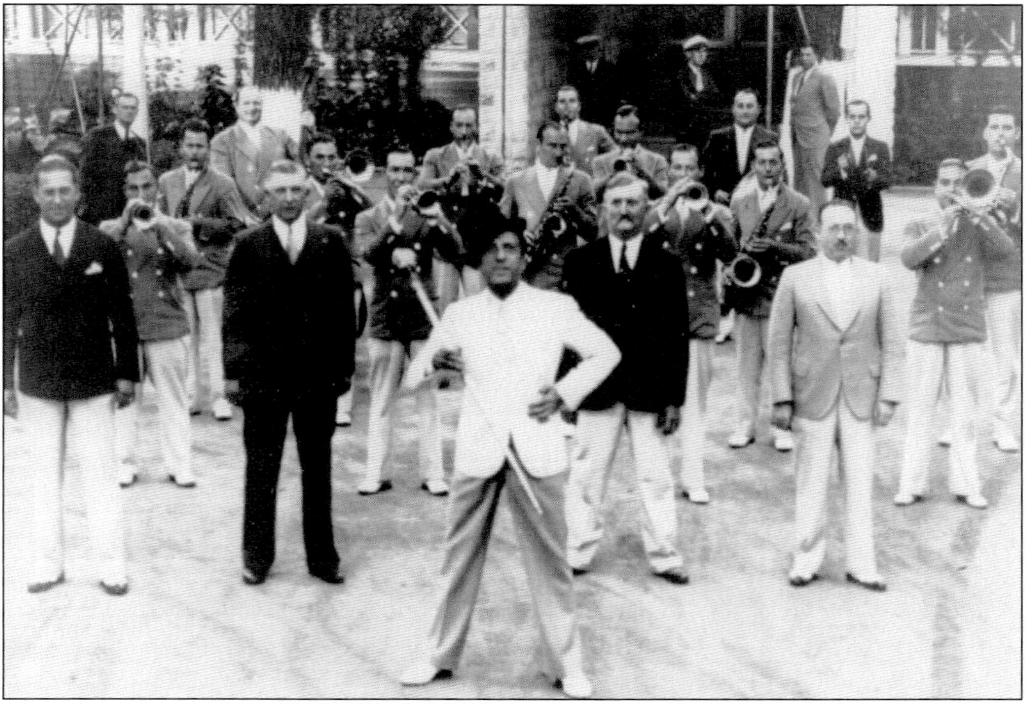

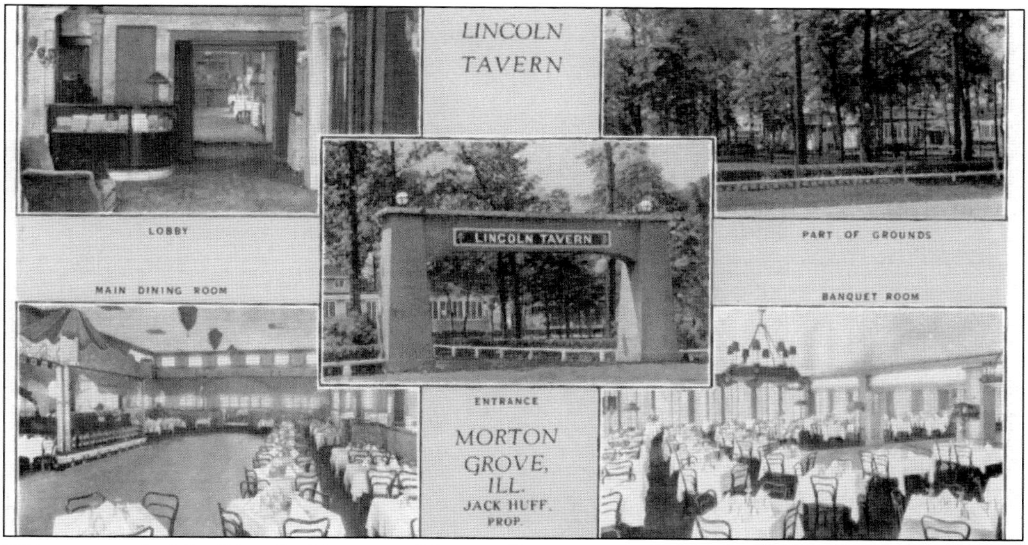

This postcard of the Lincoln Tavern in Morton Grove represents the roadhouses and entertainers that made Morton Grove a popular destination during Prohibition. Guy Lombardo, Waring's Pennsylvanians, Duke Ellington, Ted Weems, Glenn Miller, Sophie Tucker, and Sally Rand are a few of the big names mentioned in the colorful accounts of the nightclubs attracting Chicago's elite, notorious gangsters, and college men and women in raccoon coats and flapper fashions out for some jazz and burlesque kicks. (Courtesy of Lake County, Illinois, Discovery Museum, Curt Teich Postcard Archives.)

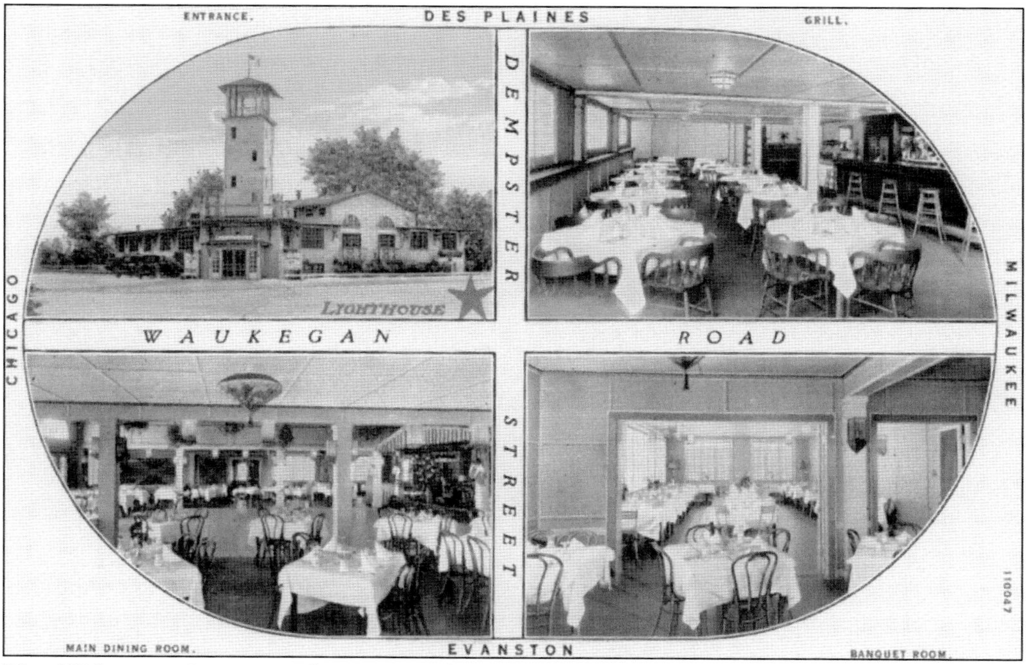

This 1926 postcard was printed to promote the Lighthouse nightclub, located on the southwest corner of Waukegan Road and Dempster Street. Well known for service at all hours with steak and chicken dinners at $1.50, as well as music, entertainment, dancing, and private dining rooms, the Light House drew customers to this rural farming community from the city of Chicago and the Northshore. (Courtesy of Lake County, Illinois, Discovery Museum, Curt Teich Postcard Archives.)

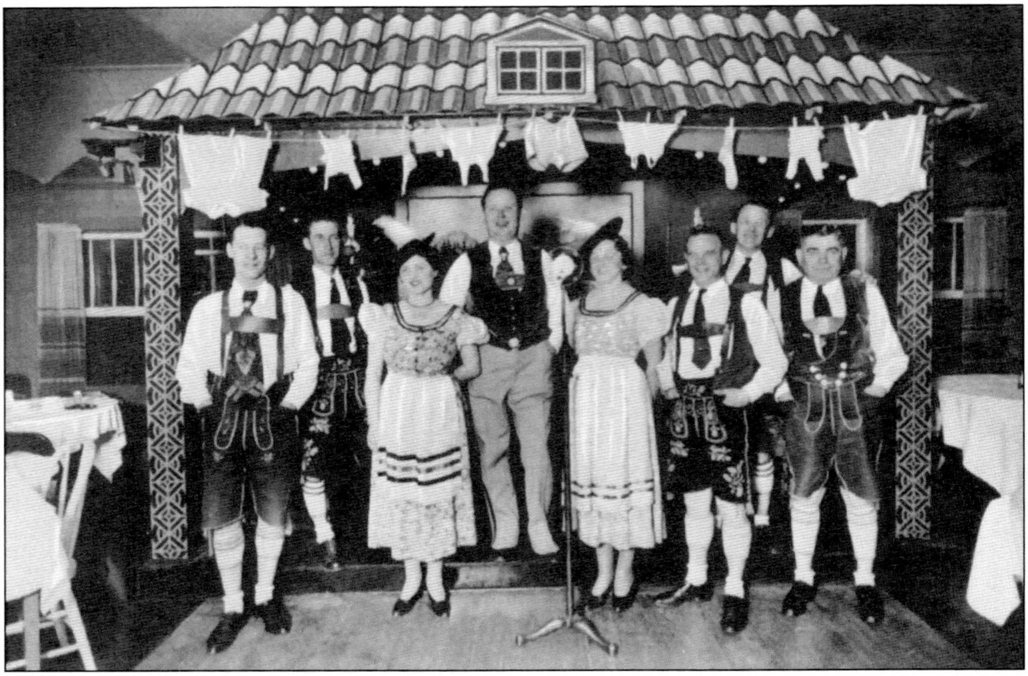

The Ferris Inn building and grounds originally operated as the Ford Children's Home on the northwest corner of Ferris and Capulina Avenues. This 1937 postcard, featuring NBC radio artist George Hessberger and his Tyrolean Ensemble, illustrates post-Prohibition-era entertainment in what was known as Chicago's finest country cafe. This club offered excellent dinners and the finest of cocktails, along with singing and dancing during the Depression. (Courtesy of Lake County, Illinois, Discovery Museum, Curt Teich Postcard Archives.)

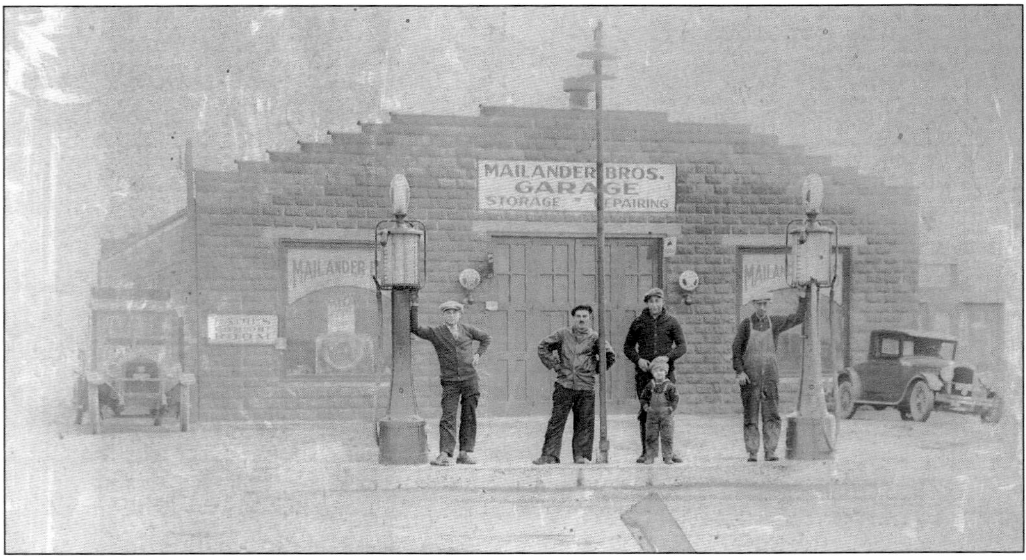

The Mailander Bros. Garage was located on what was known as North Branch Road when this photograph was taken. The Hand Car Wash operates out of this building at 9003 Waukegan Road today. Otto Mailander went into the greenhouse business with Adolph Poehlmann in 1885, which became the renowned Poehlmann Brothers Company. William Mailander continued as a contractor and builder of greenhouses during the floral industry's prime.

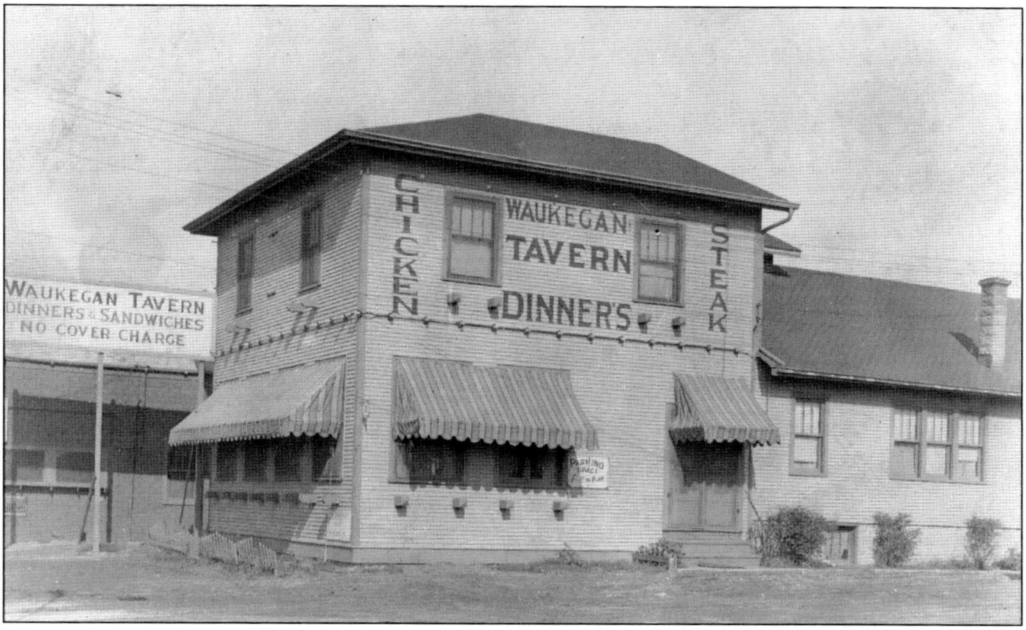

During Prohibition, proprietors such as Paul Minx were able to serve near beer from their taps. As seen in this postcard of the Waukegan Tavern, hearty meals were served with no cover charge for entertainment. Paul Minx was shut down in the 1930s during the end of Prohibition. During the following decades, Puggy Meier's, the Prairie Schooner, Rusty's, and Tommy's on Waukegan operated out of this building. Minx purchased the Sonne homestead and opened a tavern at Dempster and School Streets shortly thereafter. The tavern had been the Stumble Inn, frequented by pilots flying in and out of the Sonne Airfield. Minx sold this operation to Valentino Hoffman shortly before his death in 1951. Val's Restaurant and Tavern would later be sold to Edward O'Bradovich, former defensive end for the Chicago Bears. (Courtesy of Paul Minx.)

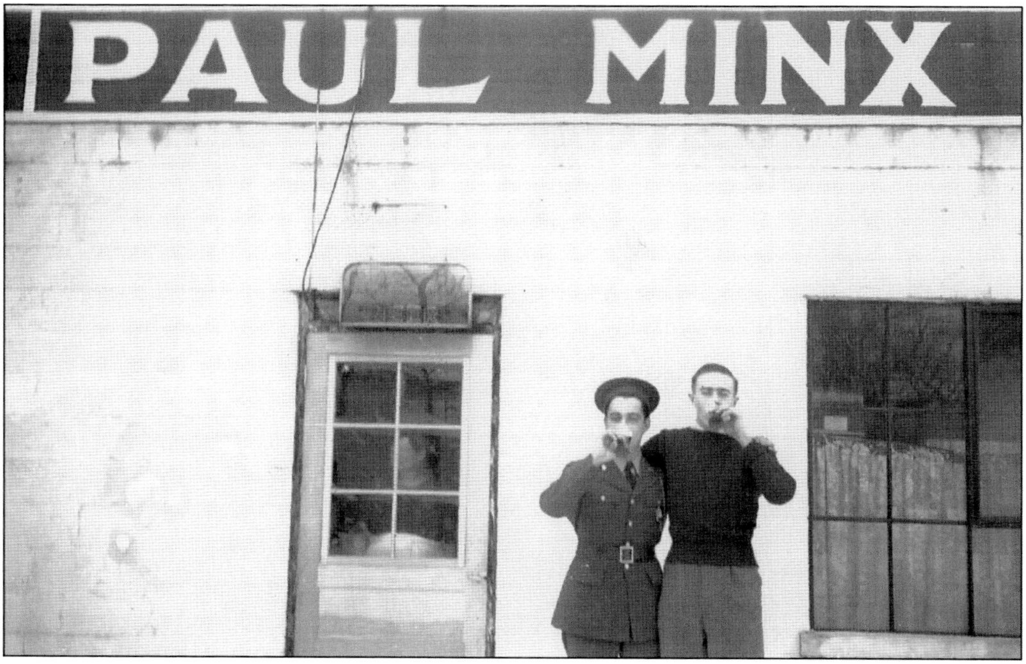

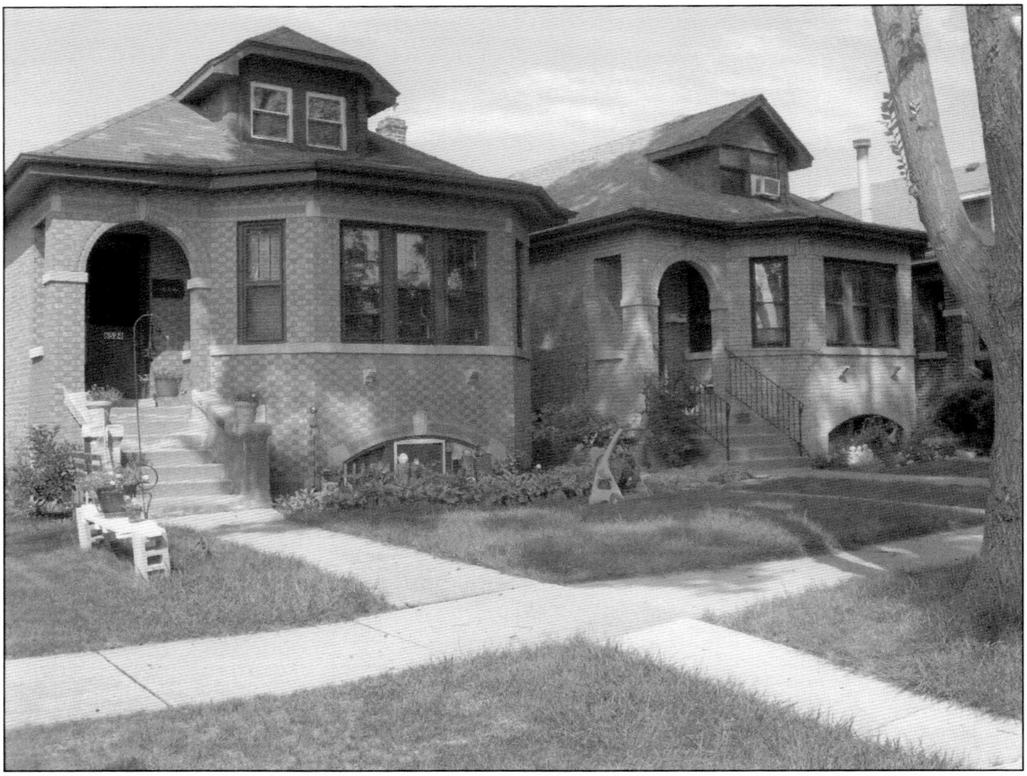

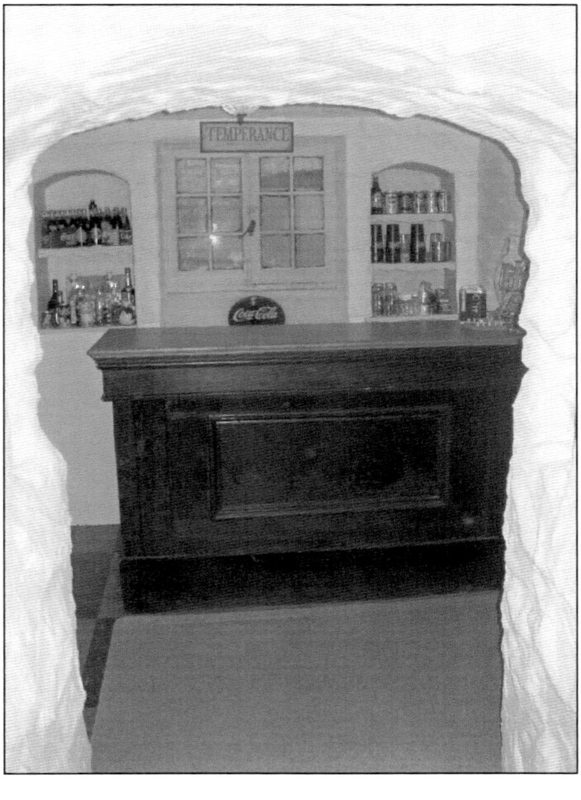

Al Cowdrey managed Club Cherie at 6021 Dempster Street in the 1920s and 1930s. He lived in a then-new bungalow on Mansfield Avenue. The Bungalow style was very popular throughout the Chicago region during the 1920s building boom. This second wave of housing development in Morton Grove coincided with the development of roadhouses and other new businesses. (Courtesy of Robert and Susan Schafer.)

The basement of Al Cowdrey's home is pictured as it exists today, with some original furnishings intact. A portion of the basement was decorated with faux fieldstone walls and likely served as an underground brewery and speakeasy during Prohibition. Elsewhere, a portion of the basement still shows scorch marks from a small fire, which neighbors at the time attributed to a distillery accident. (Courtesy of Robert and Susan Schafer.)

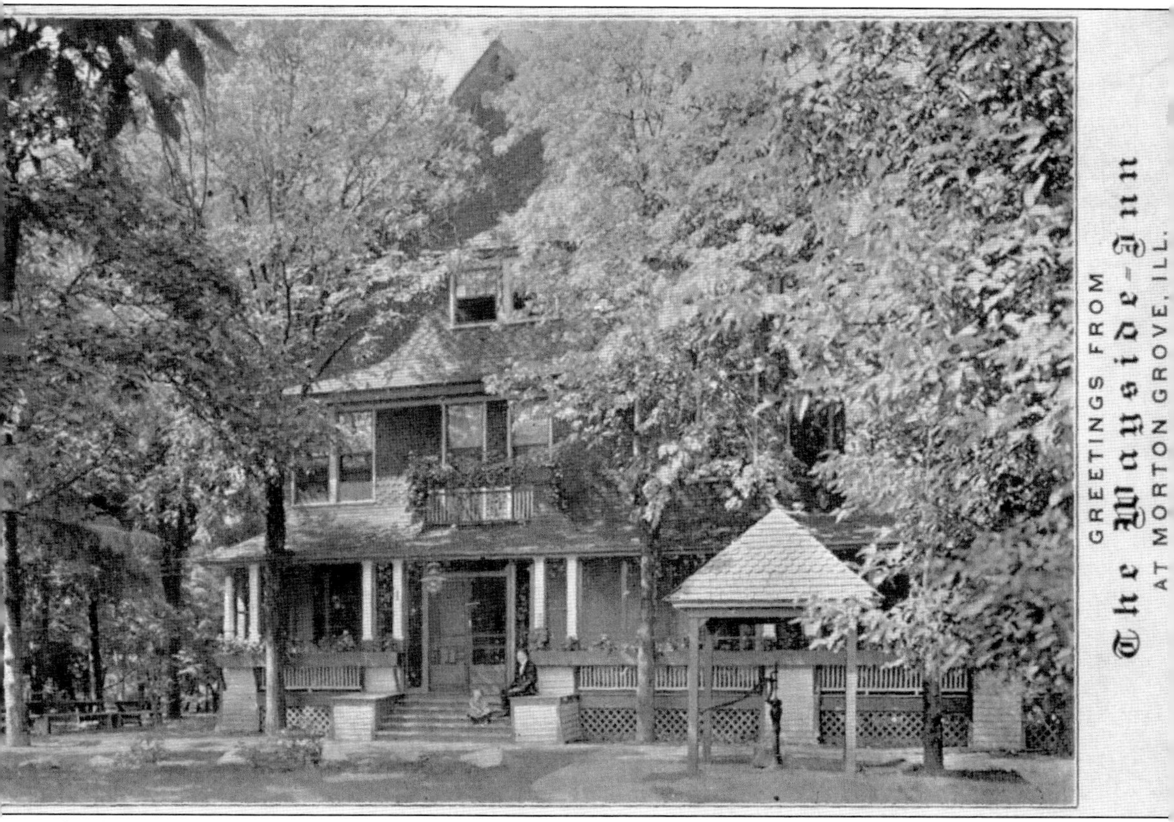

Charley Krempp's Wayside Inn was originally the home of Dr. Hotz. Emma Hotz is listed as owner of this farm in the 1910 census with daughters Lucille and Elsa. Osage orange hedgerows, commonly planted as agricultural barriers during the 1800s and early 1900s, and silver maple trees planted along the road leading to this house can be found in Linne Woods today. The Wayside Inn, famous for their chicken dinners and reputed to be a house of prostitution, operated for several years in the 1910s before it burned down in 1917.

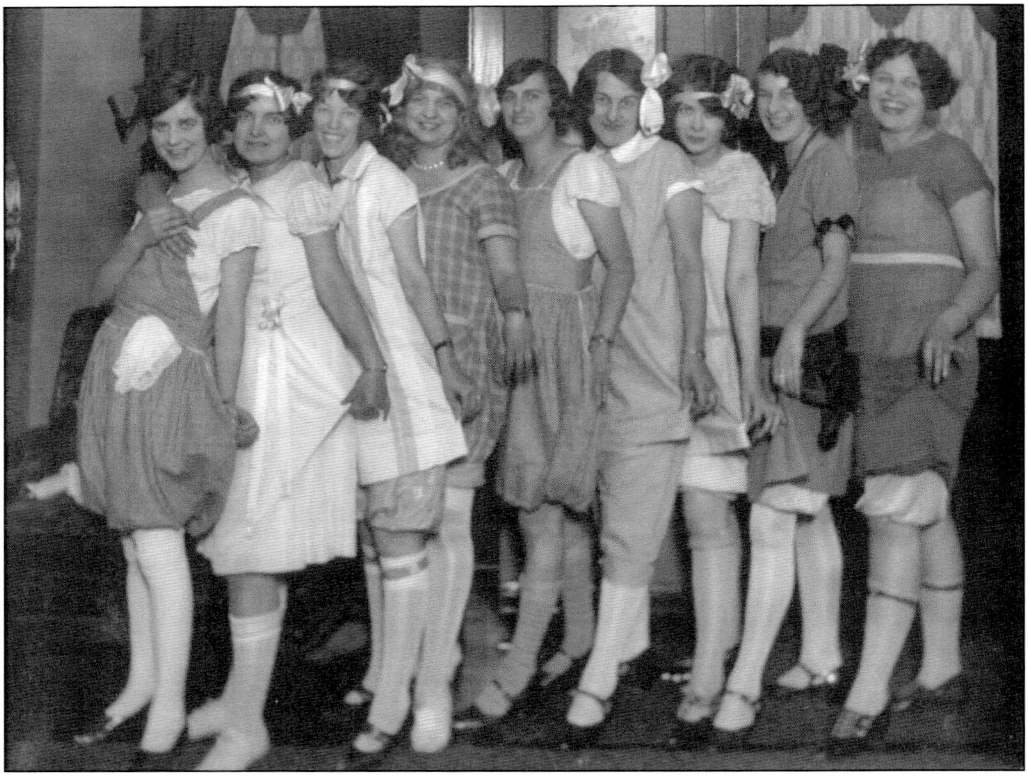

Caroline Harrer is pictured second from the right with the Sunshine Girls Club. Harrer is the youngest daughter of Morton Grove's first mayor, George Harrer and Mary (née Yehl) Harrer, born on April 17, 1904. This club often put on skits, following in the footsteps of the older girls pictured below at the Borchardt house near Waukegan Road and Dempster Street in the early 1910s. The young girls dressed in men's clothing, pictured below from left to right, are (first row) Elsie Priest, Eleanor Harrer, Matilda Priest, Clara Borchardt, Elda Brown, Erna Fluger, and Carrie Fluger; (second row) Frieda Borchardt, Olive Harrer, Alma Borchardt, and Emma Borchardt. (Courtesy of Michael A. Heuel.)

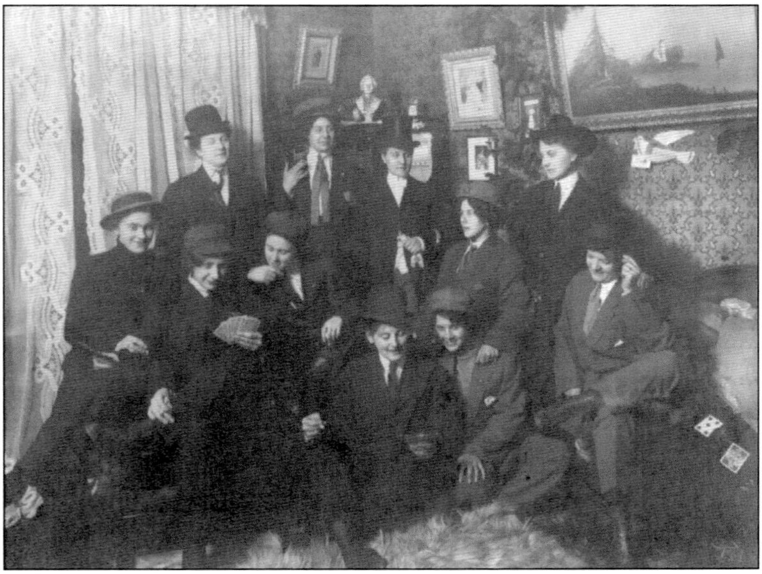

This 1923 photograph illustrates the fashions and flare of young women during Prohibition in this rural farming community. Pictured from left to right on a motorcycle are Dorothy Yehl, Ernestine Harrer, and Olive Harrer. Yehl was the last family member to reside in the Haupt-Yehl house at its original location on Lincoln Avenue before the house was donated to the Morton Grove Historical Society in 1984. (Courtesy of Larry and Judy Brod.)

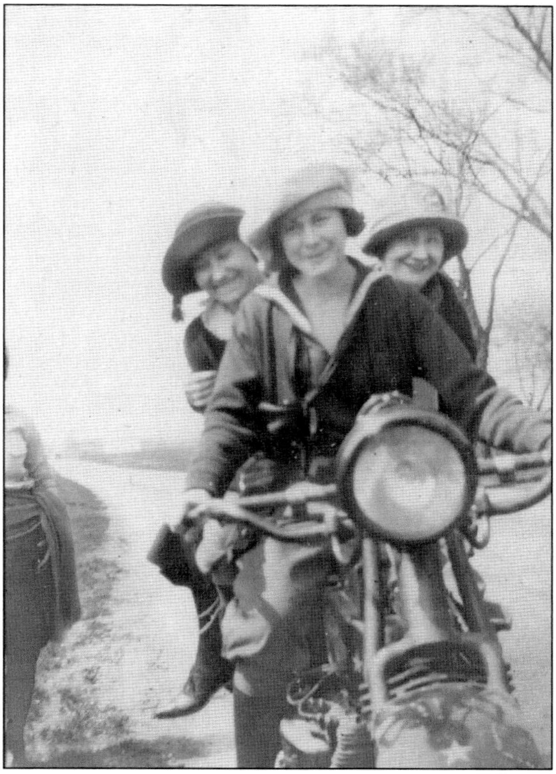

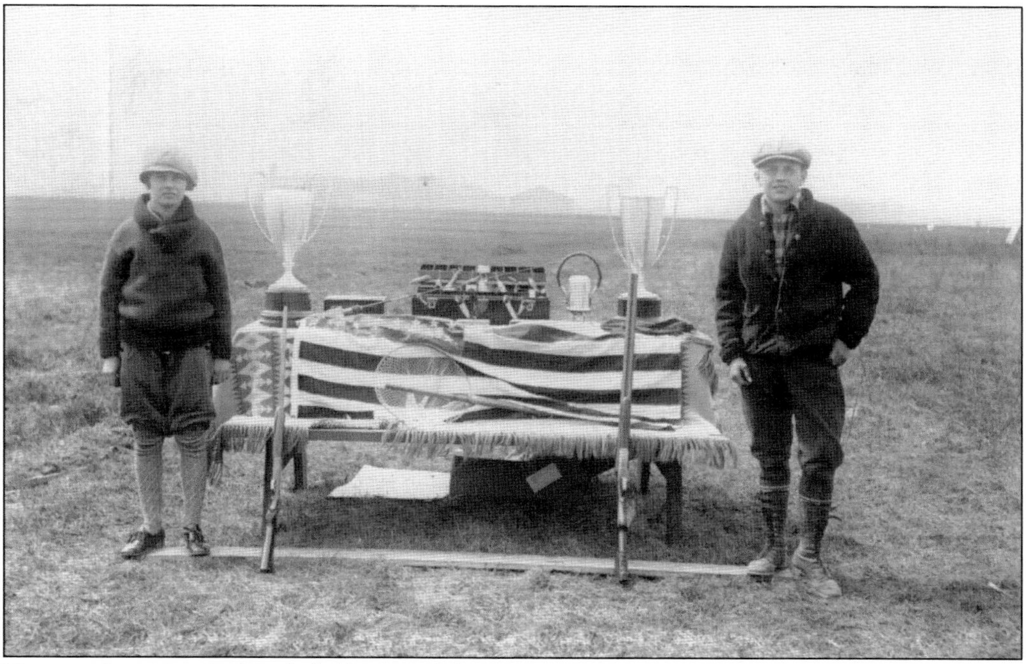

Florence (née Huscher) Raft (left) opened the event for the National Skeet Shooting Association. Raft's father, Fred L. Huscher, was among the members of the Northwest Gun Club who became state champions in this event in 1931. As a young girl, Raft would wrap a sandwich in brown paper and spend the entire day hunting for rabbit and pheasants in the local forest preserves.

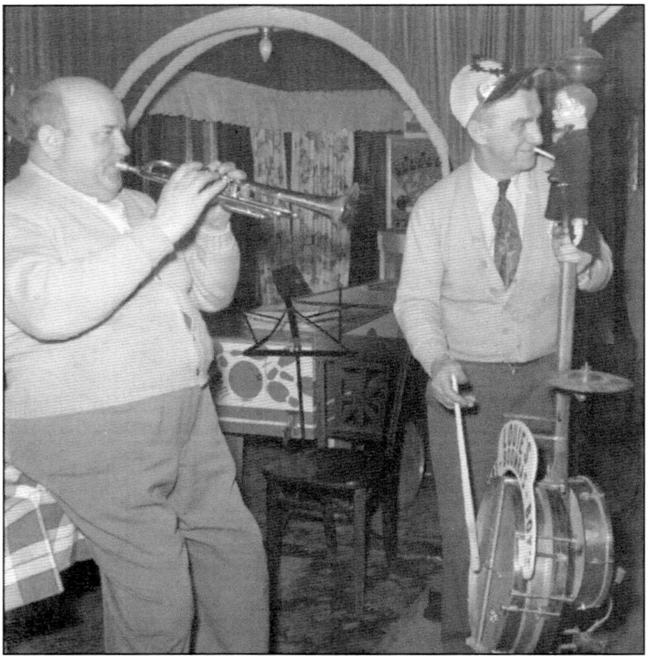

Louis "Herr Louie" and Anna "Tante Anna" Nachbauer operated Herr Louie's tavern at 8719 Ferris Avenue after Prohibition and into the late 1960s. Louis Nachbauer is shown playing trumpet in his tavern as part of his band Louie's Happy Boombas Boys. The boombas, a traditional German instrument, is made in many configurations of a staff with drumheads, cymbals, and strings played with a serrated stick. (Courtesy of the Neumann and Anzelone family.)

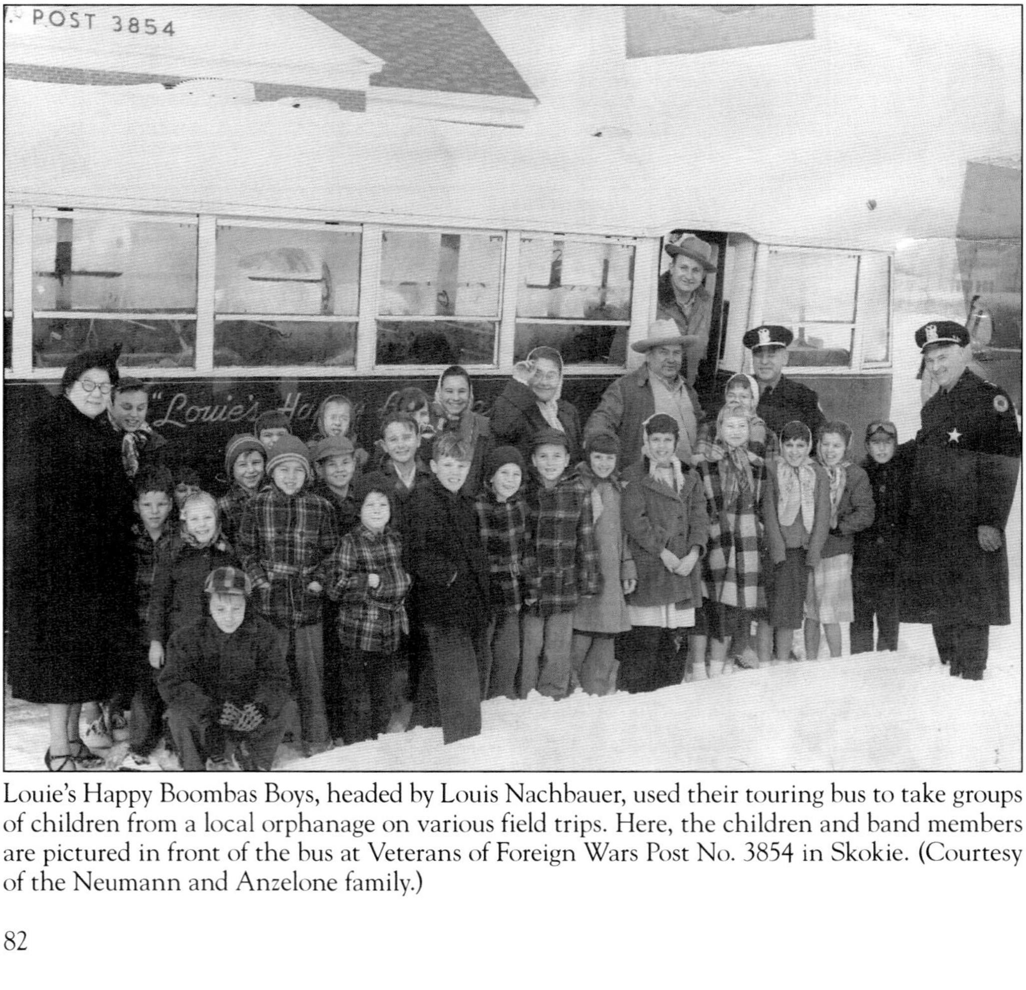

Louie's Happy Boombas Boys, headed by Louis Nachbauer, used their touring bus to take groups of children from a local orphanage on various field trips. Here, the children and band members are pictured in front of the bus at Veterans of Foreign Wars Post No. 3854 in Skokie. (Courtesy of the Neumann and Anzelone family.)

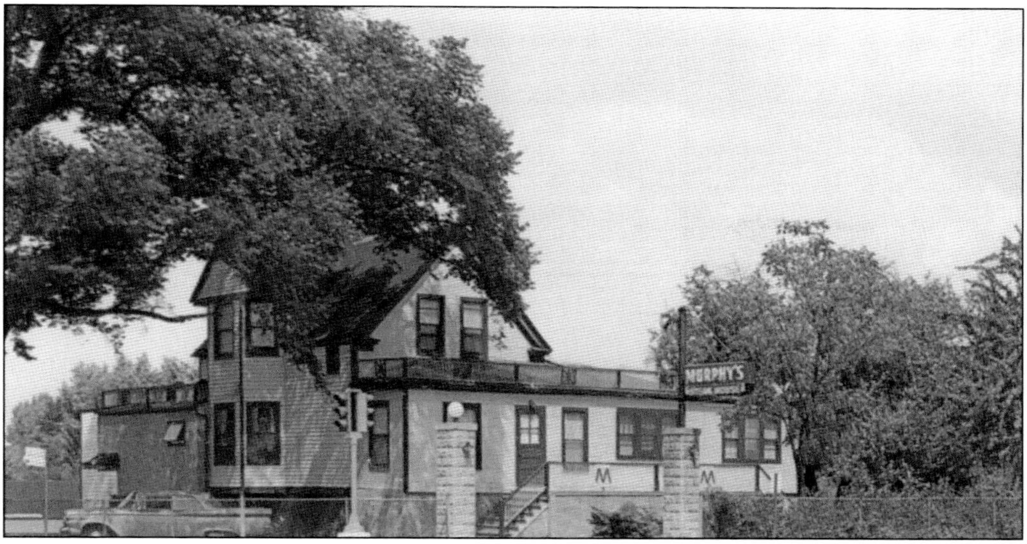

Murphy's Steak House thrived for 41 years at the corner of Austin Avenue and Dempster Street. Mildred Hugg was born in Chicago, coming to Morton Grove in 1923 to sing with Coon Sander's Nighthawks at the Lincoln Tavern after touring the country with a vaudeville act. A whirlwind romance began the night Angel "Murph" Orphan, who ran a local barbecue, was introduced to Hugg while watching her perform. Shortly afterwards, they were married, moving into a farmhouse on Dempster Street. Following a fire at the barbecue stand, they decided to turn their home into a restaurant. Hugg also recalled singing at the elegant Dells nightclub with Guy Lombardo and regularly listening to beautiful music drifting from open windows on summer evenings into their steak house next door.

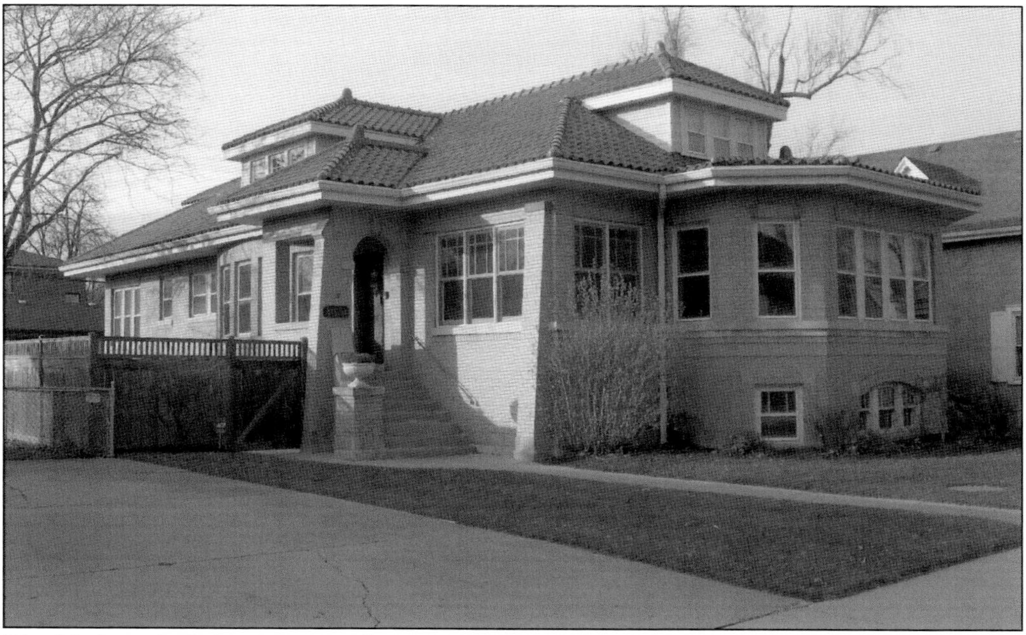

The Herbert A. Dilg House, a Chicago-style bungalow constructed in 1925 and listed in the National Register of Historic Places, is located in Morton Grove's first Bingham Fernald subdivision. Dilg, a third-generation civic leader from the Dilg family, served as mayor of Morton Grove from 1925 to 1926 and again from 1931 to 1944.

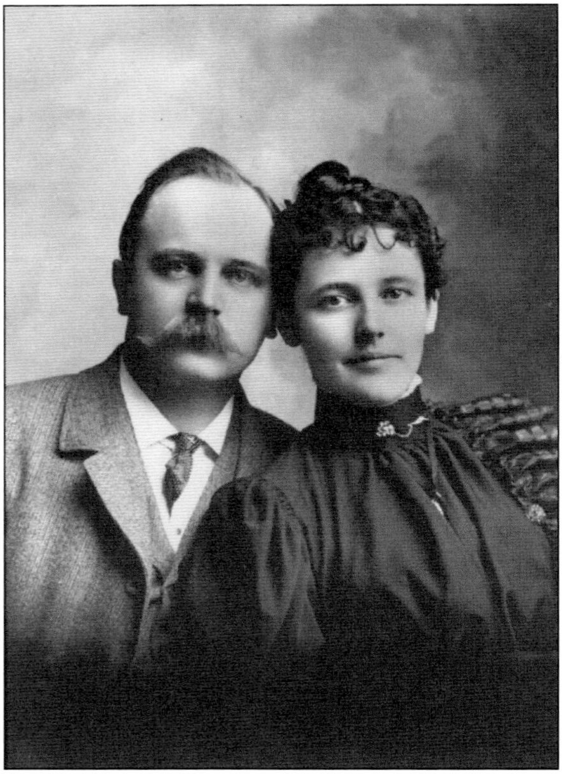

William Washington Sonne (left) was a designer, jeweler, and watchmaker. He married into one of Morton Grove's early families, moved to Morton Grove in the 1890s, and is known to have taken some of the early photographs shown in this book. He and his wife, Freida (née Huscher) Sonne (right), instilled a love of new technologies in their children.

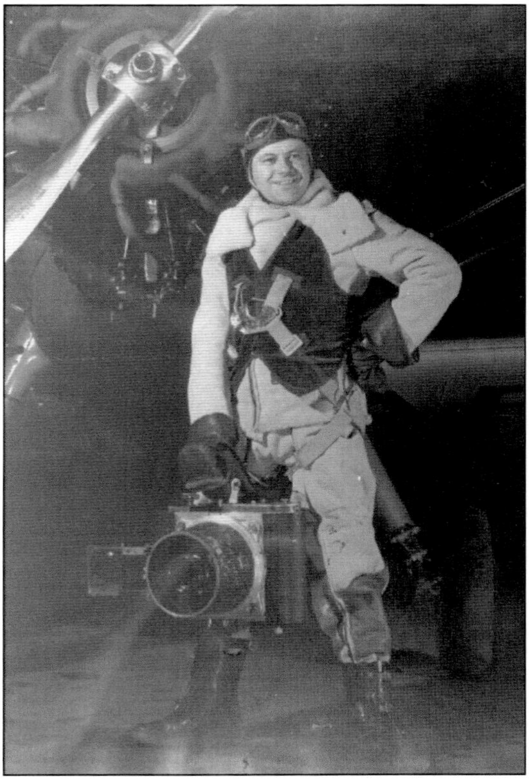

Fred Sonne, the son of William and Freida, is shown here with a plane and aerial photographic equipment. He is most famous for founding Morton Grove's Sonne Airfield and Chicago Aerial Survey Company. Fred began his interest in photography while assisting his father, and he ran the projector at Morton Grove's first silent movie theater.

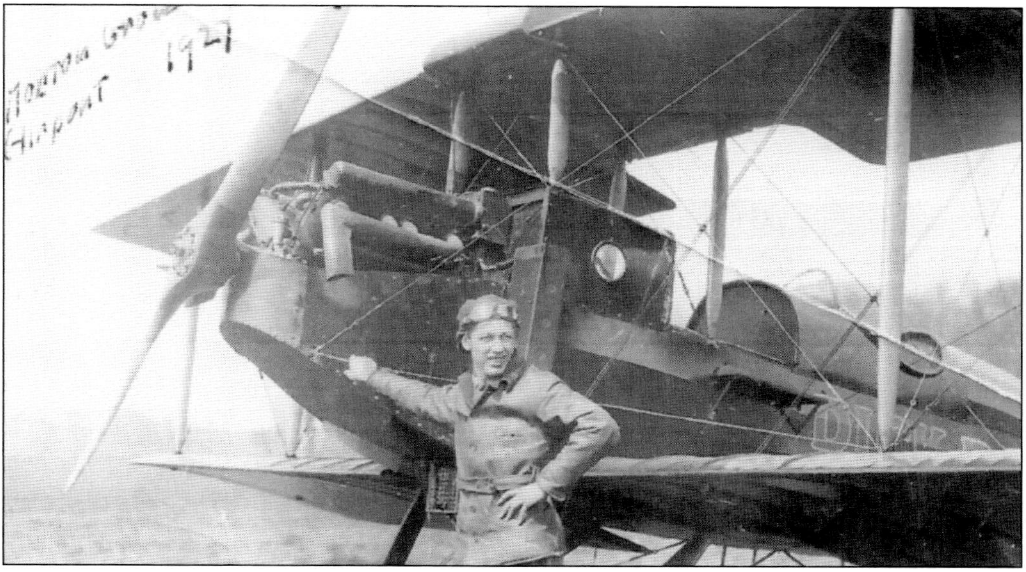

Pilot Dick Boettcher is shown with his biplane at Sonne Airfield, where he gave rides in his plane and participated in air shows. From 1919 to 1932, Sonne Airfield was located near Meade Avenue between Dempster and Lake Streets. Dick's brother-in-law Fred Sonne operated the airfield with business partner "Chance" Lawson, a World War I flying ace. Dick's wife, Hermine (née Sonne) Boettcher, was likely the first woman to go up in a plane in Morton Grove and was also known to participate in wing-walking stunts. The Boettchers moved to Arizona to train US Army Air Corps pilots during World War II and later operated other aerial businesses. Boettcher's early pilot license, signed by Orville Wright, is shown here. (Courtesy of Dorothy [née Boettcher] Voss.)

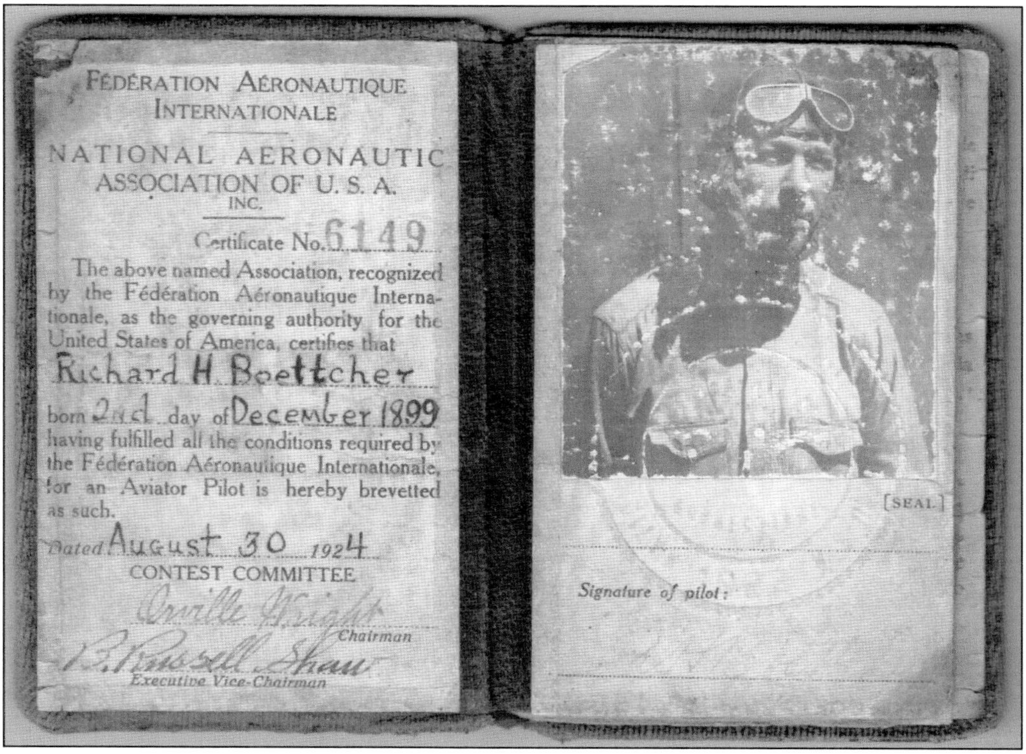
FÉDÉRATION AÉRONAUTIQUE INTERNATIONALE

NATIONAL AERONAUTIC ASSOCIATION OF U. S. A. INC.

Certificate No. 6149

The above named Association, recognized by the Fédération Aéronautique Internationale, as the governing authority for the United States of America, certifies that Richard H. Boettcher born 2nd day of December 1899 having fulfilled all the conditions required by the Fédération Aéronautique Internationale, for an Aviator Pilot is hereby brevetted as such.

Dated August 30 1924

CONTEST COMMITTEE

Orville Wright
Chairman

B. Russell Shaw
Executive Vice-Chairman

[SEAL]

Signature of pilot:

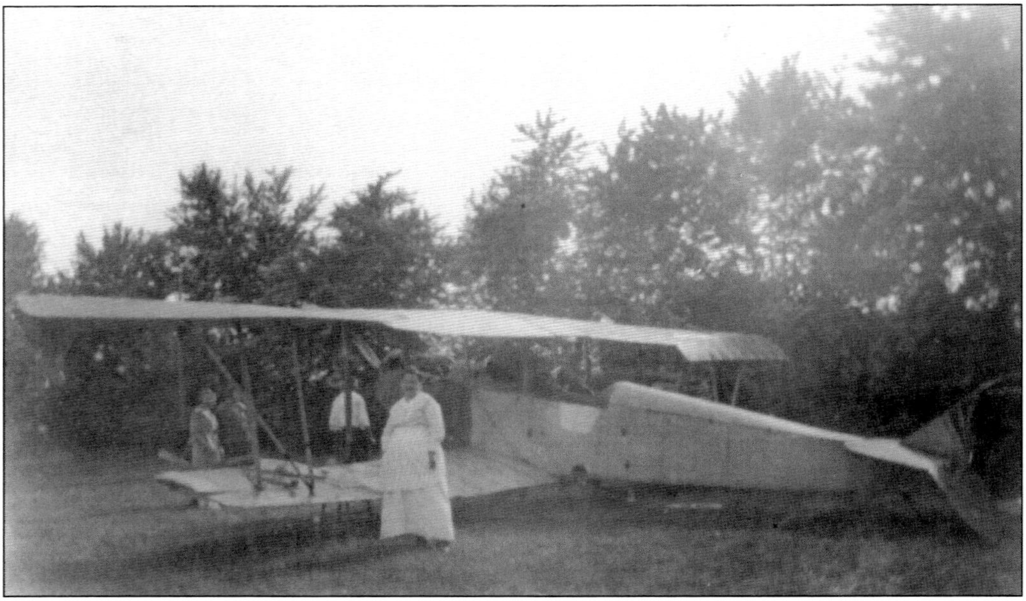

The first plane to land—or, more likely, crash—in Morton Grove was in 1919. Here, Anna Minx is pictured in front of the novelty. The plane, flown by Chance Lawson, was repaired with help from Fred Sonne. This incident is said to have led to the formation of Sonne Airfield.

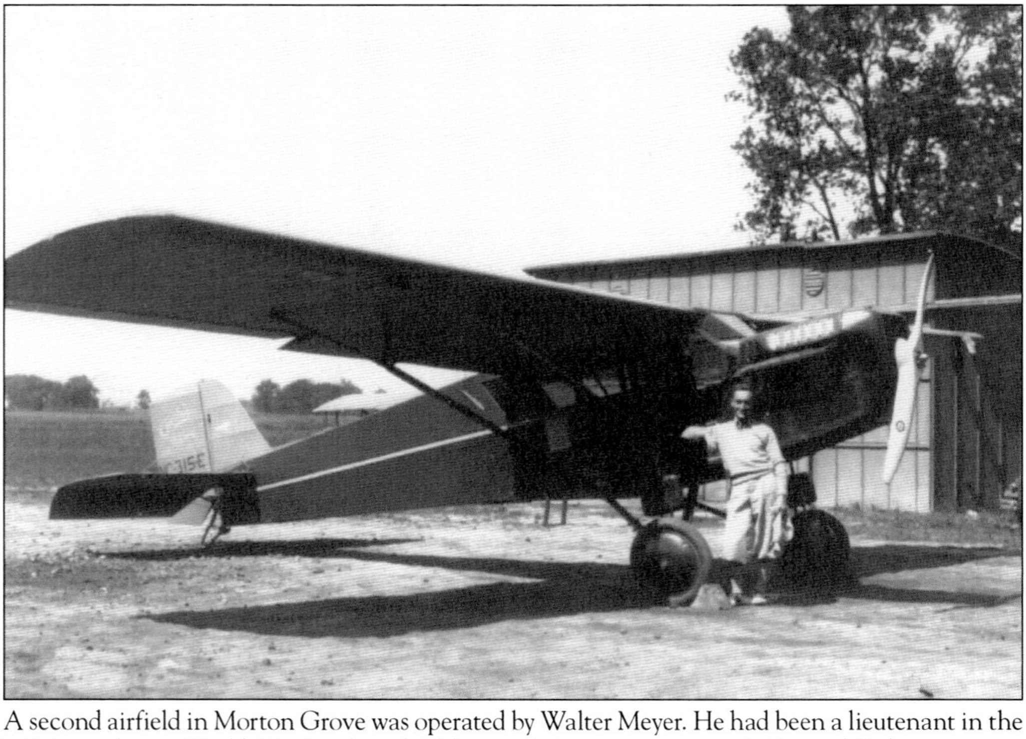

A second airfield in Morton Grove was operated by Walter Meyer. He had been a lieutenant in the US Army during World War I and was highly regarded as an experienced pilot and flight instructor. Meyer was killed in a mid-air collision with an unlicensed airplane over Northbrook, Illinois.

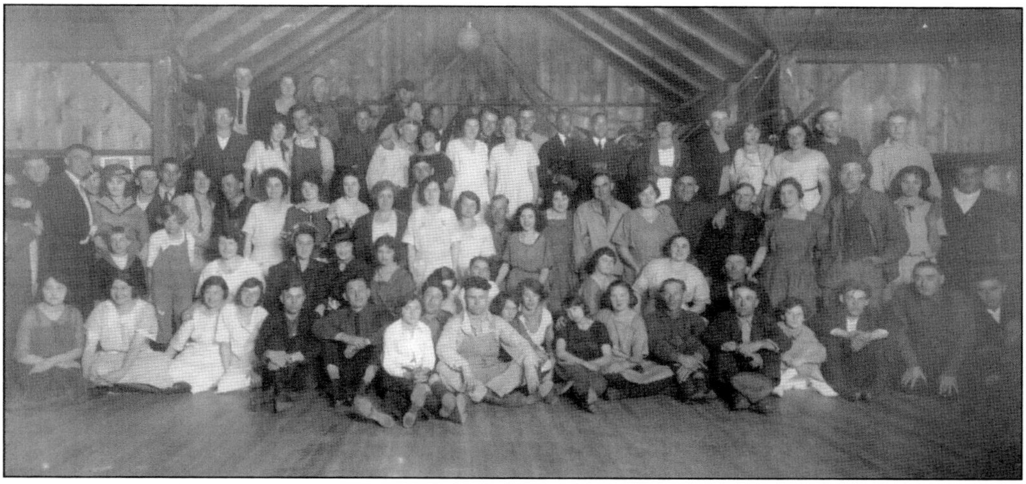

Annual "Hard Times" parties were held near Halloween to defray expenses of the Morton Grove Baseball club. On Saturday, October 20, 1934, a benefit was held in Schufreider's Hayloft on Milwaukee Avenue. Admission was 35¢, and a good time was guaranteed or money cheerfully refunded. Testimonials, a modern fan dance, novelties, music, and a parody performed by Guy Lombardi and the Royal Comedians were advertised on printed tickets.

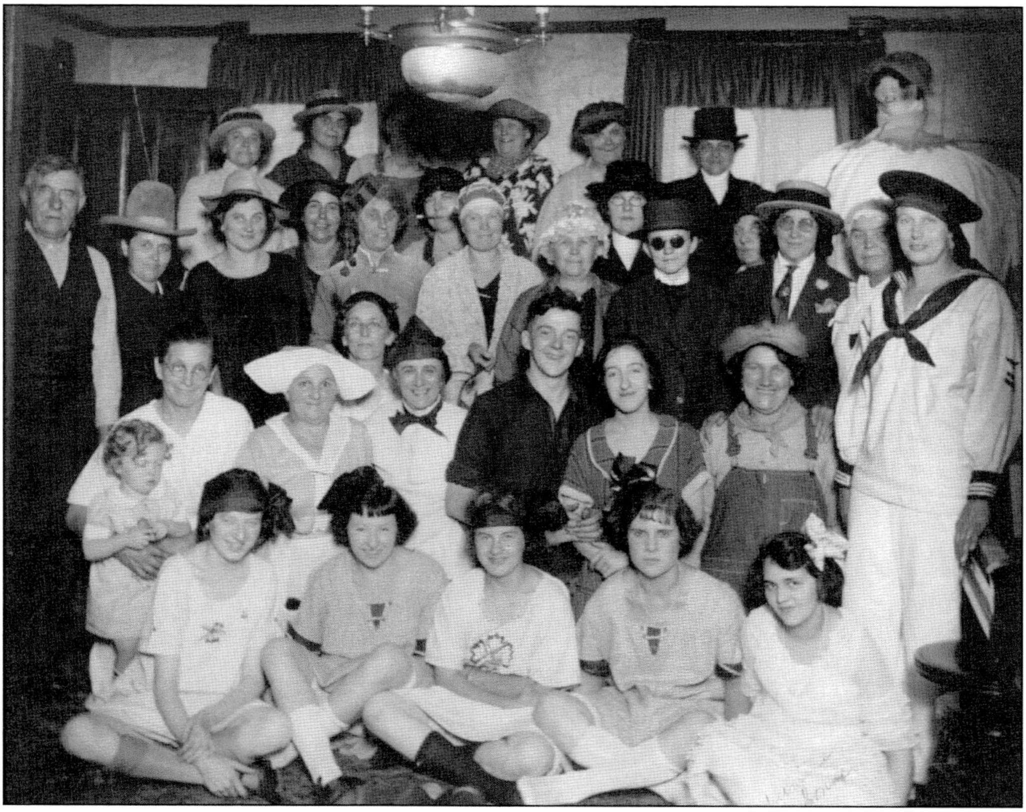

Hermine Sonne (1903–1993) is identified in the front row on the far right in this late-1910s photograph. Skits and plays were a very popular form of entertainment in Morton Grove during this time period. Church and school groups, along with clubs and volunteer organizations, put on performances in their homes, at pavilions in the parks, and in local halls and haylofts.

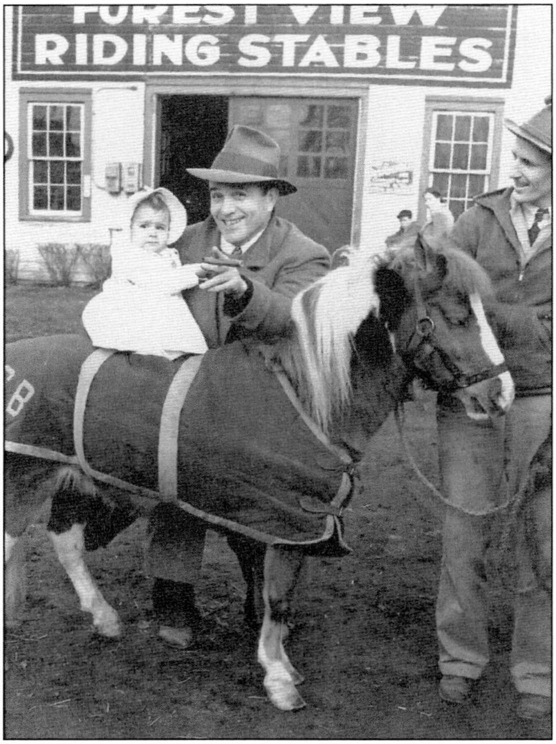

A.B. Cameron, owner of Forest View Riding Stables on the southeast corner of Harms and Golf Roads, poses with daughter Mary Cameron in 1940. Employee Dick Wager is pictured on the right. Cameron and his wife, Lillian (née Schroeder), were owners and exhibitors of show horses, including champions Dipsy Doodle and Moonlight Madonna. Annual horse shows were held in the field on the north side of Golf Road. The original clubhouse was remodeled for the family home, which they lived in until 1954. Cameron is pictured with Lillian holding newborn Michael and children, from left to right, Tony, Candy, and Mary. Elmer J. Holdorf's Riding School and Lloyd Teater Stables were operating adjacent to Forest View at this time. Morton Grove was well known for its many stables and horse farms. Northwestern Stables was located near Austin Avenue and Church Street, and the Frank Miller Riding Stable was at Railroad Avenue and Oakton Street.

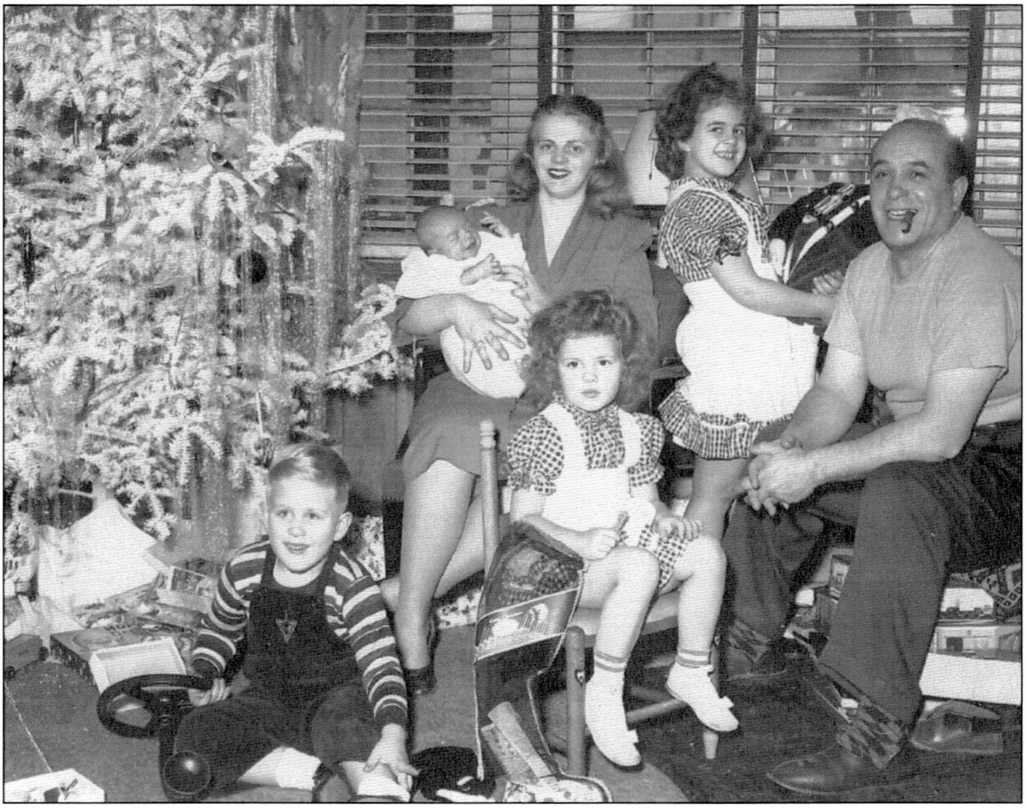

Six

Wartime and Home Front Memories

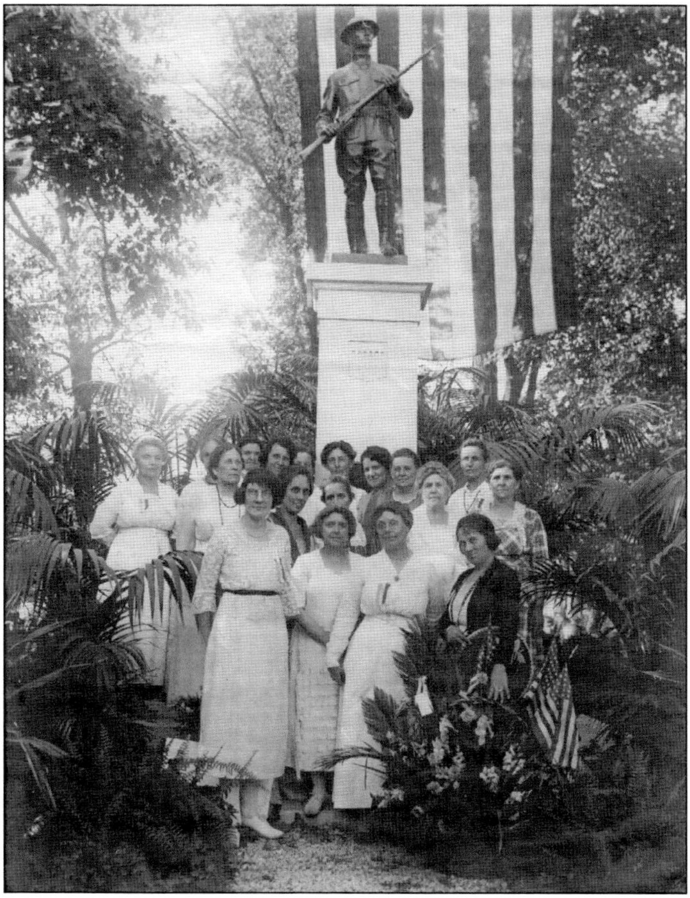

The Women's War Working Circle was a group of volunteers who worked with the Red Cross on various efforts supporting local soldiers in World War I. This interaction and mutual support between soldiers in and after wartime with their friends and relatives at home has been repeated several times throughout Morton Grove's history.

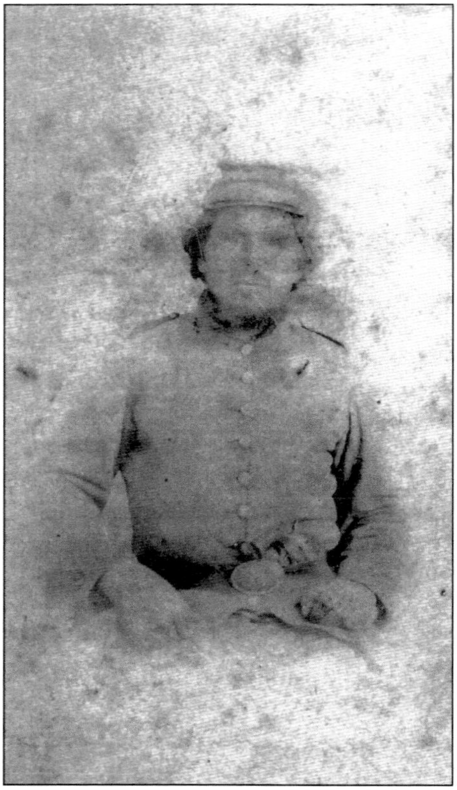

Four local men were known to have served in the Civil War. John Lochner, pictured in uniform, gave his life while representing the Union army at the 1863 Battle of Lookout Mountain. Medard Lochner returned home, becoming Morton Grove's first postmaster in 1874. August and Henry Fink were mustered in with the Illinois, US Light Artillery in 1864, both returning home in 1865. (Courtesy of the Lochner family.)

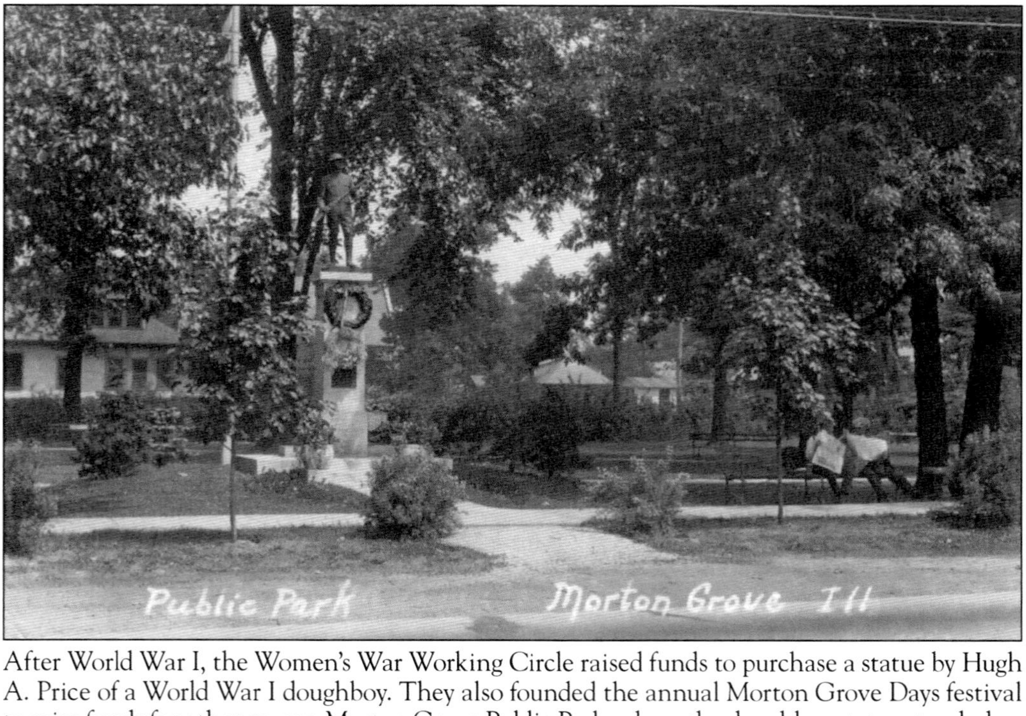

After World War I, the Women's War Working Circle raised funds to purchase a statue by Hugh A. Price of a World War I doughboy. They also founded the annual Morton Grove Days festival to raise funds for other causes. Morton Grove Public Park, where the doughboy statue stands, has since been replaced by the Morton Grove Public Library, although the statue remains in place.

By World War I, Morton Grove's population had grown and an increasing number of residents participated. Here, three local soldiers pose with a fourth unidentified man (sitting) who is noted as not being from Morton Grove. Standing from left to right are August Sturn, Henry Sturn, and Harry Loutsch.

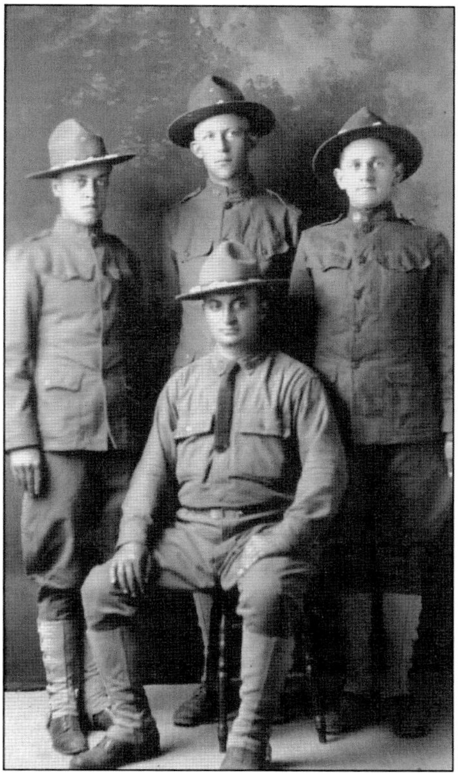

Here, several young people are on a truck advertising Louie's Tavern at the Morton Grove Days parade in the early 1940s. Louis Nachbauer, owner of the tavern, is in the middle of the group, wearing lederhosen and a hat. The young man in white pants and shirt is Bernard Stellar Sr. who, along with some of the other young men, served in World War II shortly after this time.

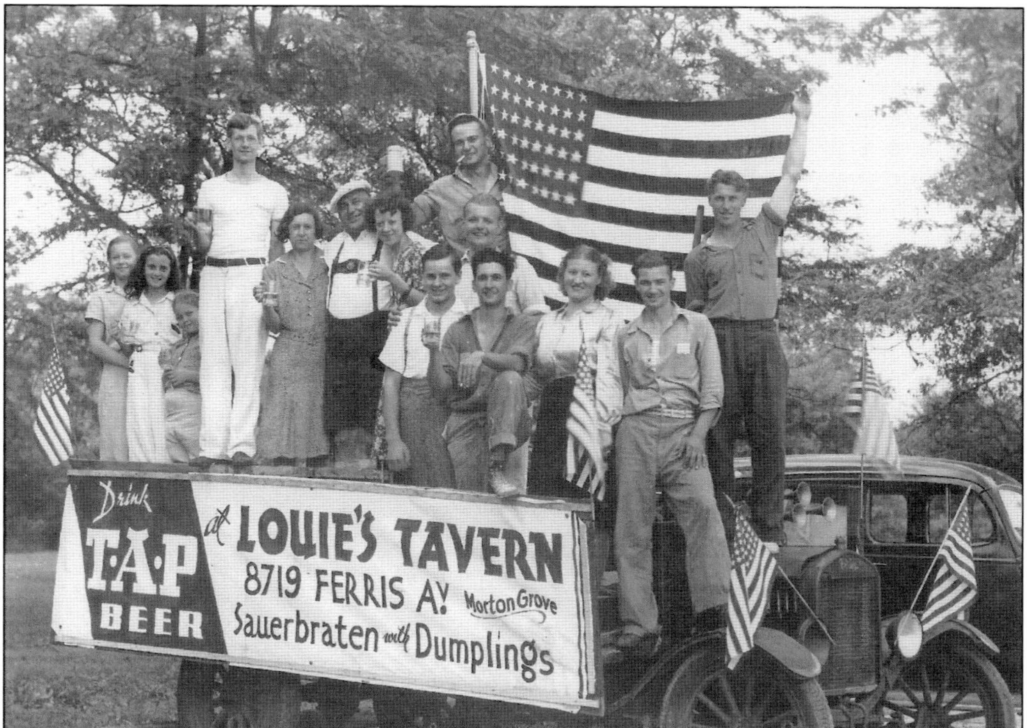

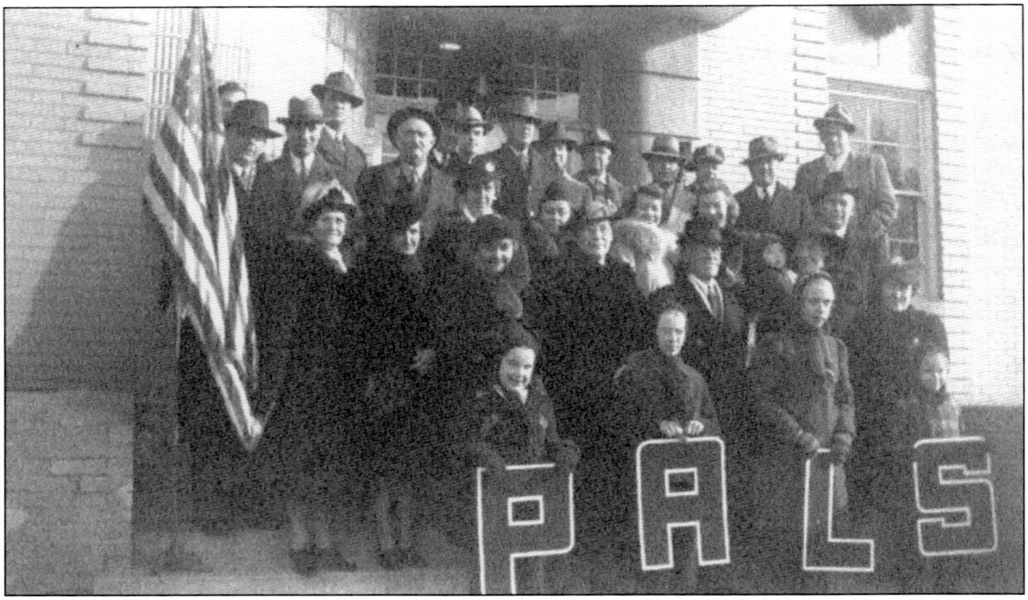

The Program to Aid Local Servicemen was formed in 1941 to support local residents serving in World War II. Members are pictured on the steps of the Village Hall. Letters and packages were sent out, while a billboard in Memorial Park, newsletters, and articles in local papers were maintained on the home front to share any news. This group disbanded in 1945 following a welcome-home party at Deckert's Hall.

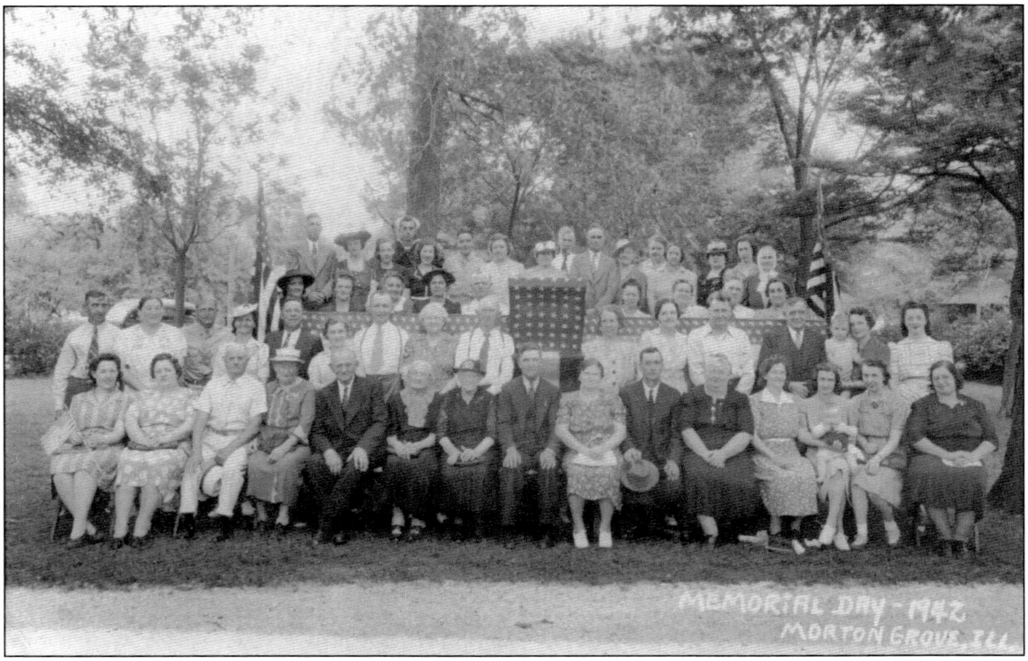

The families of local servicemen gathered on Memorial Day in 1942 in support of those serving in World War II. Service flags were displayed, representing the number of local men in the armed forces at the time. Morton Grove sent 313 young men to serve in this war, with all but nine returning home. The fallen are remembered and have been memorialized in several locations in Morton Grove.

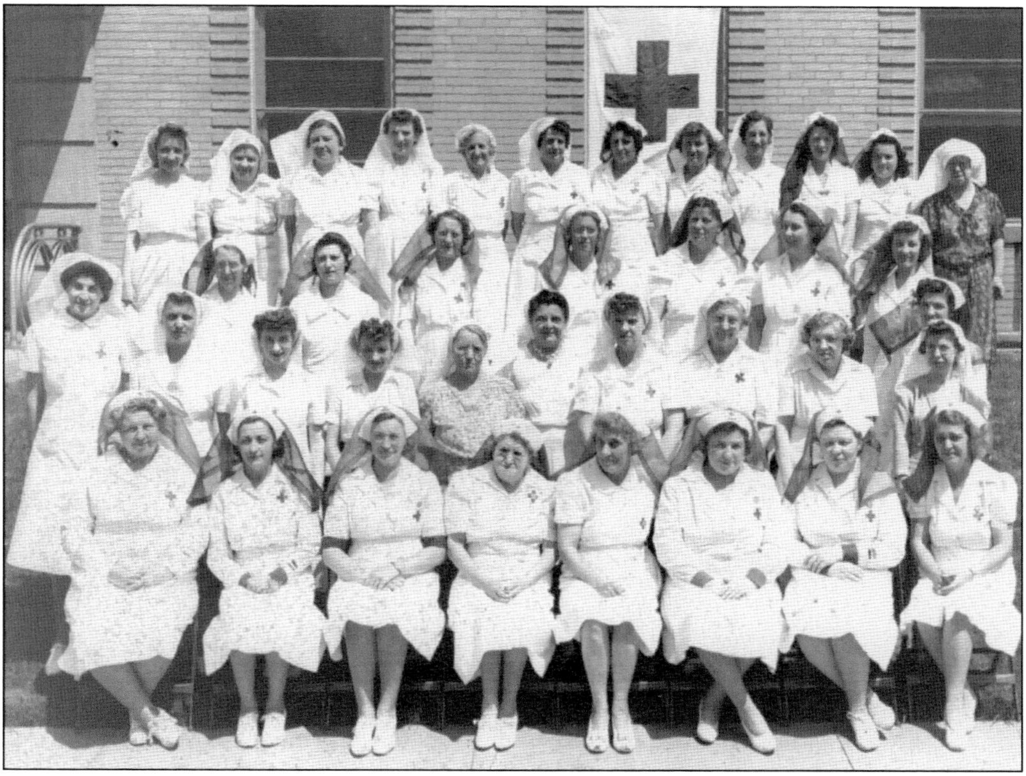

Several women residing in Morton Grove following World War II have served in the US Army and US Navy, and the local women have supported war efforts in numerous other ways over time. Red Cross volunteers, pictured in front of the Village Hall, assembled medical packages and supplies that were sent overseas and organized blood drives for our armed forces as part of a national effort.

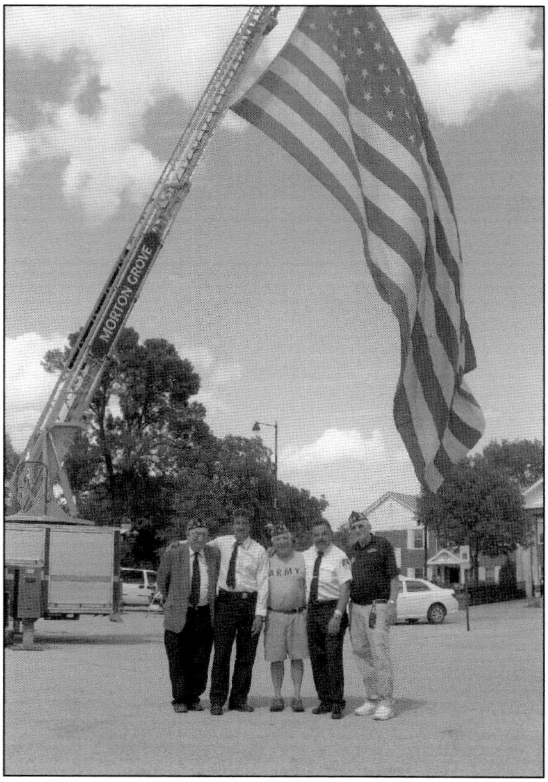

The Patriot Flag flew from Morton Grove's fire engine No. 4 on June 16, 2011, at the American Legion Memorial Civic Center. Traveling across the country on its way to New York City is part of an effort that was originated by firefighter Mitch Mendler of the San Diego Fire-Rescue Department, as a tribute to the first responders, second responders, the 9/11 families, and the fallen of the attacks on America. Pictured from left to right are Joe Hedrick, firefighter Mitch Mendler, Joe Gesicki, spokesperson and FDNY retired lieutenant Joe Torrillo, and Casey Bachara.

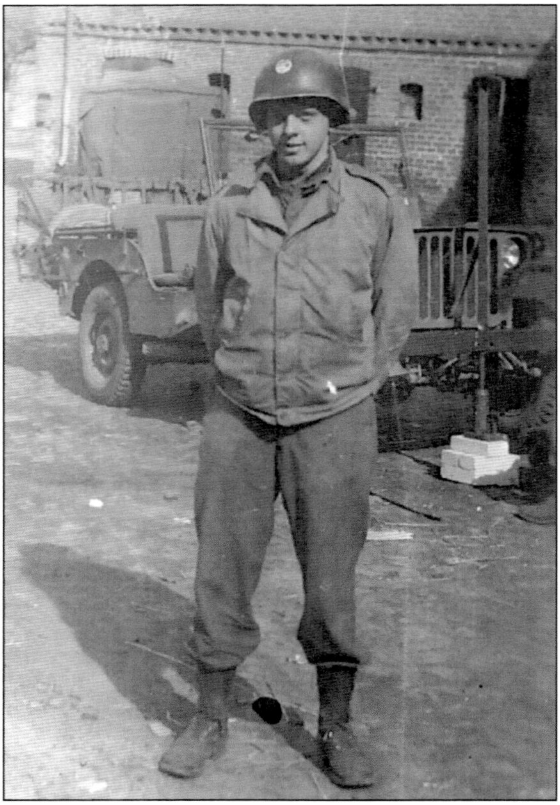

Dan Scanlon (1924–2010) entered the US Army at Camp Grant, Illinois, in March 1943. He joined the 84th Infantry Division at Camp Claiborne, Louisiana, and served under Capt. James B. Grace in the Cannon Company of the 335th Infantry Regiment. This division began fighting in the Siegfried Line, was called to fight in the Ardennes, advanced to the Rhine River, and joined the race to the Elbe River at the conclusion of World War II. After being discharged, Scanlon joined Local 134 of the International Brotherhood of Electrical Workers. Scanlon married Morton Grove girl Betty DuMont and settled down to raise a family, serving two terms as mayor of Morton Grove (1996–2005).

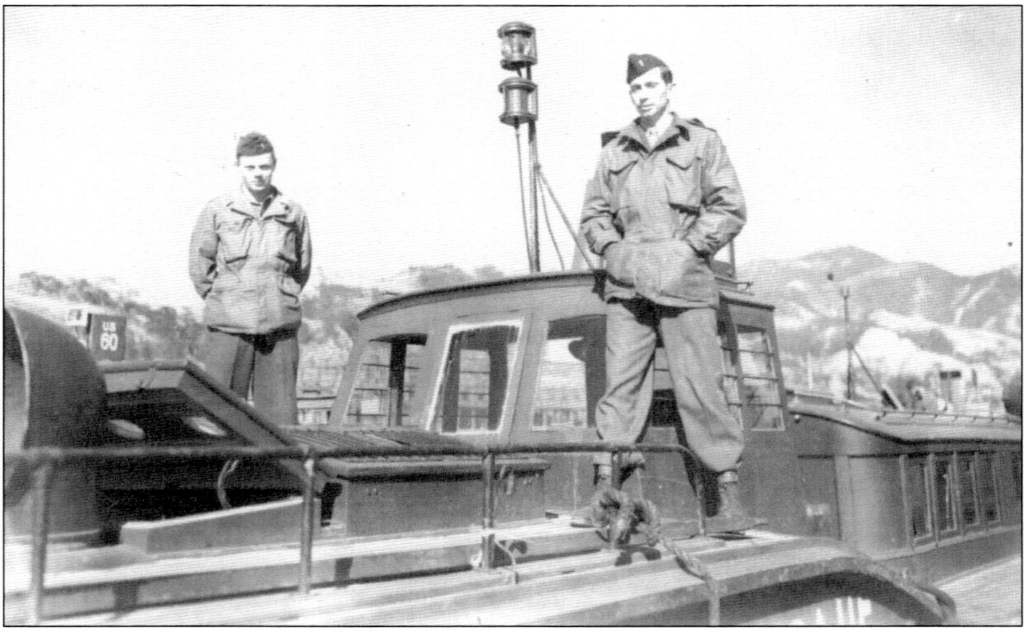

John Slater (right) is pictured aboard a Japanese ship during the occupation in Kure, Japan, following the dropping of the atomic bomb on Hiroshima. Slater served in the Pacific Theater during World War II with the US Army Corps of Engineers, 242nd Engineer Combat Battalion, 77th Infantry.

Bette Horstman, born in Hibbing, Minnesota, resided in Morton Grove for over 50 years and served in the Army Medical Corps during World War II. Horstman, a captain in the 5th Army at the 22nd Station Hospital on Saipan, served as a physical therapist to wounded American soldiers and Japanese prisoners of war and at Brooks General Hospital, Texas. Horstman's oral history interview is available through the Morton Grove Historical Museum.

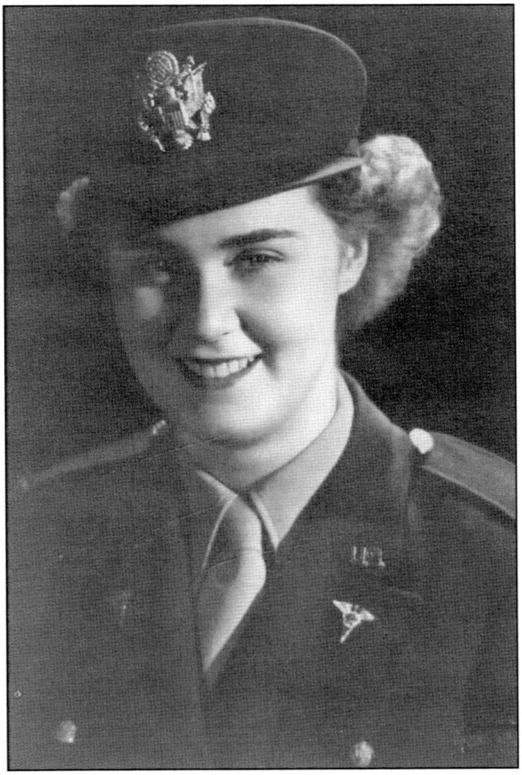

Thomas Stockenberg, a Morton Grove resident for over 57 years, served in the US Navy during World War II. Pictured from left to right are Stockenberg with Chick Morrison and Herb Rogers, who were butchers aboard the USS *Topeka*, CL 67. "The Order of the Silver Cleavers, Manila, 1946," is noted on the back of this photograph.

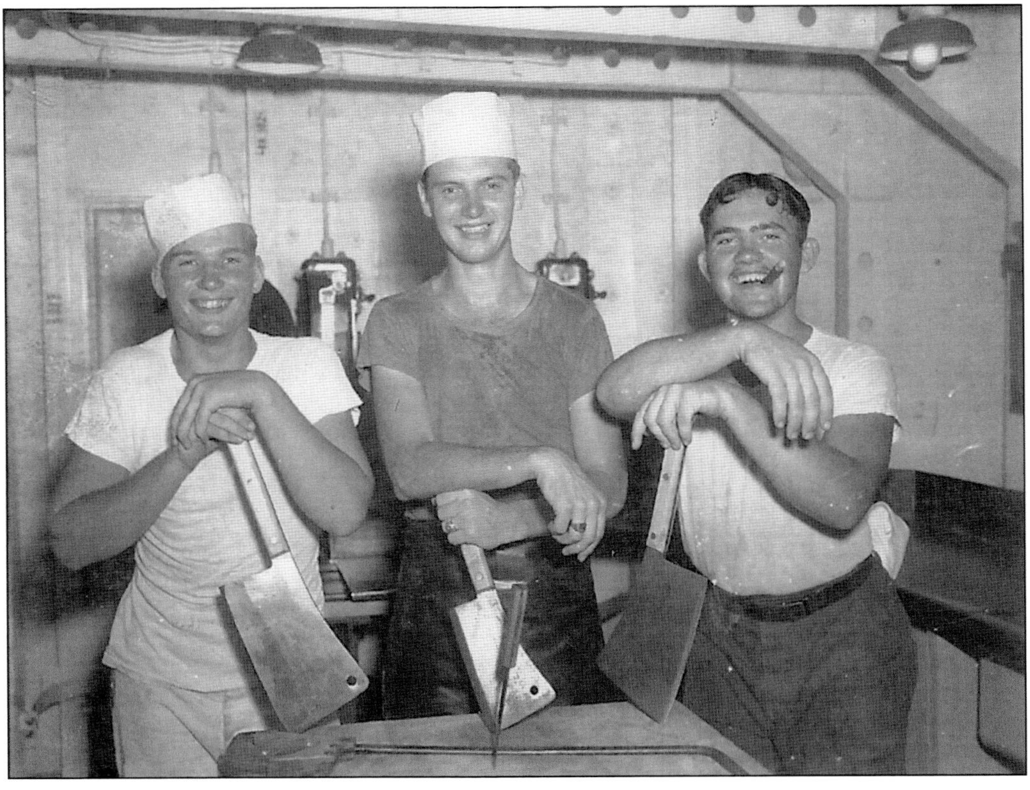

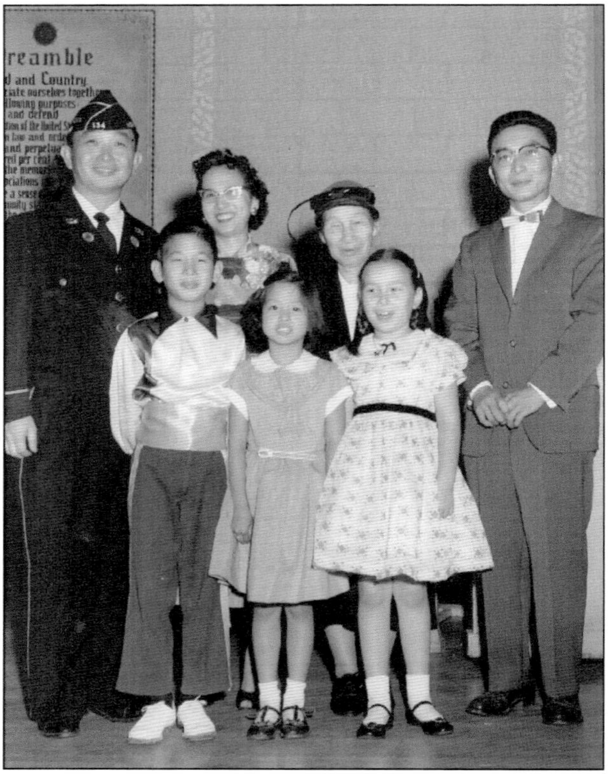

Tadao "Tad" Kimura is pictured with family members during his installation ceremony as commander of American Legion Post No. 134 in 1959. Pictured from left to right are (first row) Stanley, Teresa, and Judy Kimura; (second row) Tad, Susie, Kuga, and Steve Kimura. Tad was the first Japanese American commander of the post and was among the heroic men serving as translators, personal interpreters, and prisoner of war interrogators with the Military Intelligence Service during World War II. Congress passed a public law, signed by Pres. Barack Obama on October 5, 2010, conferring the Congressional Gold Medal to Japanese American World War II veterans of the 100th Battalion, the 442nd Regimental Combat Team, and the Military Intelligence Service. Tad is pictured below in uniform.

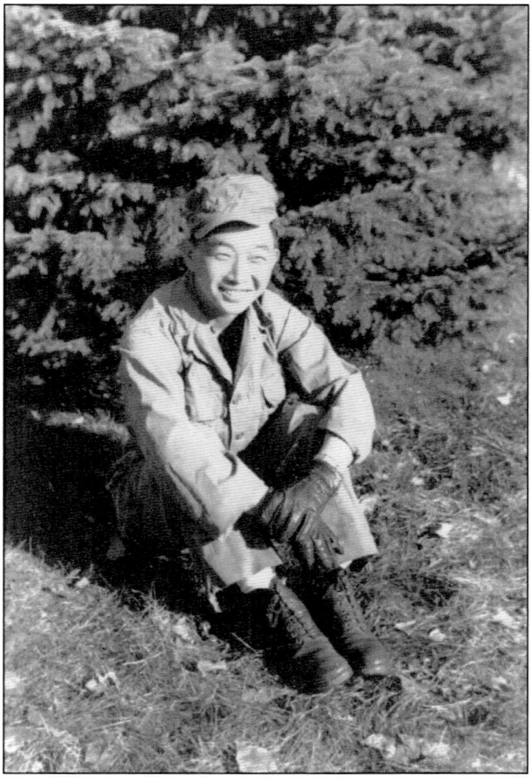

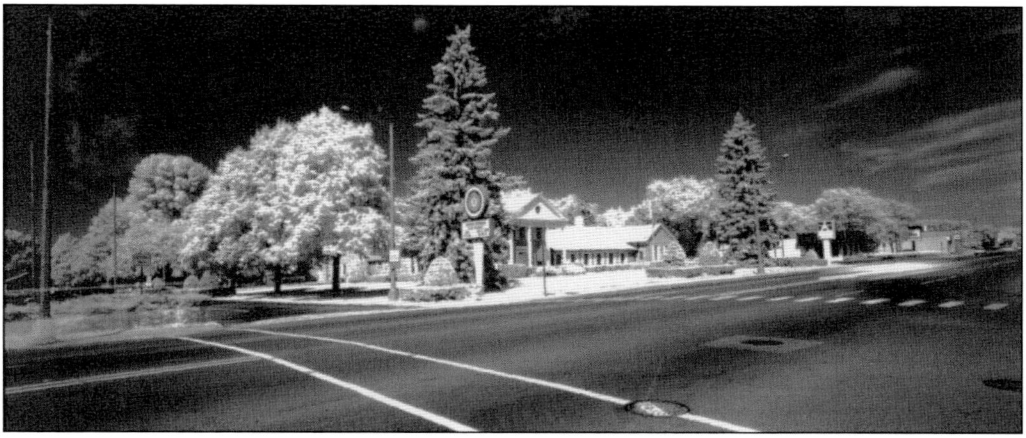

This infrared photograph by Roland Weigt shows American Legion Post No. 134 at 6140 Dempster Street in 1991. The post was formed in 1924 and met at various locations until this building was constructed in 1949. The legion has since sponsored many other groups and community activities. The building is now the American Legion Memorial Civic Center, which is owned by the village and used for senior services and other civic activities in addition to its use by the American Legion.

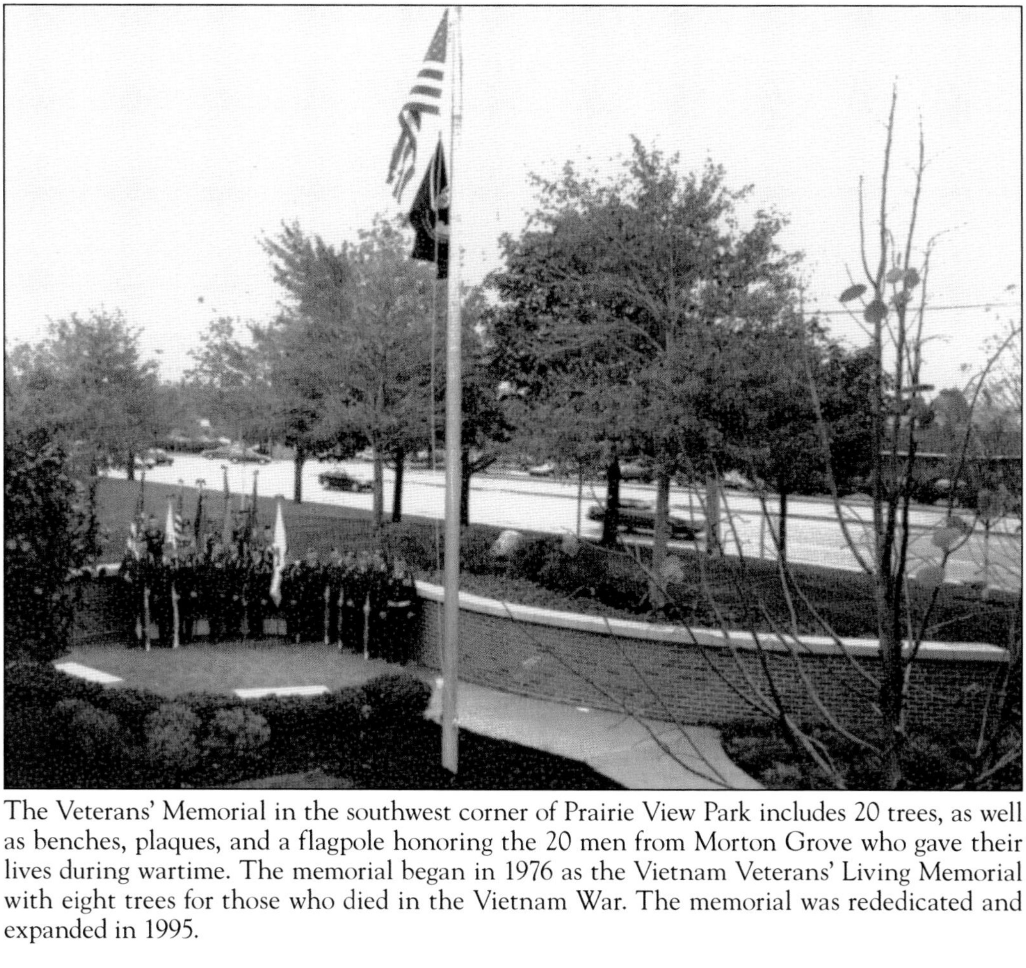

The Veterans' Memorial in the southwest corner of Prairie View Park includes 20 trees, as well as benches, plaques, and a flagpole honoring the 20 men from Morton Grove who gave their lives during wartime. The memorial began in 1976 as the Vietnam Veterans' Living Memorial with eight trees for those who died in the Vietnam War. The memorial was rededicated and expanded in 1995.

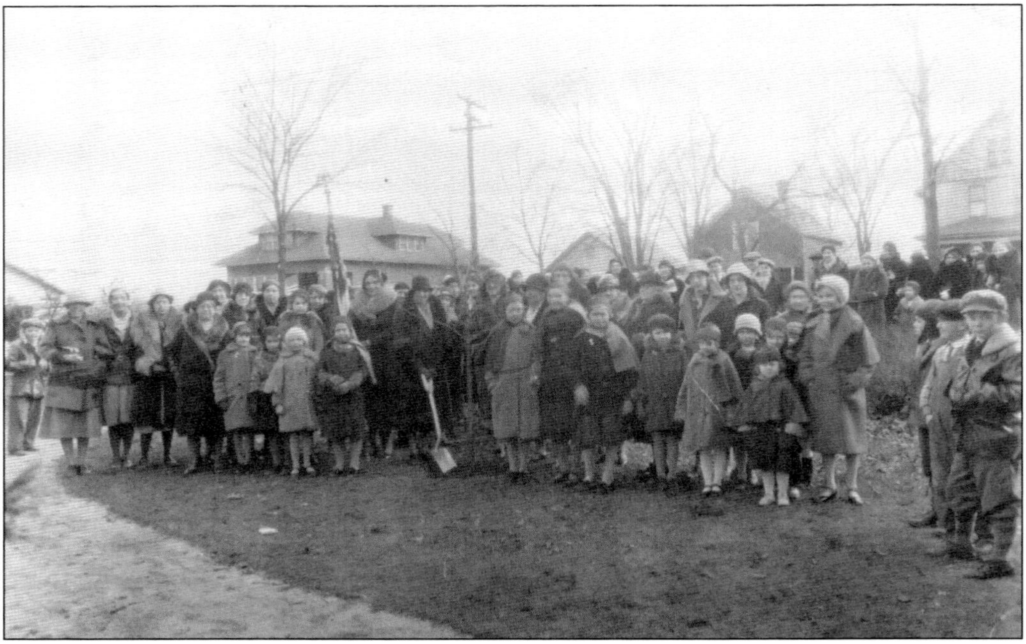

Josephine L. Gebel of Morton Grove, a Niles Township unit member, was elected president of the 7th District American Legion Auxiliary of Illinois in 1931. Above, Gebel is pictured with a shovel beside the 7th District Washington elm planted on February 22, 1932, in Morton Grove's Public Park, joined by unit members, junior members, and a Wilmette Girl Scout troop. Below, a group of American Legion Auxiliary members are shown in a car decorated with flowers for the 1931 Morton Grove Days parade. St. Martha's Catholic Church can be seen behind the women. (Both, courtesy of Morton Grove American Legion Auxiliary.)

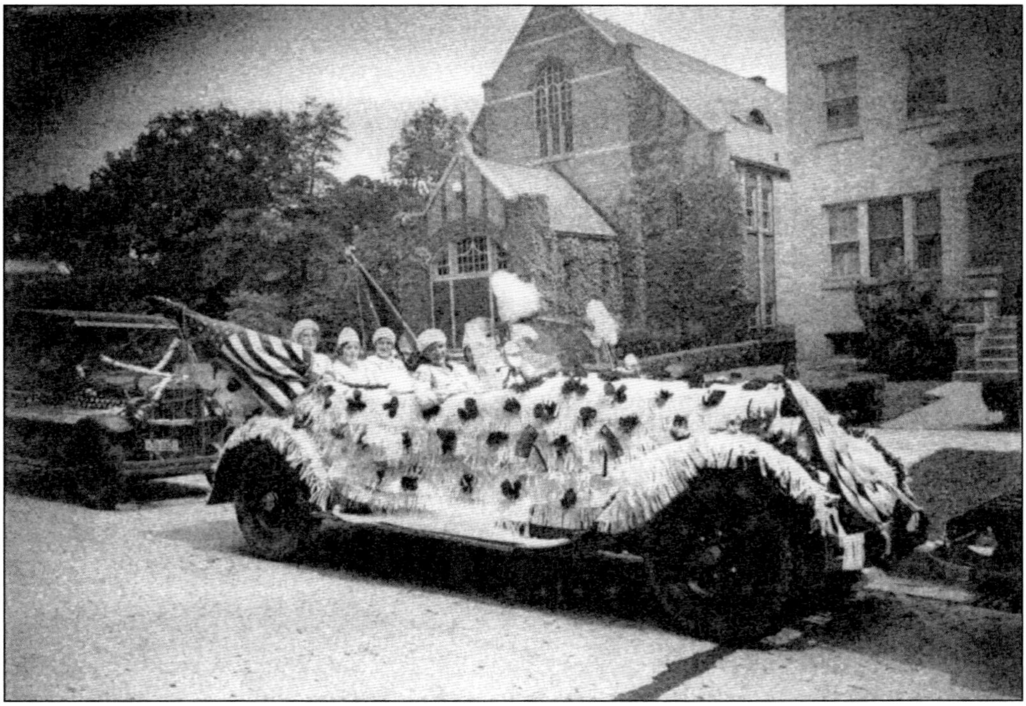

Seven

COMMERCE AND INNOVATIONS IN INDUSTRY

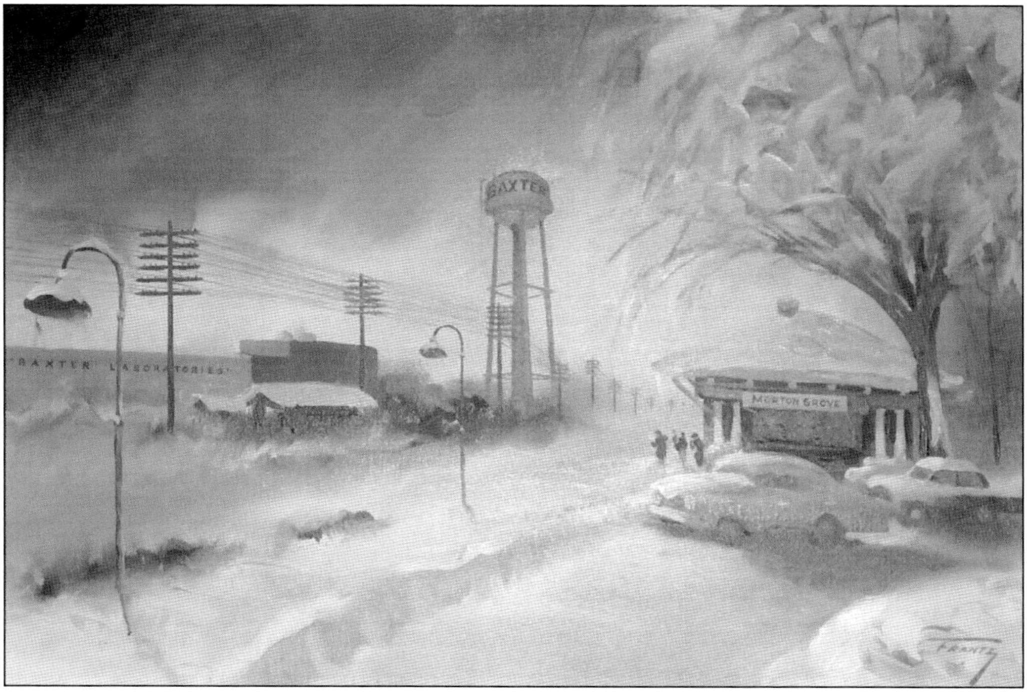

This painting of Baxter Laboratories by Frantz was donated by Margaret Graham Caswell, the daughter of William B. Graham, who was the company's vice president in 1945 and chief executive officer from 1953 to 1980. Baxter moved from Glenview to a larger plant and headquarters in Morton Grove in 1947 and pioneered development of some of the most important medical products of the century. The first flexible intravenous container system as well as the first artificial kidney and blood collection system were among their accomplishments.

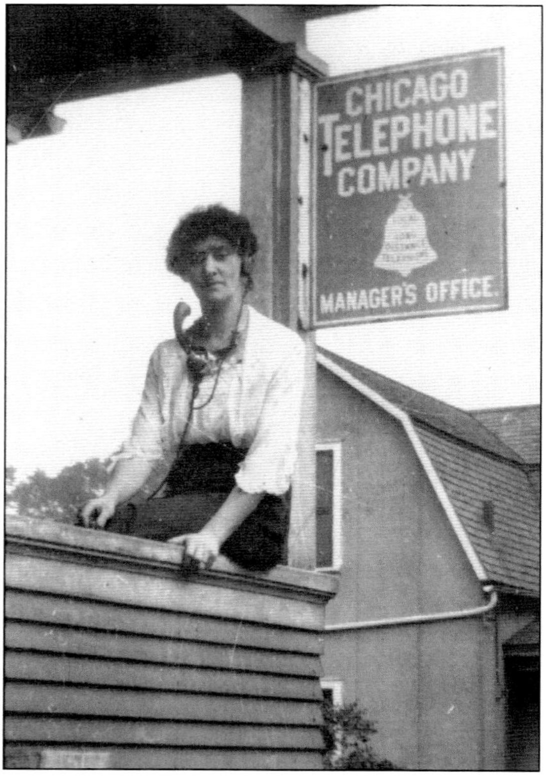

Eleanor Engels is shown here in 1918 outside of the Chicago Telephone Company office in Morton Grove. She was the first switchboard operator at this station. Engels's handwritten telephone book from that year includes about 50 entries for businesses and a few individuals in Morton Grove, notably skipping no. 4, which had belonged to the Wayside Inn before it burned down the year before.

Fred L. Huscher went into business with his brother-in-law Peter Haupt in 1912 along the railroad tracks south of Dempster Street. Starting out in the ice business, Huscher soon bought out Haupt and expanded to include coal, gravel, and sand. Huscher began excavation work with a team of horses, evolving into trucking. His sons Carl and Fred joined the family business upon returning from the Navy in World War II.

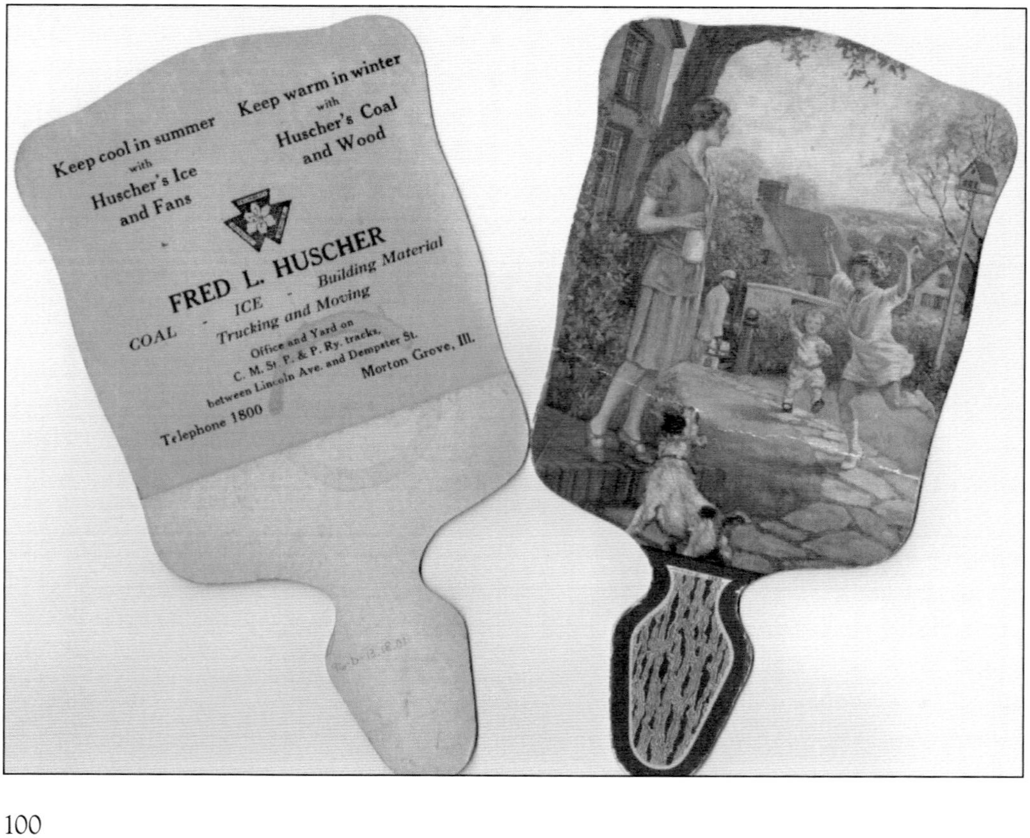

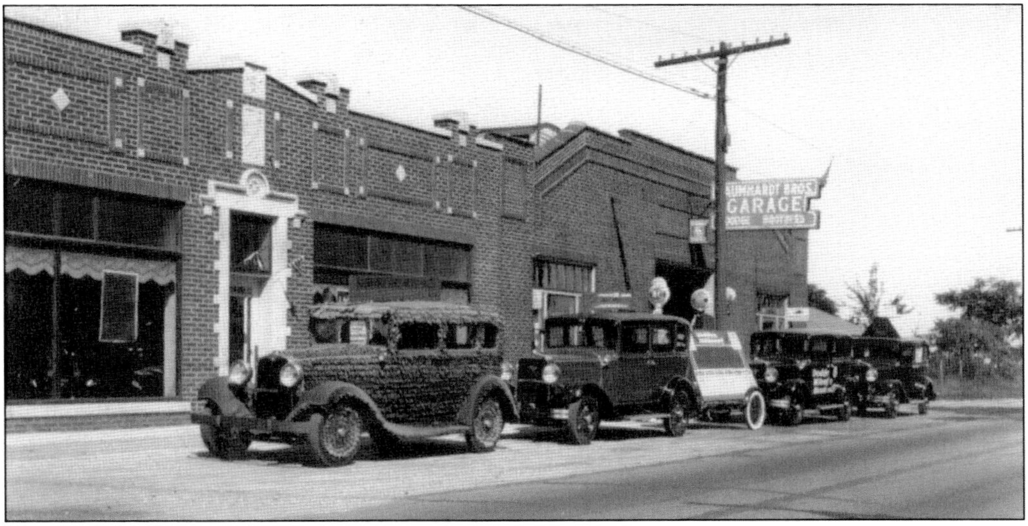

Baumhardt Bros. Garage, at 5844 Lincoln Avenue, is shown in approximately 1930. The cars, prepared for a parade, include the Dodge Eight Marathon, an automobile that performed a long-distance stunt to demonstrate the qualities of the new model. On its many paths across the United States, the marathon car visited as many Dodge dealers as possible.

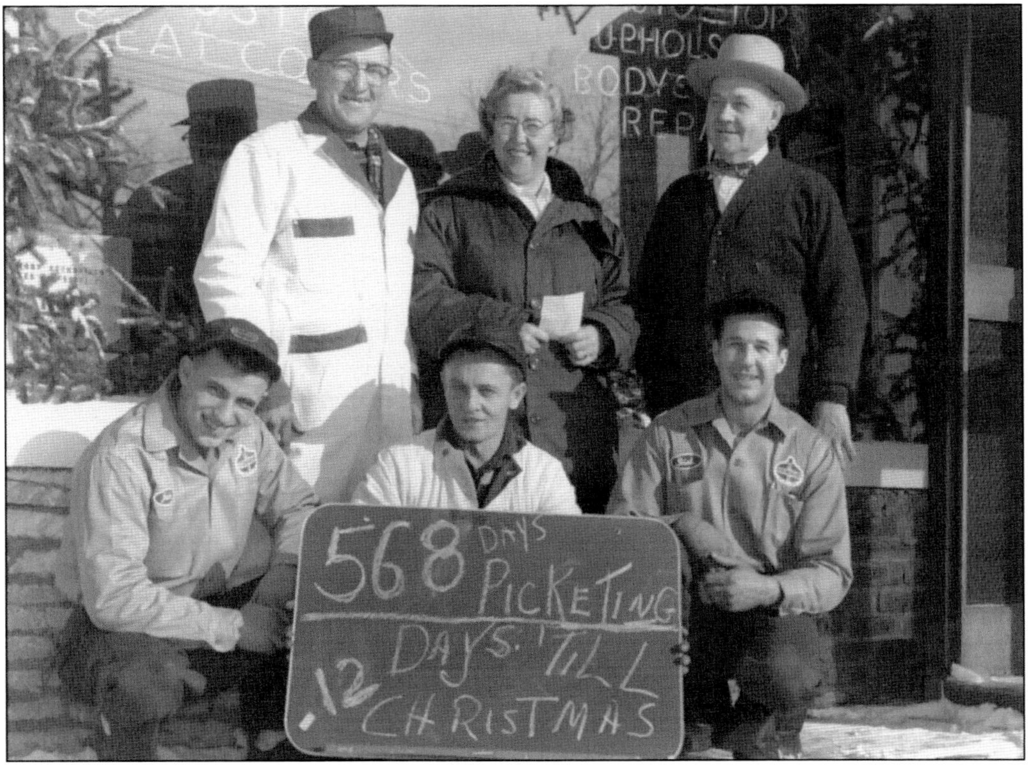

Carl Eckhardt's Standard Oil station opened in 1940 at Austin and Lincoln Avenues, closing temporarily while Eckhardt served in the Army during World War II. Eckhardt battled the Teamsters Union, Local 705, from 1955 to 1958, standing firm with employees refusing to join the union. Pictured from left to right are (first row) John Heinz, unidentified, and Dick Wolflick; (second row) Carl Eckhardt, Helen Eckhardt, and unidentified.

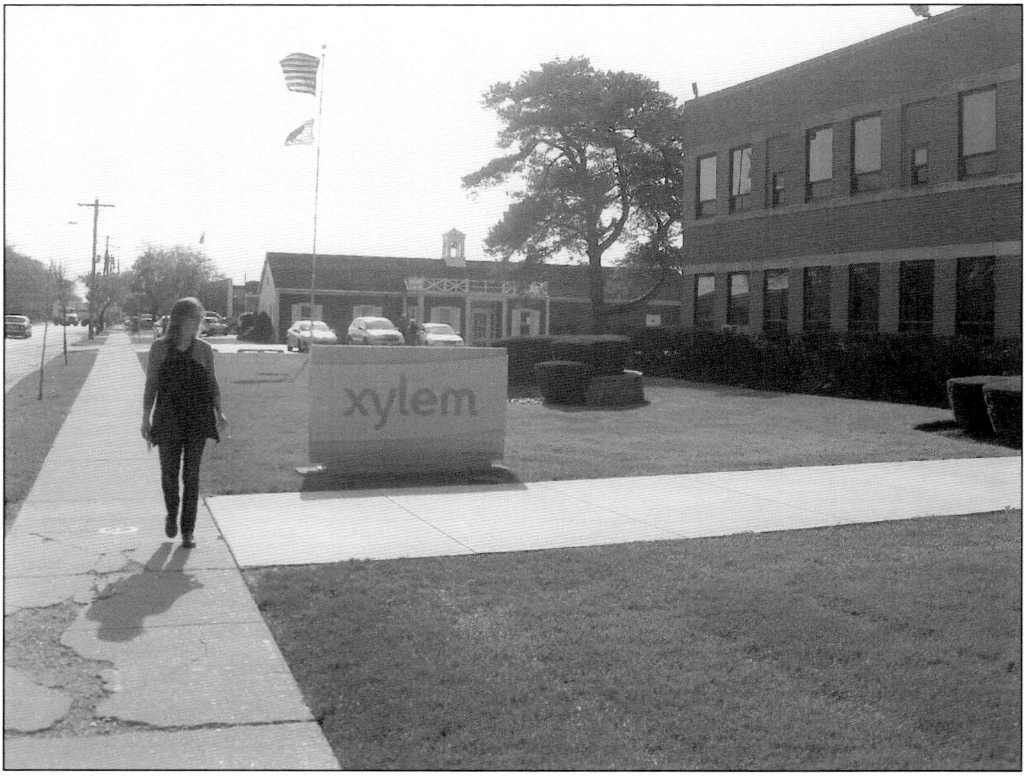

Bell and Gossett (now Xylem) moved its heating, cooling, and water equipment offices and factory to a 20-acre plot in Morton Grove on December 7, 1941, the day of the attack on Pearl Harbor, and immediately adjusted its production to make parts for tanks and ships used in World War II. Today, the facility manufactures parts and trains installers on equipment for residential and industry uses.

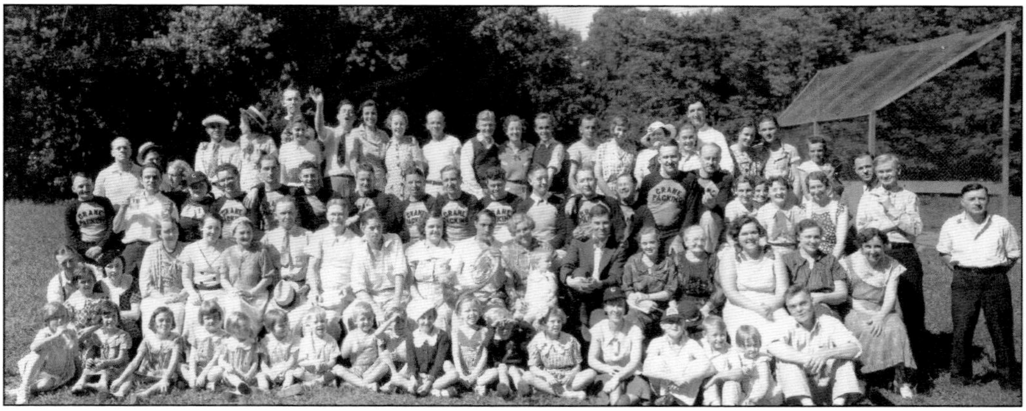

John Crane moved to its current 26-acre site on Oakton Street in Morton Grove in the early 1950s. John Crane is a world leader in the manufacturing of mechanical seals and mechanical packings. This group photograph of the annual John Crane packing company picnic was taken in 1935. The company was known for open houses over the holidays and athletic events for employees, including golf, bowling, and softball.

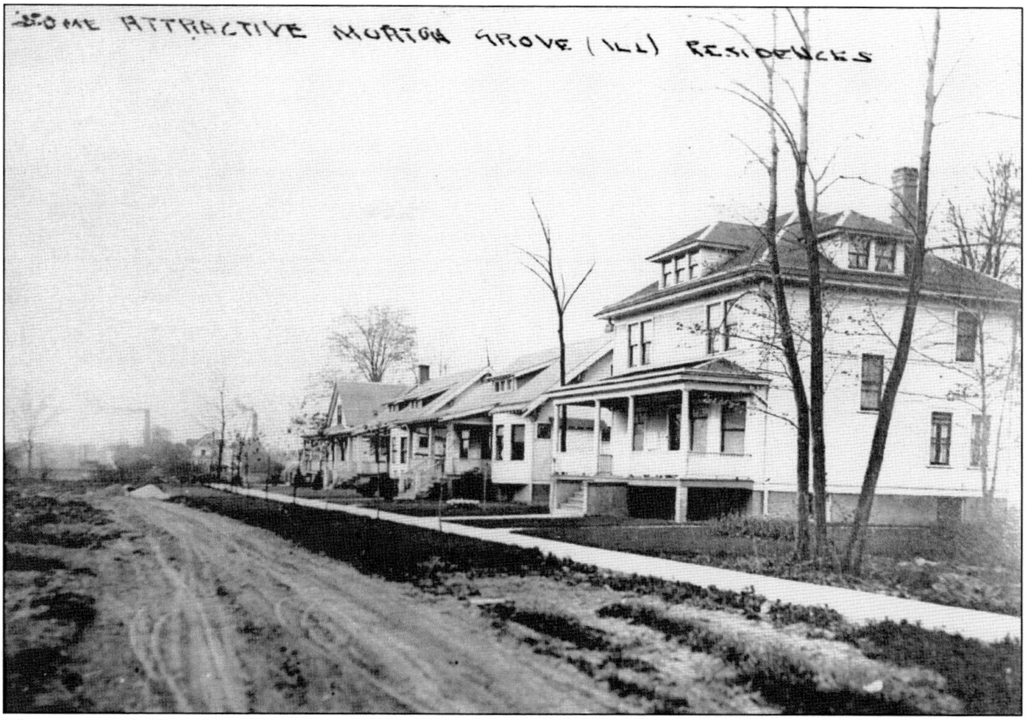

Houses on Callie Avenue are shown here, including some Sears kit homes. Sears, Roebuck and Co. sold many models of homes to be assembled by the purchaser, coinciding with the early-20th-century housing boom between the world wars. A few of these homes, although somewhat modified, are still in use today.

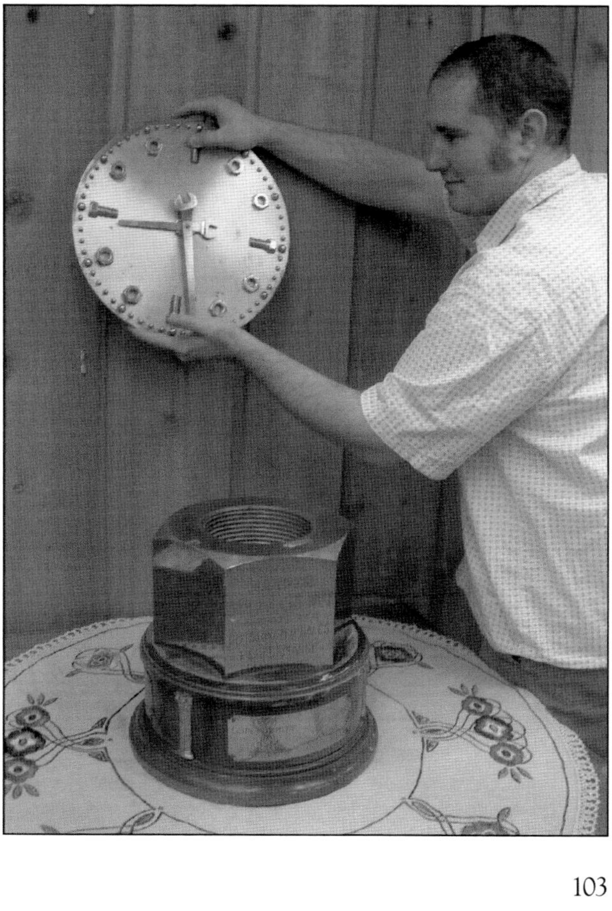

H.M. Harper Company was located at Lehigh and Oakton Avenues from 1946 to 1982. The company produced lightweight, high-strength fasteners and parts for the airline industry. The "Big Brass Nut" sales trophy, as well as the clock that once hung in Harper's break room, are now held in the Morton Grove Historical Museum. Assistant curator Tim Mayse-Lillig is shown placing these items for exhibit.

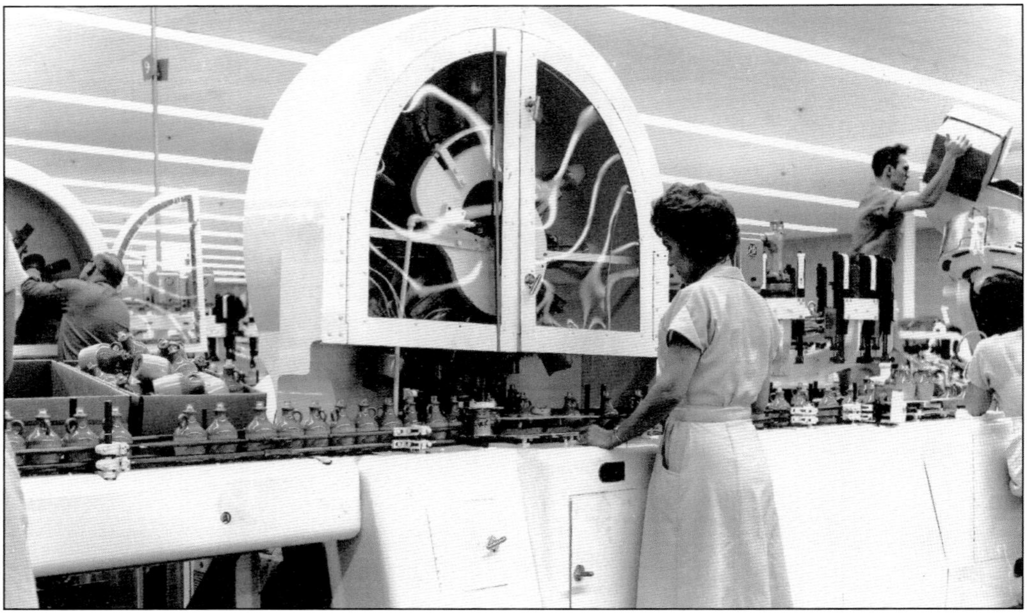

Avon Products is one of the world's largest cosmetics and direct sales companies. It created its facility at Waukegan and Golf Roads in 1956. Later, a second building was constructed slightly farther north on Waukegan Road in Glenview. Here, workers are shown on Avon's assembly line packing products for distribution. (Courtesy of Avon Products.)

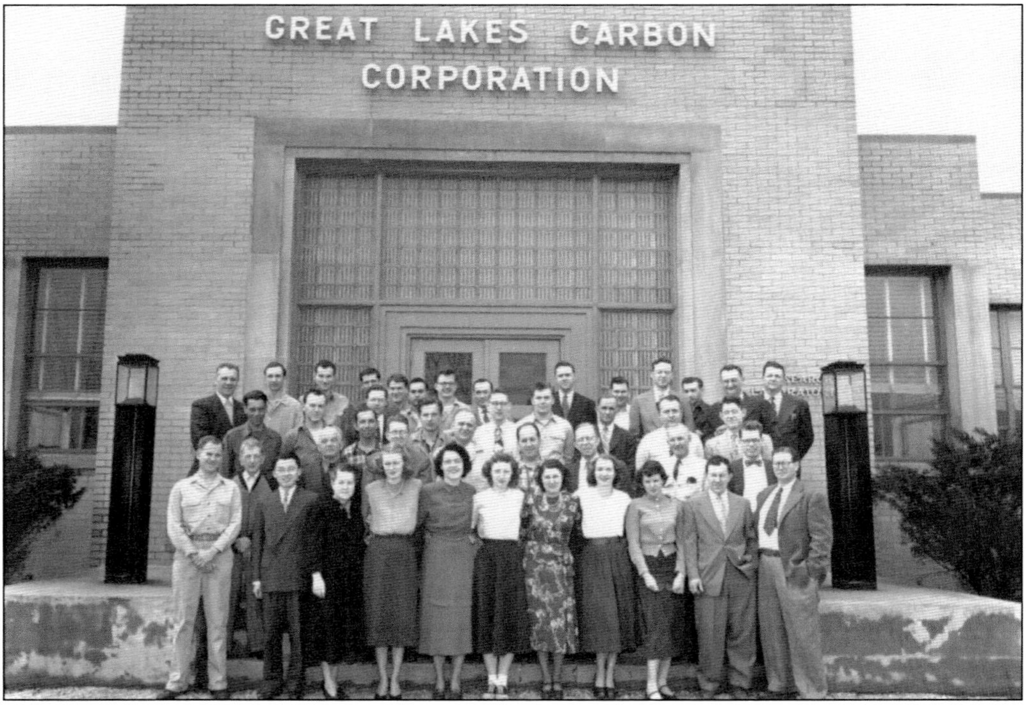

The Great Lakes Carbon Corporation was founded in Chicago in 1919. Employees are pictured in front of the firm's research and development laboratories at 8201 Austin Avenue in Morton Grove in the late 1950s. Elizabeth Fink of Morton Grove was a long-standing employee and is pictured in the front row, third from the left.

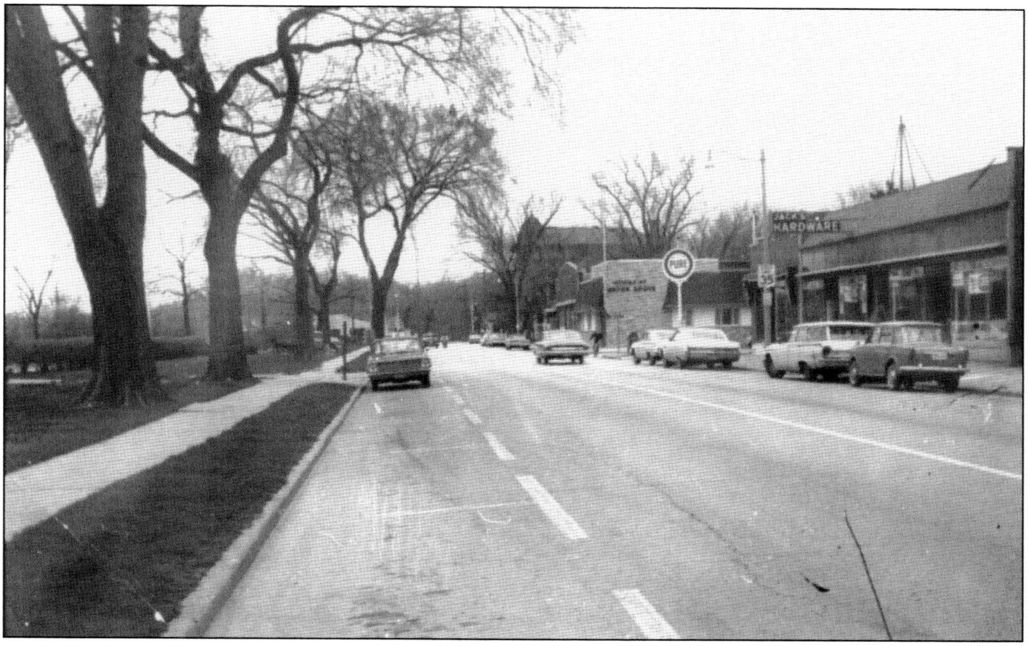

This view of Lincoln Avenue in the 1960s shows the Dilg Building in the background and Jack's Hardware at 6244 Lincoln Avenue. Jack Koller, the store's owner, also served as Morton Grove's mayor from 1957 to 1960. He was the son of John Koller, who operated Koller Exchange in the 1880s and 1890s.

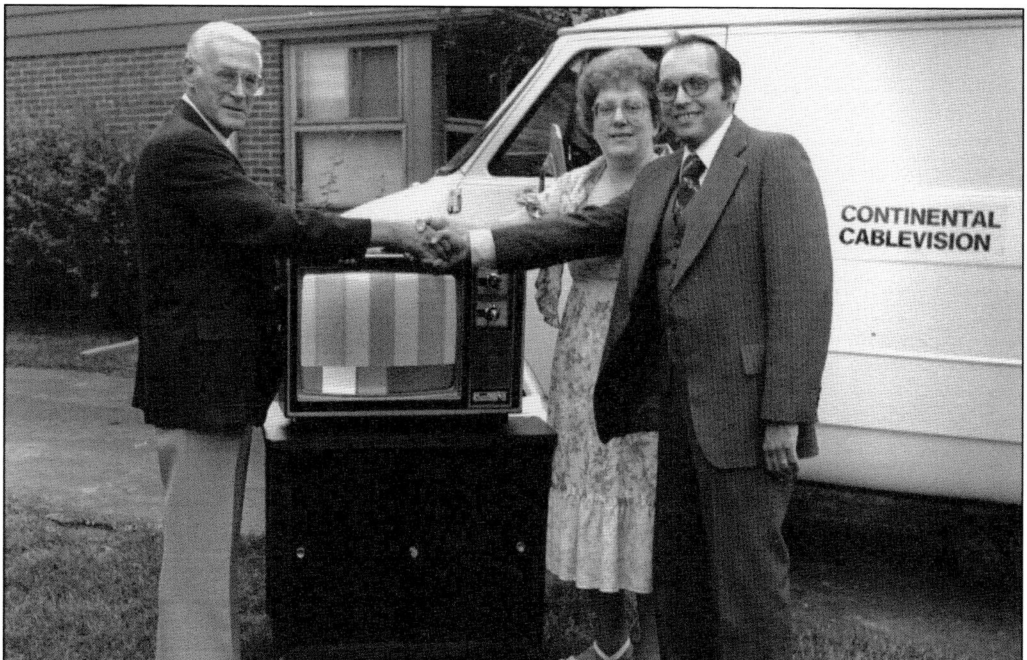

The Goldberg family of Morton Grove became the first family in Chicago's North Shore suburbs to receive cable television in August 1980. Pictured from left to right are Morton Grove mayor Richard Flickinger, Vicki Goldberg, and Sheldon Goldberg. The service from Continental Cablevision provided 36 channels for $6.95 per month at that time.

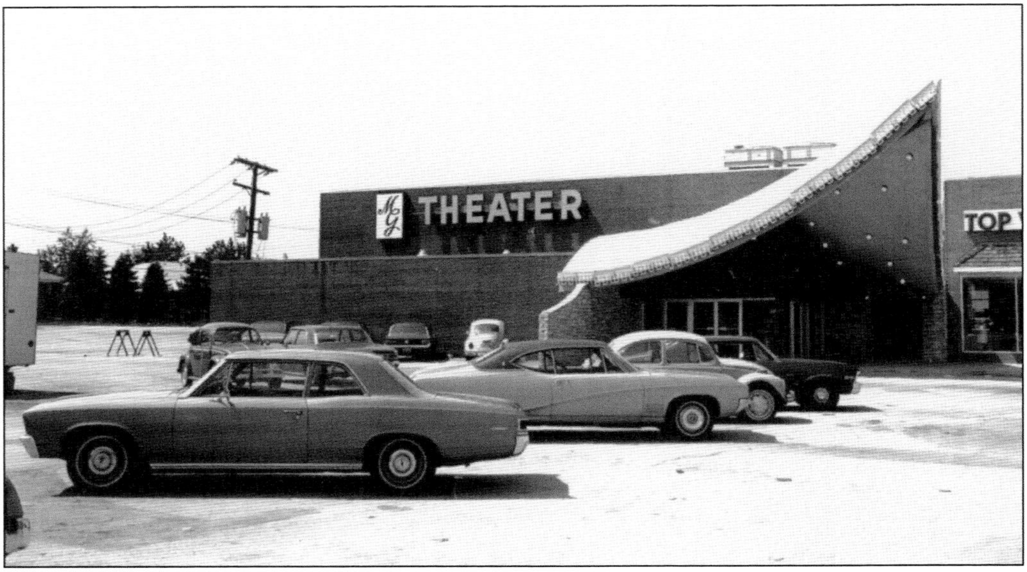

The Morton Grove Theater, located in the shopping plaza at the northwest corner of Harlem Avenue and Dempster Street, was situated next to the Topp's department store. This modern indoor theater opened in 1966, seated 1,800, and boasted the finest in comfort and technical quality in projection and sound at the time. This building was razed in 2002.

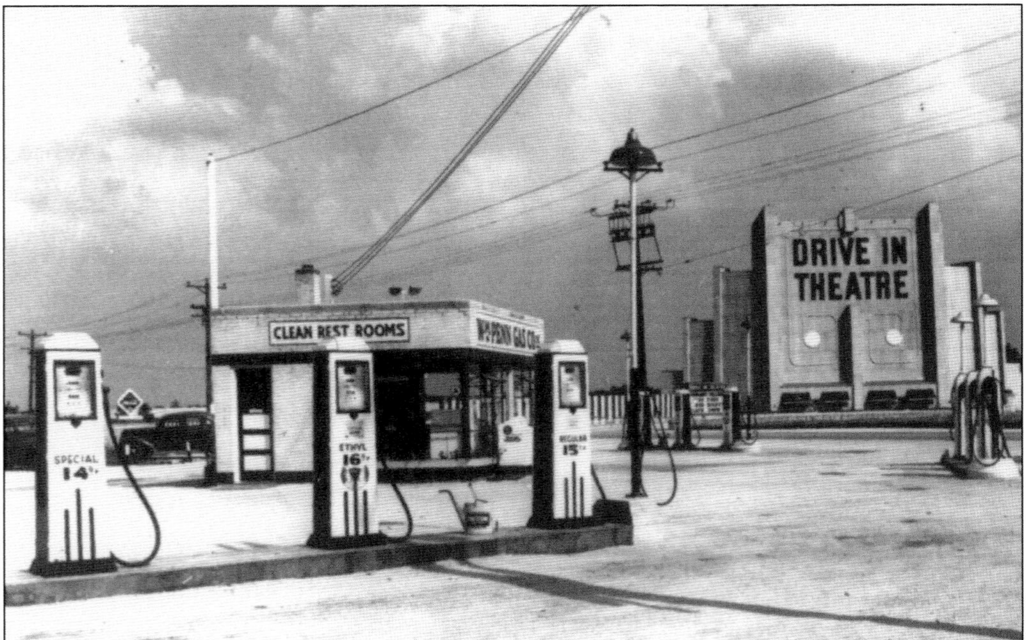

Morton Grove's Drive-In Theatre opened in 1941 on the southeast corner of Golf and Waukegan Roads. Residents nicknamed it "the Passion Pit." Programs listing major motion pictures showing here in 1943 and 1944 include *Keeper of the Flame* with Spencer Tracy and Katherine Hepburn; *It Ain't Hay* with Abbott and Costello; *Now, Voyager* with Bette Davis, Paul Henreid, and Claude Rains; and *When Johnny Comes Marching Home* with Gloria Jean and Allan Jones.

Eight

Suburban Development and Modern Diversity

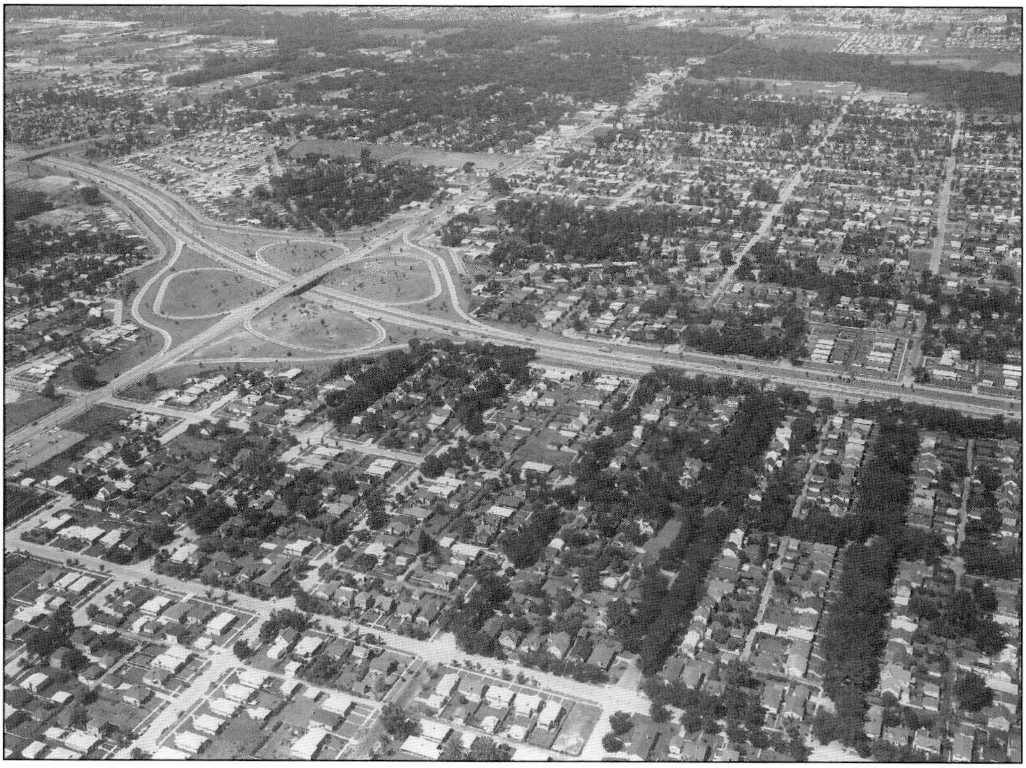

The completion of the Edens Expressway in 1951 contributed significantly to the postwar building boom. Industrial development and the growth of retail businesses in the region provided new job opportunities and evoked a migration from Chicago to suburban areas, as well as from further locations. People from around the world have made Morton Grove home in recent decades, and the village has become exceptionally diverse.

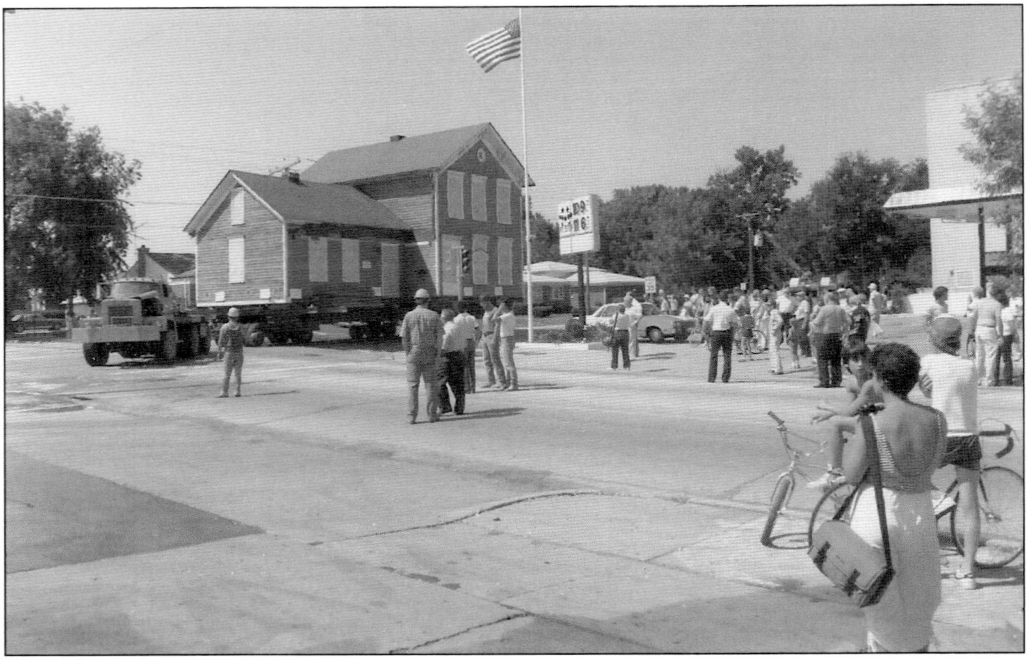

The Morton Grove Historical Society got its start through the Village of Morton Grove Senior Citizens Organization in 1976, with its first meeting held at the old fire station, later moving to the lower level of the Village Hall. Members held open houses for the public to view multi-themed exhibits at this location up until the Haupt-Yehl House was purchased from the Abbey Builders for $1 in 1984. A fundraising campaign was held, which raised $50,000 for the old farmhouse located at 6025 Lincoln Avenue to be relocated to a small parcel of land donated by the Morton Grove Park District at 6240 Dempster Street. The house moving drew crowds of residents as it made its way down Austin Avenue to Dempster Street.

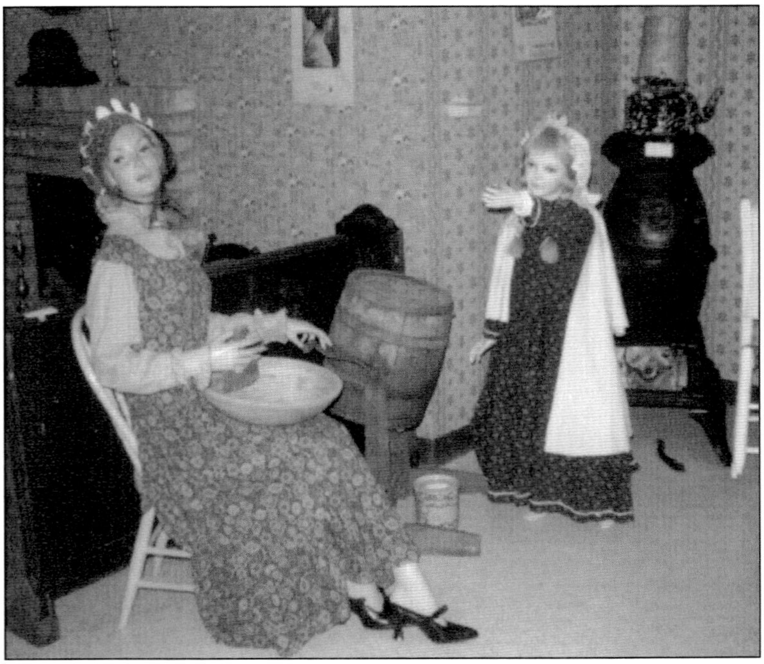

Jayne (née Wible) Barry, a descendant of the Hoffman family who settled near Beckwith Road and Lehigh Avenue in 1868, is pictured painting inside the Haupt-Yehl House museum. Barry was one of many who contributed artifacts, photographs, and documents on her family history, as well as donating her time as a volunteer and assisting with refurbishing the museum.

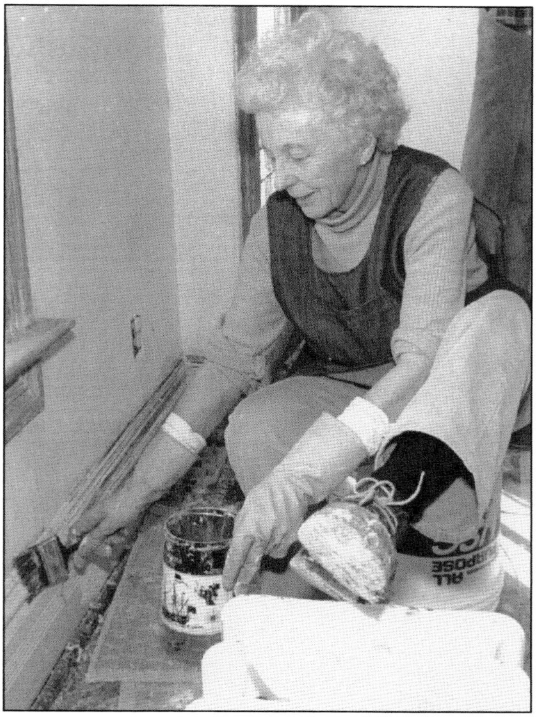

The bronze plaque placed on the Morton Grove Historical Museum grounds states, "In observance of the bicentennial (1787–1987), we rededicate ourselves to uphold and defend the Constitution of the United States, the citizens of Morton Grove, September 13, 1987." Pictured below from left to right are Fred N. Huscher, museum curator; John Tamraz and Celine Timchuck, Americanism officers for American Legion and Auxiliary Post No. 134; village administrator Larry Arft; Post No. 134 commander; John Slater; and park district director Gary Balling.

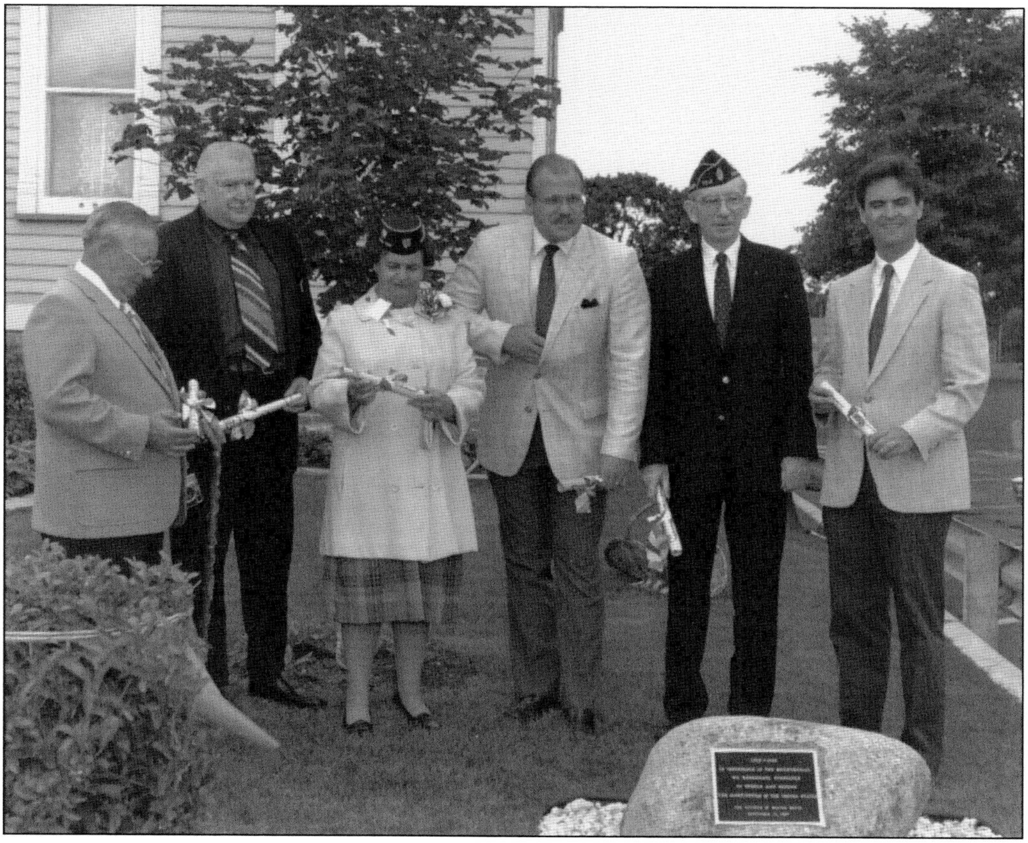

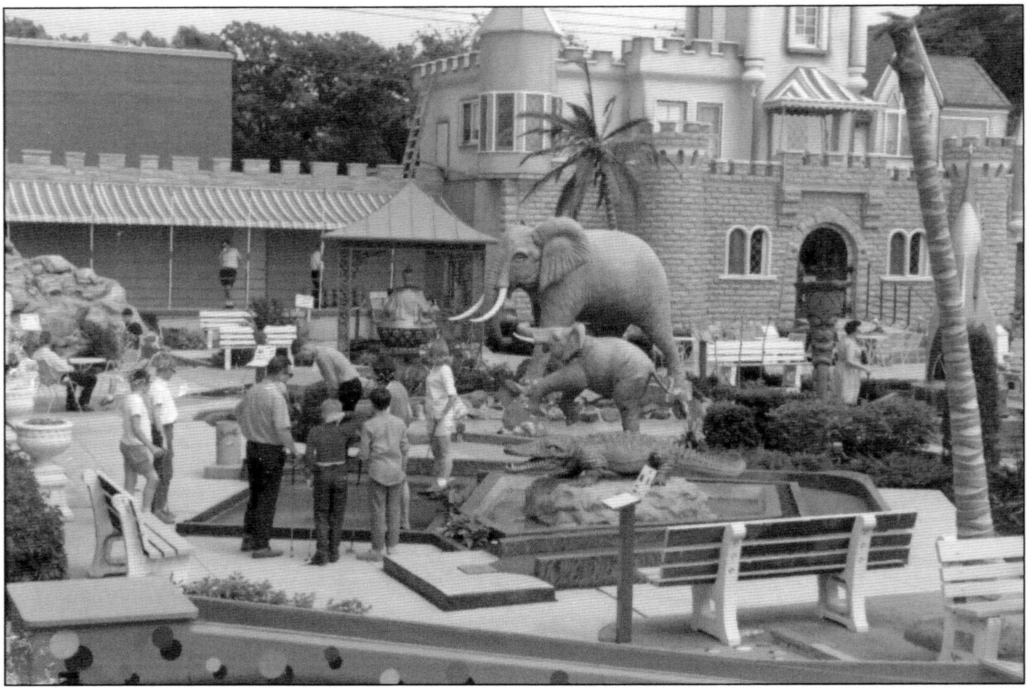

The Boznos family ran several businesses on their property at Waukegan Road and Dempster Street over several decades. In the 1950s, this included 4G Practice Fairway, a golf driving range. This was accompanied by Par King Skill Golf, a miniature golf course. In the early 1960s, the Boznos family sold all but one acre of their land for the E.J. Korvettes shopping center, keeping only Par King. The miniature golf course gained an excellent reputation for its imaginative and colorful challenges, including roller coasters for golf balls, as well as many mechanical and sculptural elements. Above, an overview of the course shows several holes and the large pink castle building that served as a backdrop. Below, teenagers at Par King Skill Golf's 18th hole are watching to see if they've won a free game on the roulette wheel.

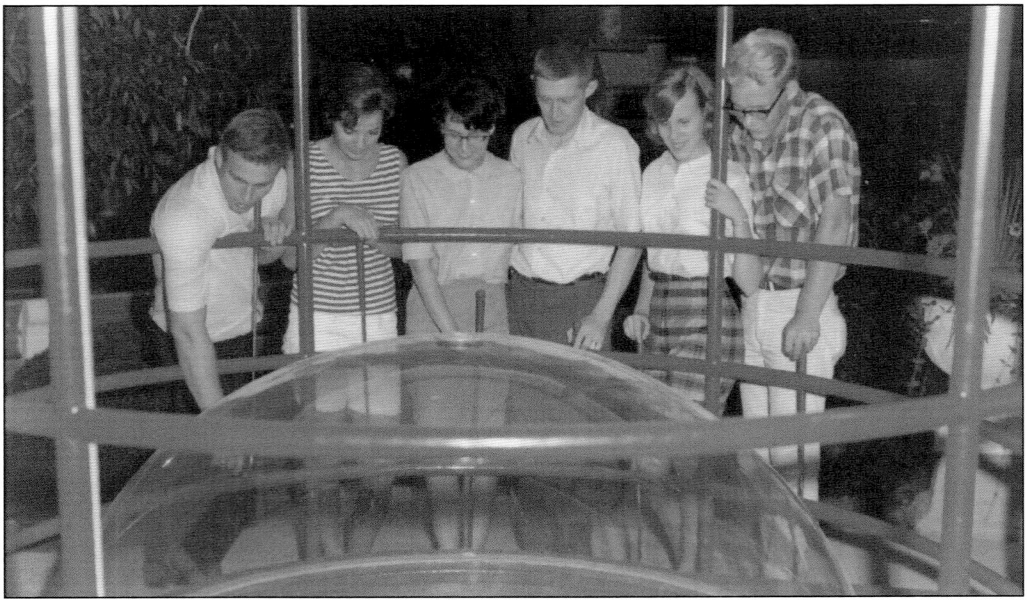

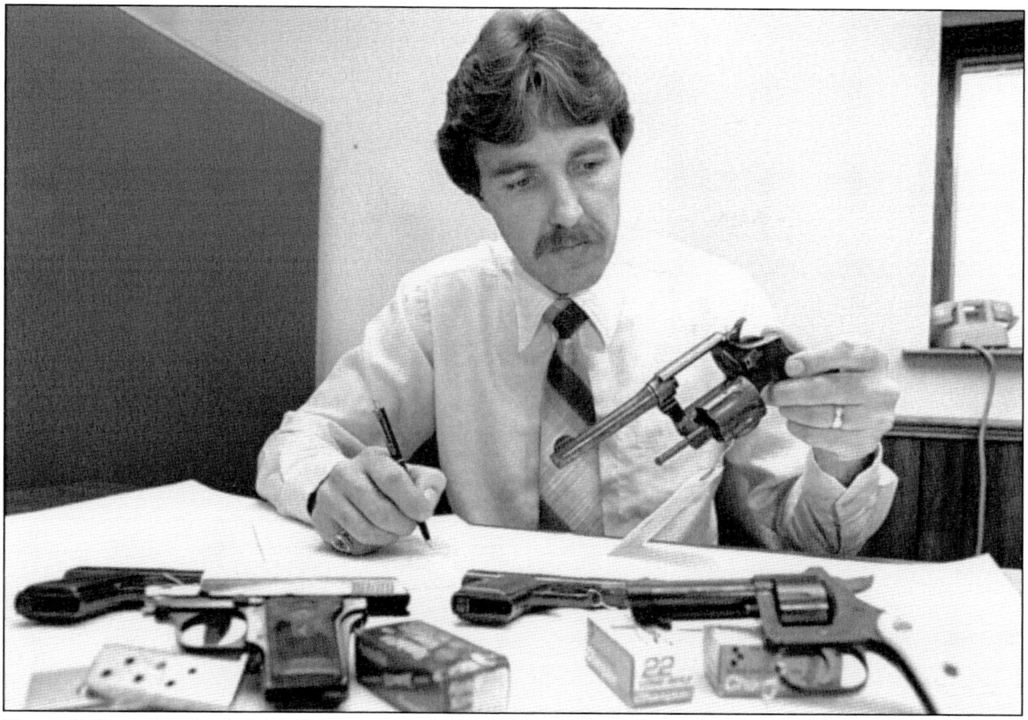

Here, Robert Jones of the Morton Grove Police Department catalogs guns turned in by citizens after the ban took effect early in 1982. Morton Grove passed ordinances relating to prohibiting the sale of handguns within the village and restricting the possession of handguns after residents requested that a gun store be prevented from opening in their neighborhood. In 2008, the law restricting possession of handguns was repealed.

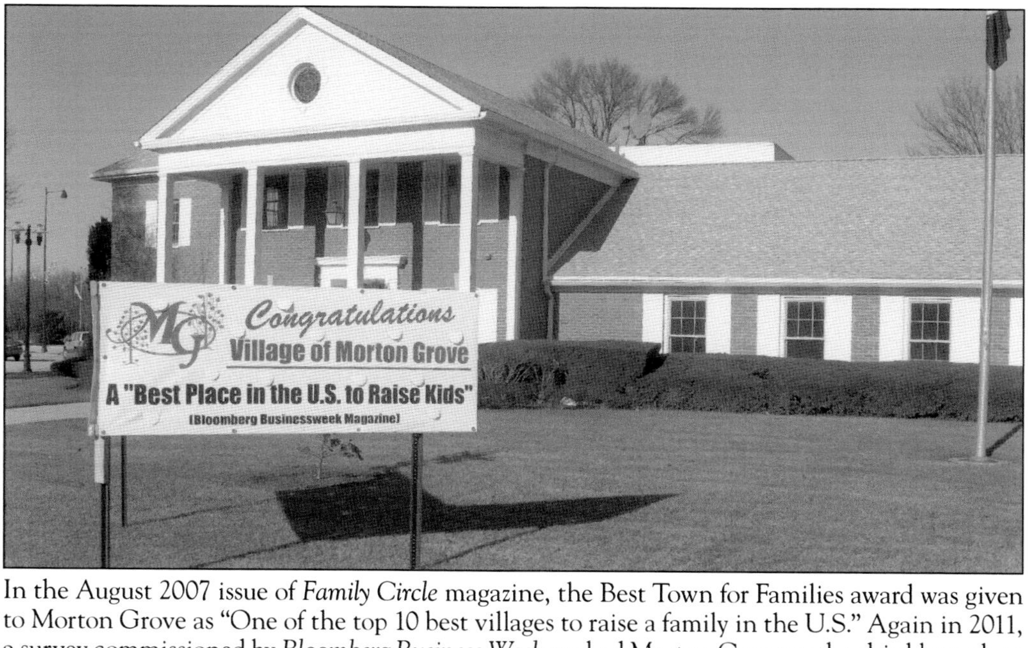

In the August 2007 issue of *Family Circle* magazine, the Best Town for Families award was given to Morton Grove as "One of the top 10 best villages to raise a family in the U.S." Again in 2011, a survey commissioned by *Bloomberg Business Week* ranked Morton Grove as the third-best place in the country to raise kids.

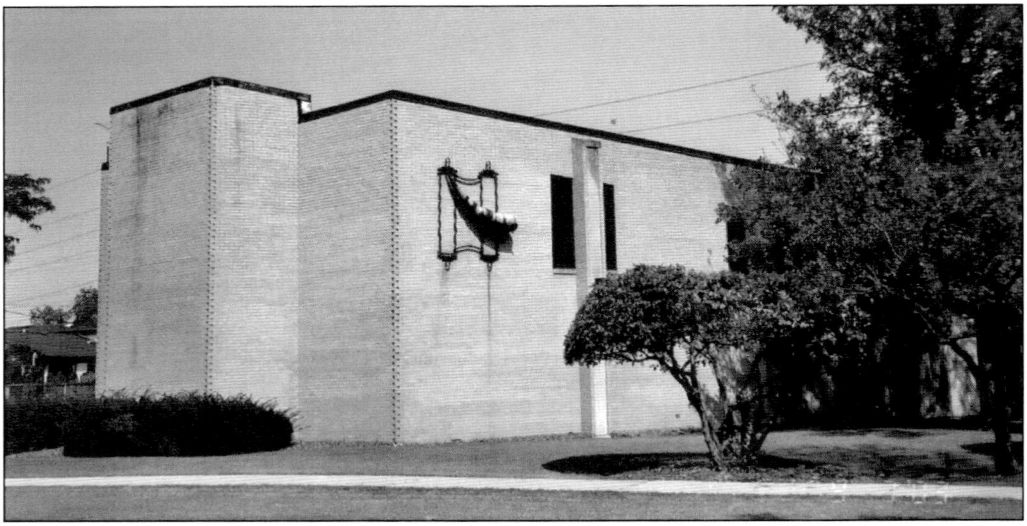

Northwest Suburban Jewish Congregation was formed in 1957 to serve families in Morton Grove, Niles, Des Plaines, and Glenview with services in a private residence. Rabbi Lawrence H. Charney began to serve as their spiritual leader in 1958. The synagogue and school building at 7800 Lyons Street, shown here, was opened on January 6, 1963. "After experiencing declining membership, the synagogue officially closed in 2010, and this building was transformed by St. Mary's Knanaya Catholic Parish of Chicago."

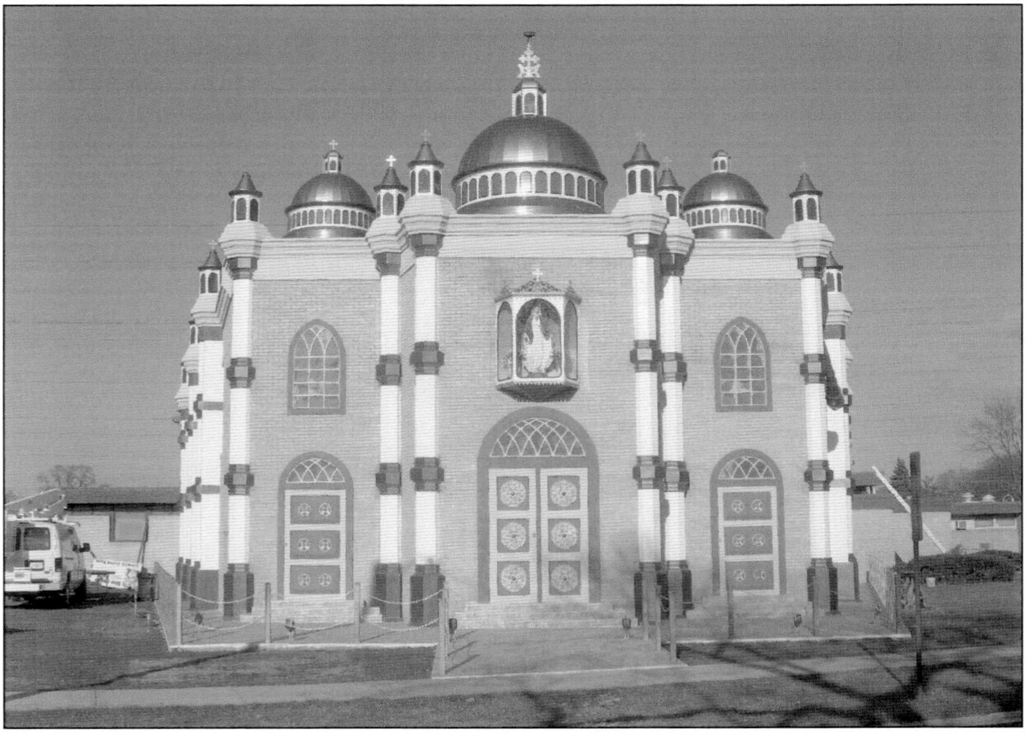

St. Mary's Knanaya Catholic Parish of Chicago was consecrated to serve members of this community, originally from southern India, with a place for worship, education, and events. The local Knanaya community worked from the early 1980s with their bishops in Kottayam, India, and the Archdiocese of Chicago to establish parishes in Maywood in 2006 and Morton Grove in 2010.

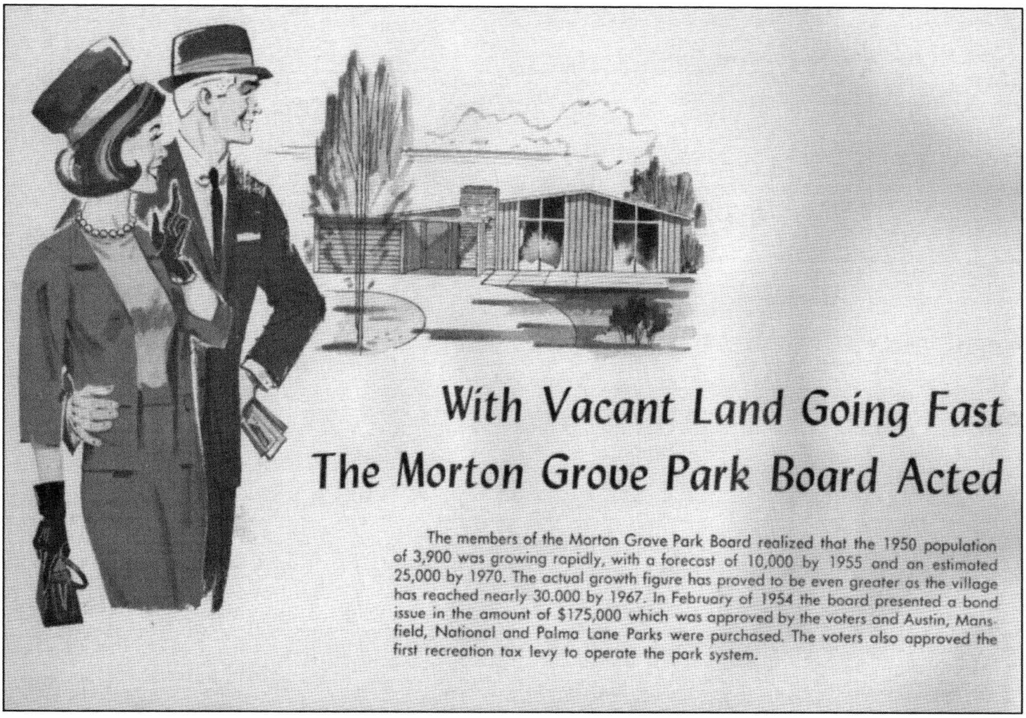

In 1935, the Morton Grove Days committee opened negotiations for a 32-acre parcel belonging to the Poehlmann Brothers Company. Foreseeing a need to set aside land for a public park, the property was finally purchased for $52,000 in 1940. After 8 acres were sold to School District 70 and 4 acres to the Forest Preserve District of Cook County, 20 acres remained that would become Harrer Park. The Morton Grove Days committee donated this land to the newly formed Morton Grove Park District in 1951. When the building boom hit in the early 1950s, Austin, Mansfield, National, and Palma Lane Parks were purchased. Today, the park district boasts 14 beautiful parks.

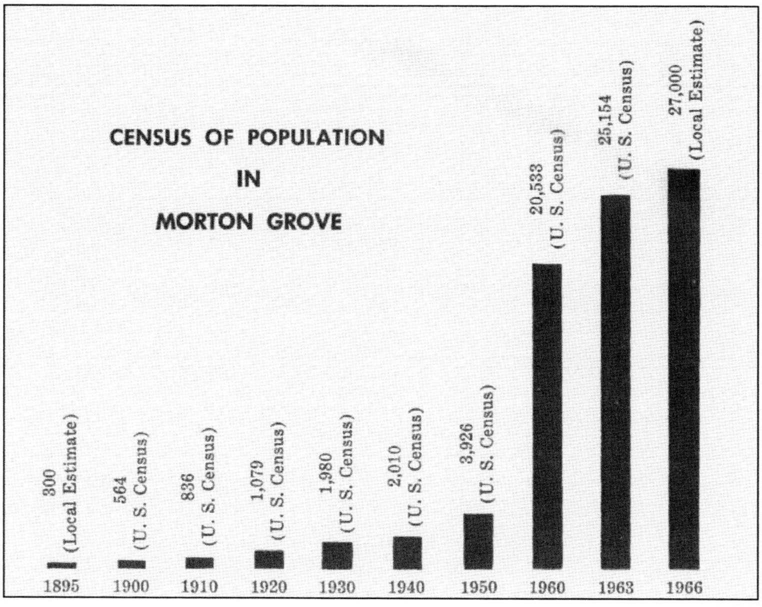

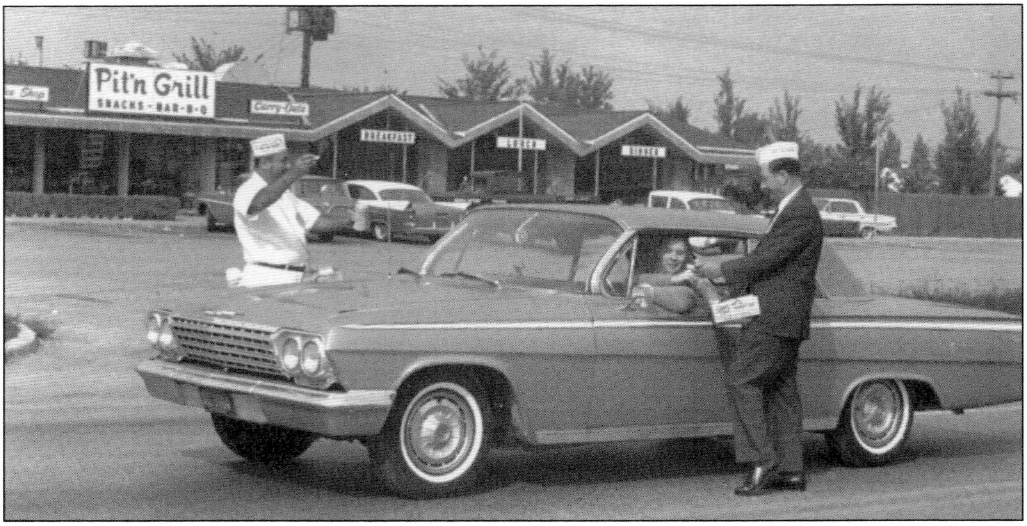

Members of the Lion's Club are pictured in front of the Pit'n Grill restaurant and cocktail lounge on Candy Day. Pit'n Grill, located at Waukegan and Beckwith Roads, was known for its barbecue ribs, chicken, beef, and pork. Jim Kavooras is remembered by the community as the host of this local establishment.

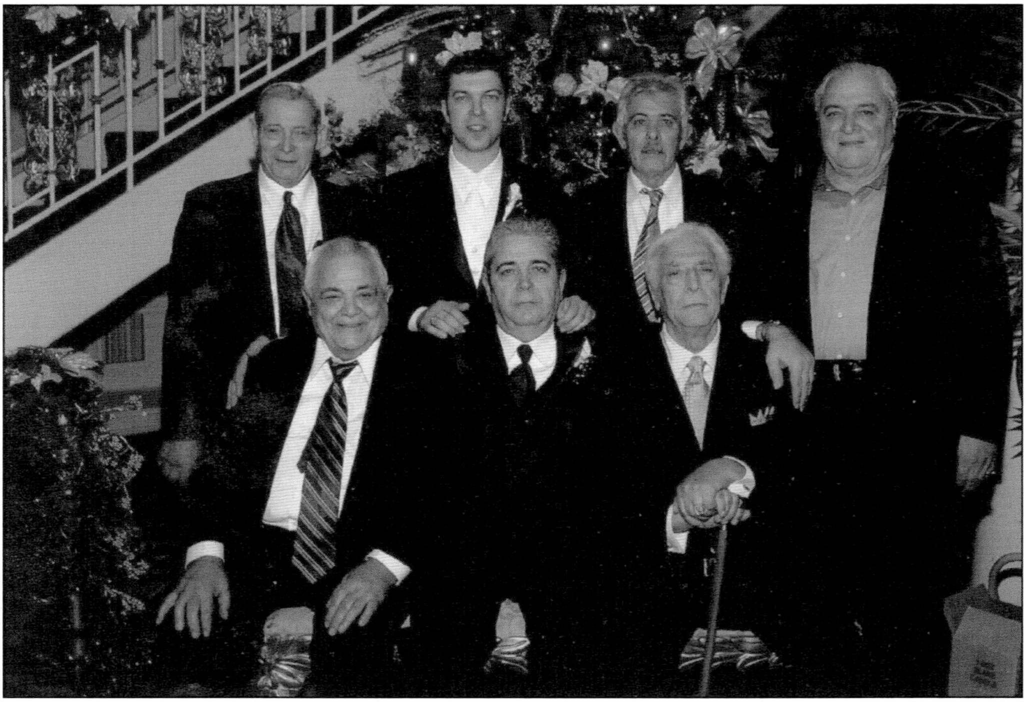

Seven brothers purchased Manda's Restaurant, located just north of their current location at 9300 Waukegan Road in 1966. After using the name Manda's for their famous family-style restaurant for nearly eight years, they officially renamed the restaurant Seven Brothers. In 1989, they moved to their current location, formerly the Pit n' Grill. Pictured from left to right are (first row) Bill, John, and Pete; (second row) Sam, Angelo, Mike, and James Tsagalis. Nephew Angelo is included in the family photograph, and the seventh brother George is not pictured. The seven brothers come from the Nestani and Tripoli region of Greece.

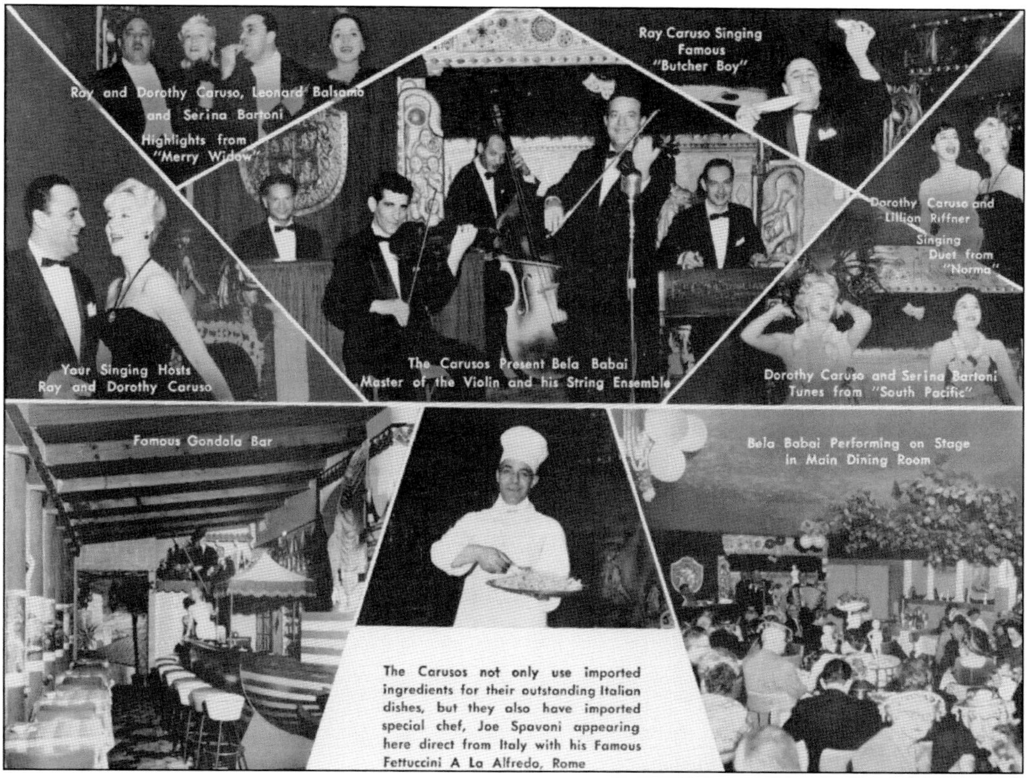

This 1961 postcard of the Caruso's Restaurant, located at 9110 Waukegan Road, illustrates the continental atmosphere that made this restaurant and gondola bar internationally known for its Italian American cuisine. Hosts Ray and Dorothy Caruso sang nightly, and their operatic ensemble performed selections from the grand opera. Featured artists such as Bela Babai and his string ensemble offered Hungarian, Gypsy, Viennese, and American selections. (Courtesy of Lake County, Illinois, Discovery Museum, Curt Teich Postcard Archives.)

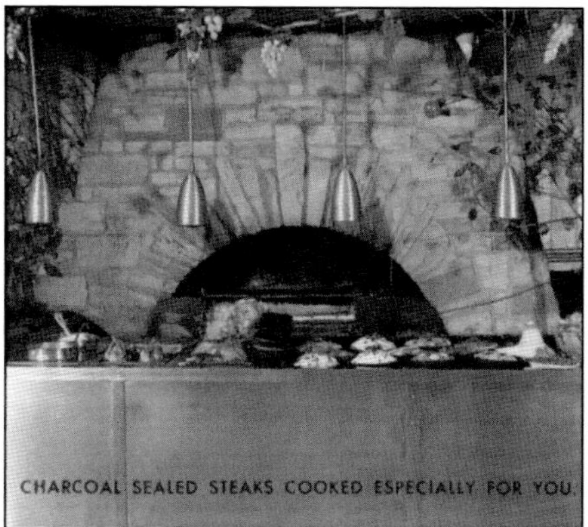

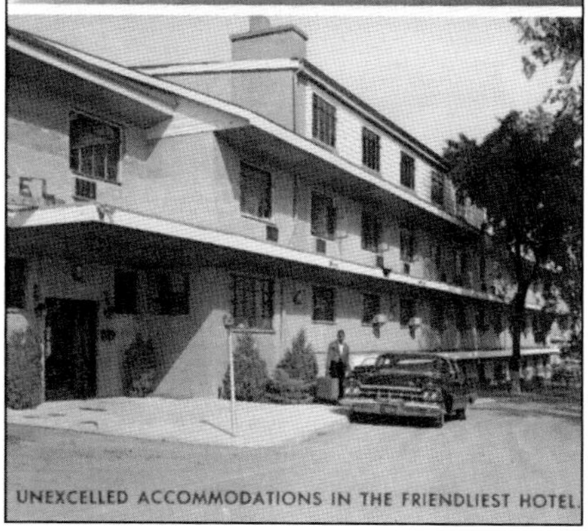

Ed Robert's Colonial Restaurant and Hotel was famous for charcoal-sealed steaks, conventions, and trade shows. The original building was constructed by George Gable in 1847 and served as a homestead, stagecoach stop, and Indian trading post. It was sold to his son-in-law John Dilg in 1856. The Dilg Homestead restaurant and lodge flourished for nearly 100 years. The Fireside Inn did business at this location following Ed Roberts' Colonial Restaurant and Hotel. The building was razed in 1999 for the redevelopment of the Waukegan Road Corridor. (Courtesy of Lake County, Illinois, Discovery Museum, Curt Teich Postcard Archives.)

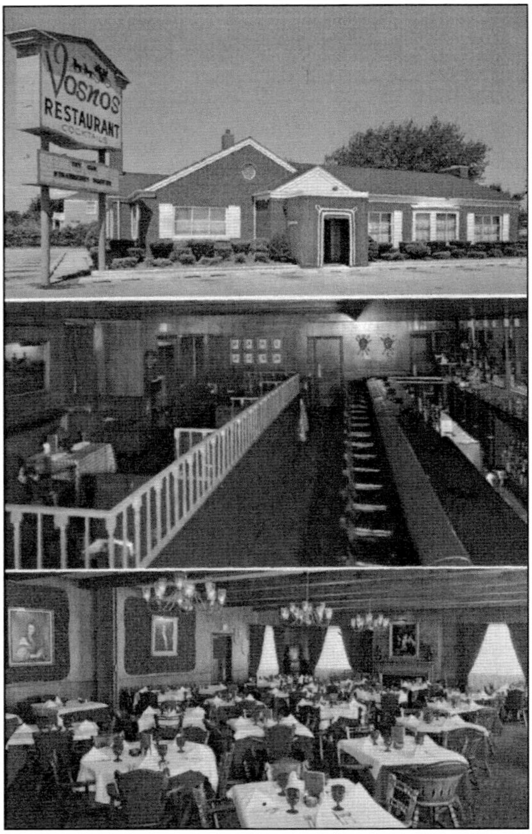

Vosnos Restaurant and Cocktail Lounge was located at the northwest corner of Waukegan Road and Dempster Street. Many local groups and families held special events here from 1949 and for decades after. The back of this postcard describes the restaurant as "Known the world over for seafoods and prime steaks."

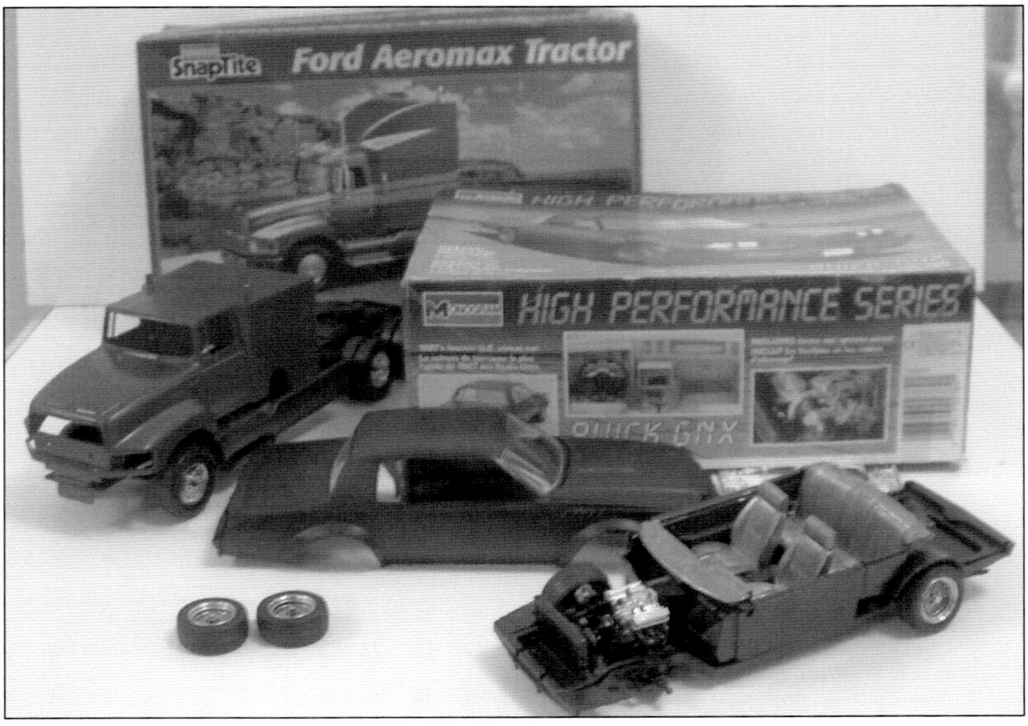

Monogram Models moved into its new Morton Grove headquarters at 8601 Waukegan Road in 1961 and became known as Revell-Monogram Inc. when the two companies merged. Designed to accommodate model development, molding, and packaging, this plant operated until the beginning of the 21st century. In 2004, the company moved to Northbrook, with the silos that were used to hold raw plastic pellets being the last to go before the building was razed in 2006. (Courtesy of Joe and Ginny Jung.)

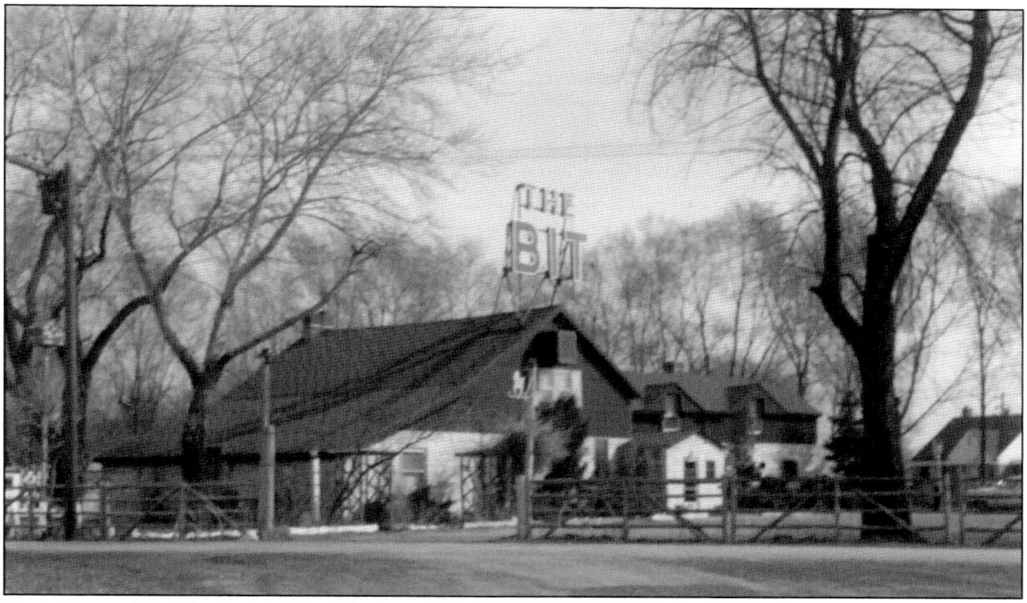

Bix's Bit and Bridle, later called the Bit under a second owner, was located on Harms Road north of Dempster Street. The restaurant was situated in a large remodeled stable and riding school that had been built some years before the restaurant opened in 1934. Al and Myrtle Bixler, the original owners, also lived in a small apartment in the same building.

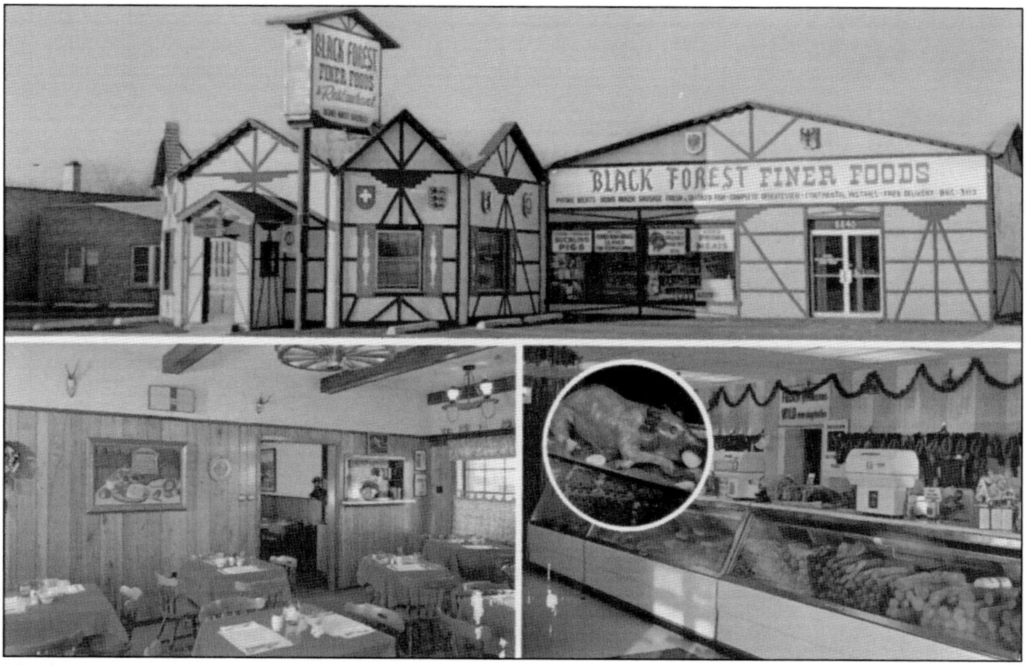

Black Forest was opened as a meat market in Morton Grove in the early 1960s by Robert Tschurtz, who operated a meat market of the same name near Lincoln and Belmont in Chicago. As seen in this 1968 postcard, Tschurtz expanded to include the Black Forest Finer Foods & Restaurant, as well as a gift shop. Management and ownership changed hands several times before the business closed in 2005. Peter and Rob Tschurtz currently own and operate Fritzl's European Restaurant and Pub in Lake Zurich, established by their father and named for their grandfather Fritz in 1985.

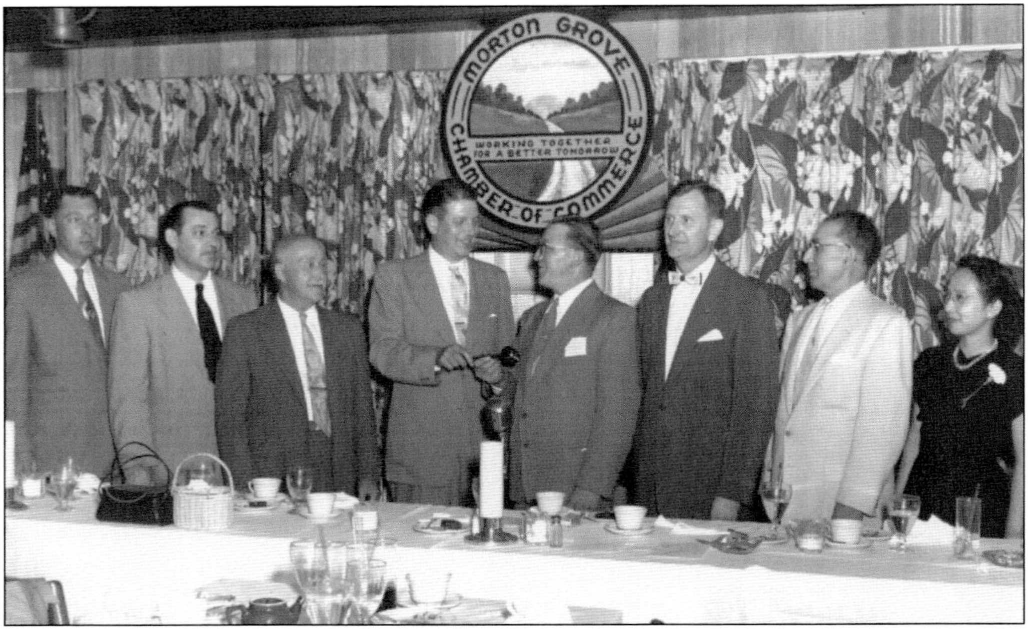

"Working Together for a Better Tomorrow" is the slogan on the Morton Grove Chamber of Commerce logo in the background during a banquet in the 1950s. Pictured from left to right, chamber members include two unidentified men, village president Max Finke (1945–1956), unidentified, Carl Eckhardt, Art Loutsch, unidentified, and Susie Kimura. Mayor Max Finke was also well known as the local plumber in the village.

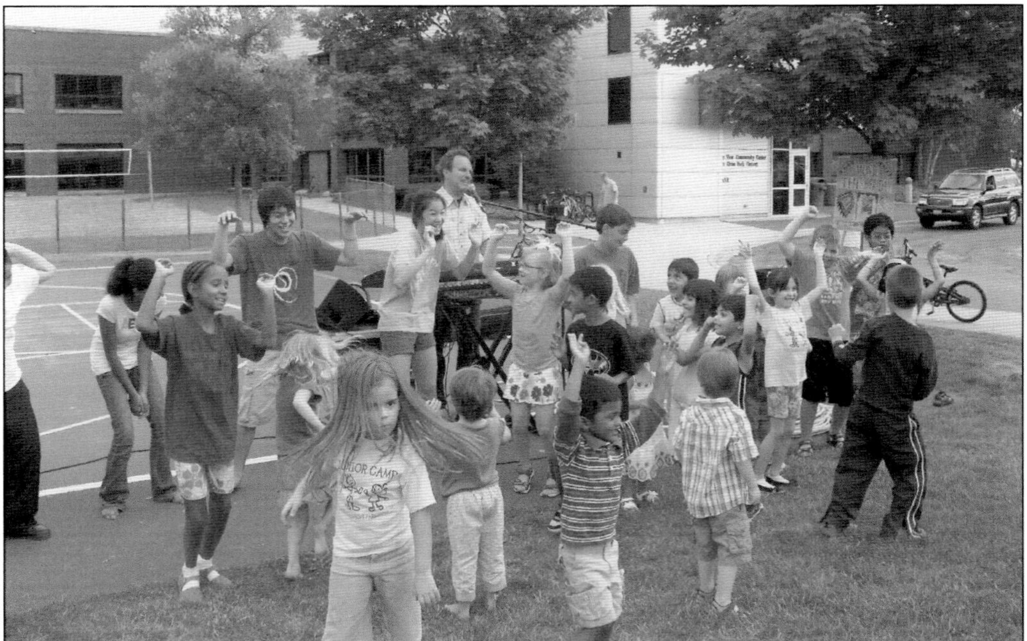

Children of all ages come out to enjoy music and dancing at Party in the Park in the summer. These parties, started in 2001, are free family events held at three neighborhood parks each summer. Ice cream is served to all in attendance, and families can enjoy a wide variety of activities planned by the Morton Grove Park District recreation staff.

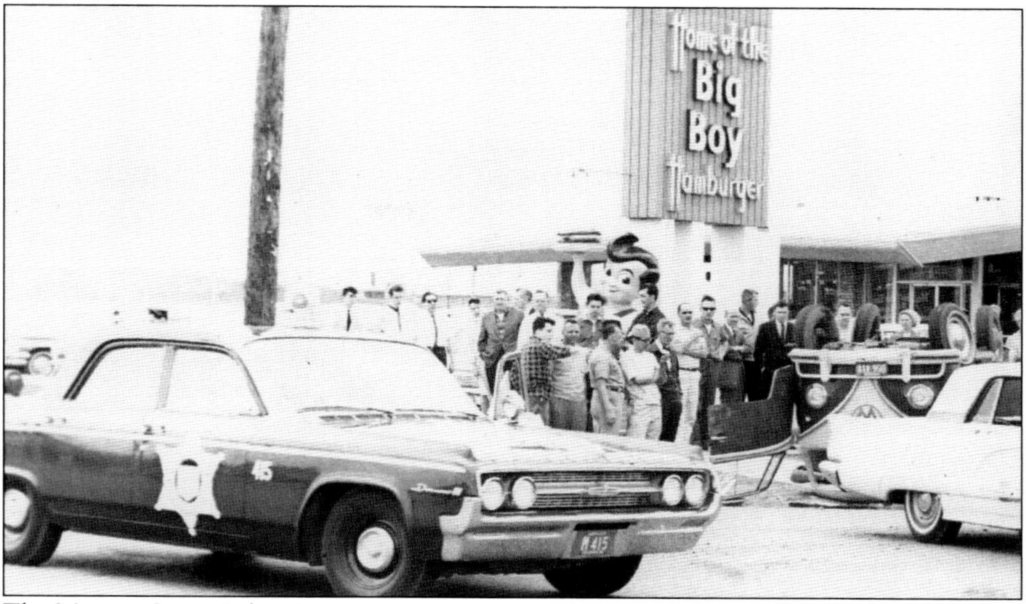

The Morton Grove Police Department captured a classic image of Tops Home of the Big Boy at the scene of a Volkswagen bus accident. Big Boy's, known for its fiberglass figure and popular comic book for customers, did business at the northwest corner of Dempster Street and Harlem Avenue, where Kappy's Restaurant has become a favorite today. Started in California in 1936, Tops did business in Illinois from 1966 to 1993 as a regional franchise. (Courtesy of Mark Erickson, chief of Morton Grove Police Department.)

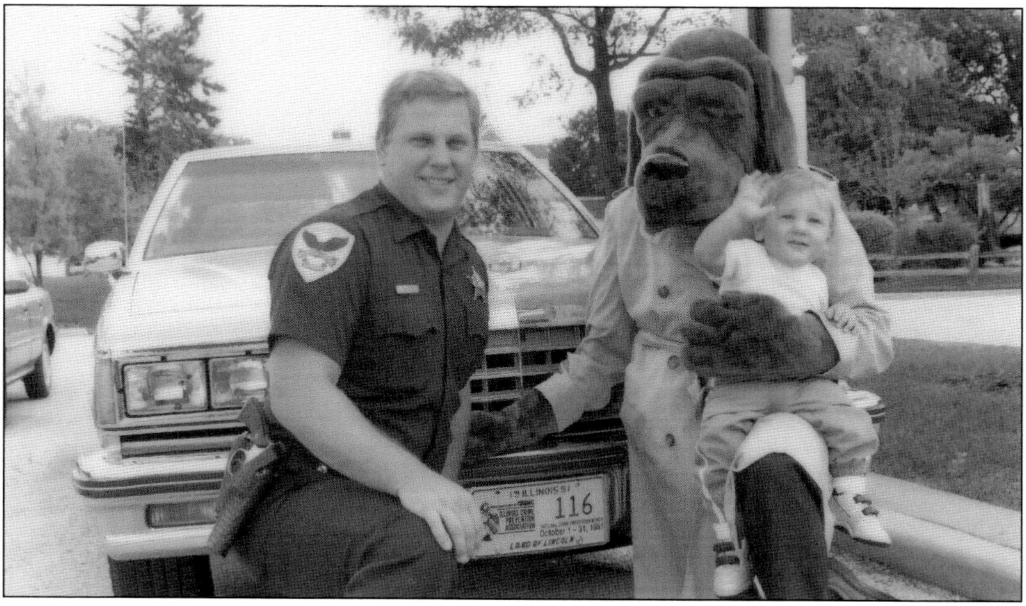

Mark Erickson, now chief of police for the Morton Grove Police Department, is pictured with his son Ricky and McGruff the Crime Dog (Sgt. Matthew Pankow). The National Crime Prevention Council was founded in 1982, with McGruff making his first public service announcement to "Take A Bite Out Of Crime" shortly after. Drug Abuse Resistance Education (DARE), the highly acclaimed program that gives kids the skills they need to avoid involvement in drugs, gangs, and violence, was also part of their crime prevention education at that time.

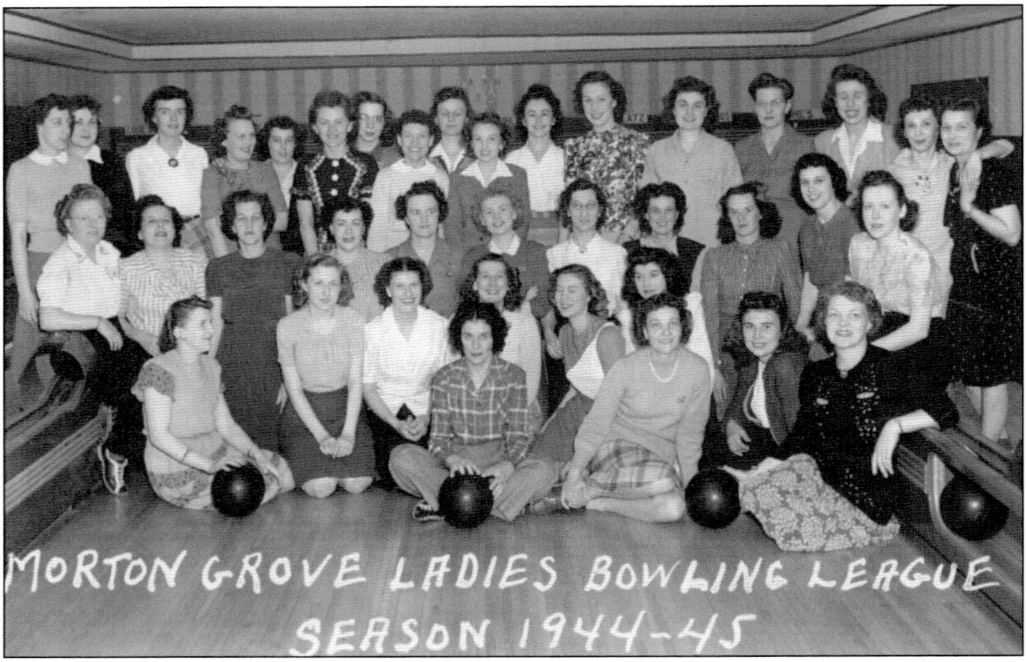

The bowling lanes operating at 6309 Dempster Street were started by Norbert Happ in 1941 and taken over by Charley Poss in 1945 after a fire. In 1954, Jack Schaul took over the business until it was replaced by a McDonald's in 1979. Many local bowling leagues, such as the Morton Grove Ladies Bowling League, the Moose Lodge, and St. Martha's youth organizations, have bowled these lanes through the years. Pictured below in 1962, from left to right, are Annie (née Nachbauer) Neumann (who worked in the lanes over 33 years), Jack Schaul, unidentified, Dave Ford, Jim Kaferly, Rudy Follman, two unidentified, Dick Flickinger (village president from 1977 to 1988), Andy Paul, and Lu Flickinger.

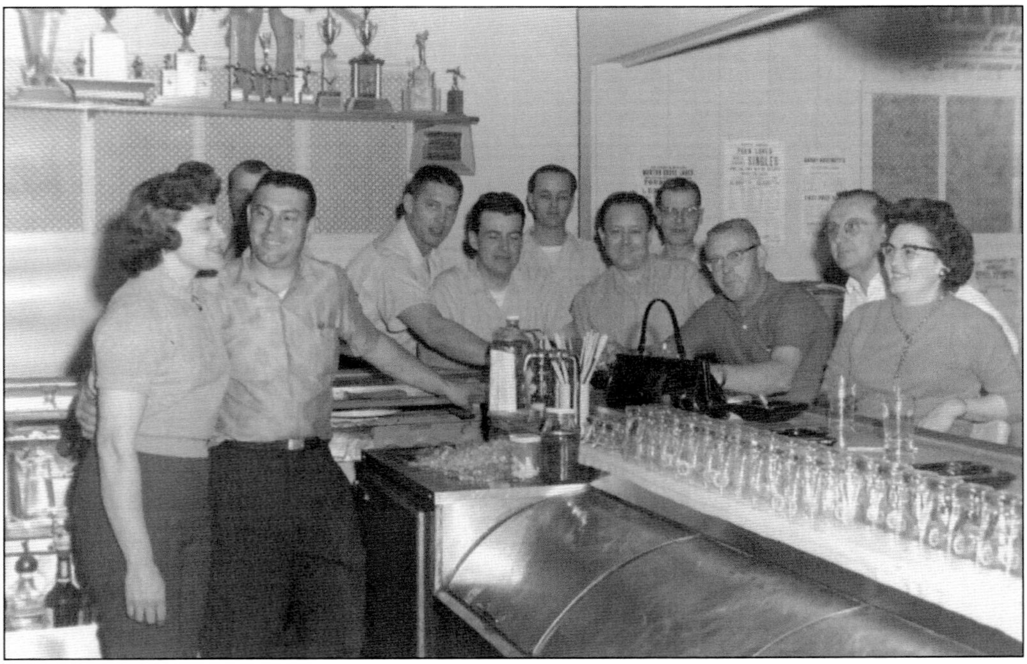

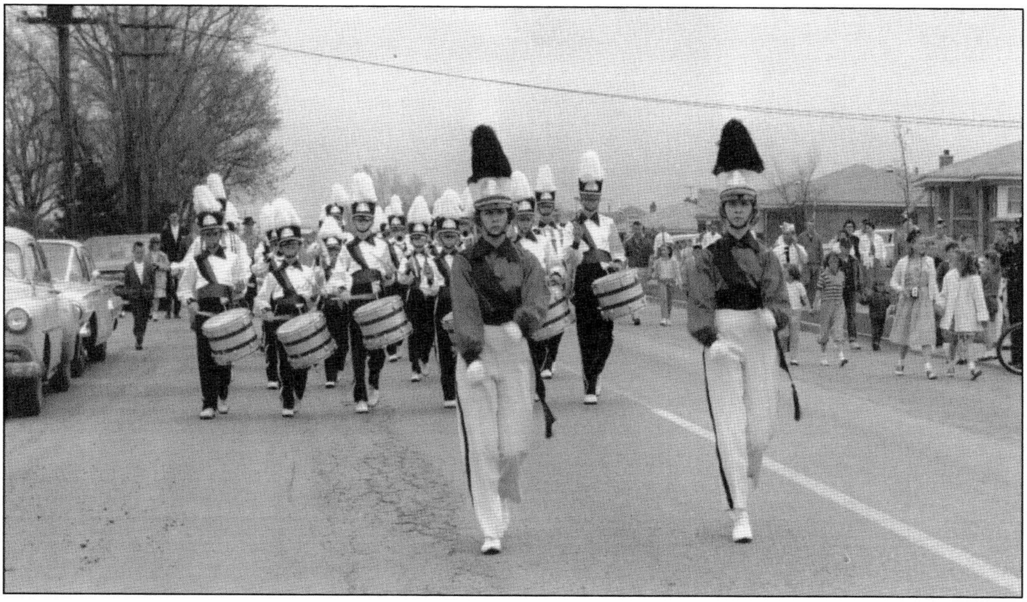

The Morton Grove Cougars Drum and Bugle Corps, sponsored by Post No. 134, Sons of the American Legion (SAL), are pictured with their color guard on parade. Organized in the mid-1950s and becoming state champions in the SAL bracket at the Illinois American Legion convention in Chicago in 1960, they went on to merge with the St. Michael's Chicago "Chi" Angels, becoming the Chicago Spartans Drum and Bugle Corps in 1964. The Spartans competed on a national level. Spartan bugler Michael Drehobl recalls being among the top 20 corps in the nation, competing against Chicago rivals the Blue Knights and the Cavaliers and setting a goal to reach the nationals that year. Just short of qualifying for the finals in Cleveland, the Spartans disbanded in 1965, with many members migrating to the Chicago Royal Airs.

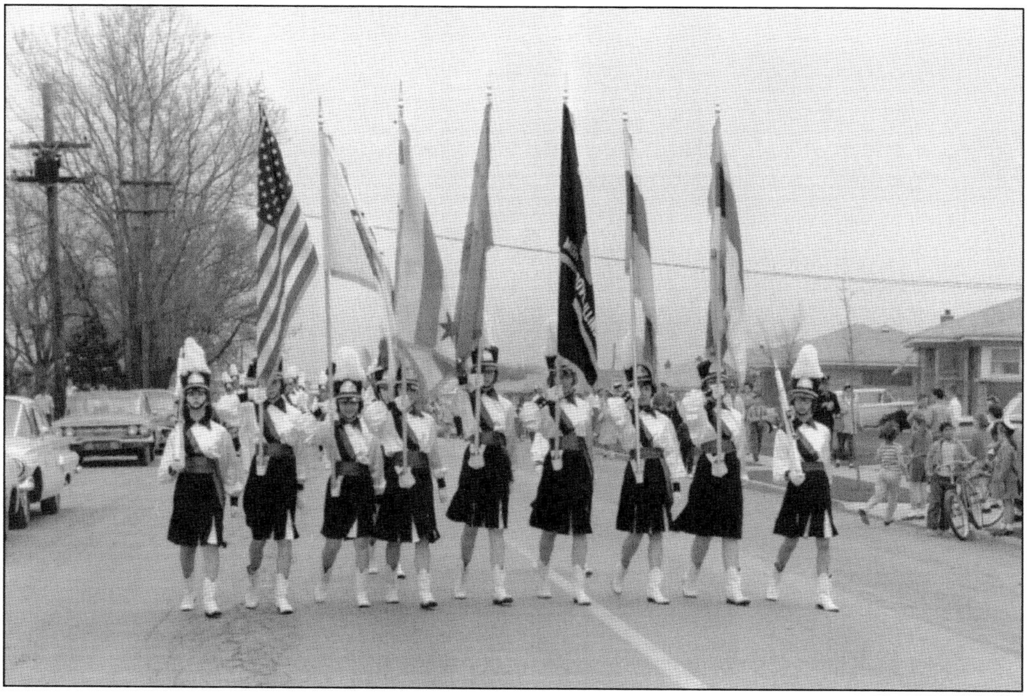

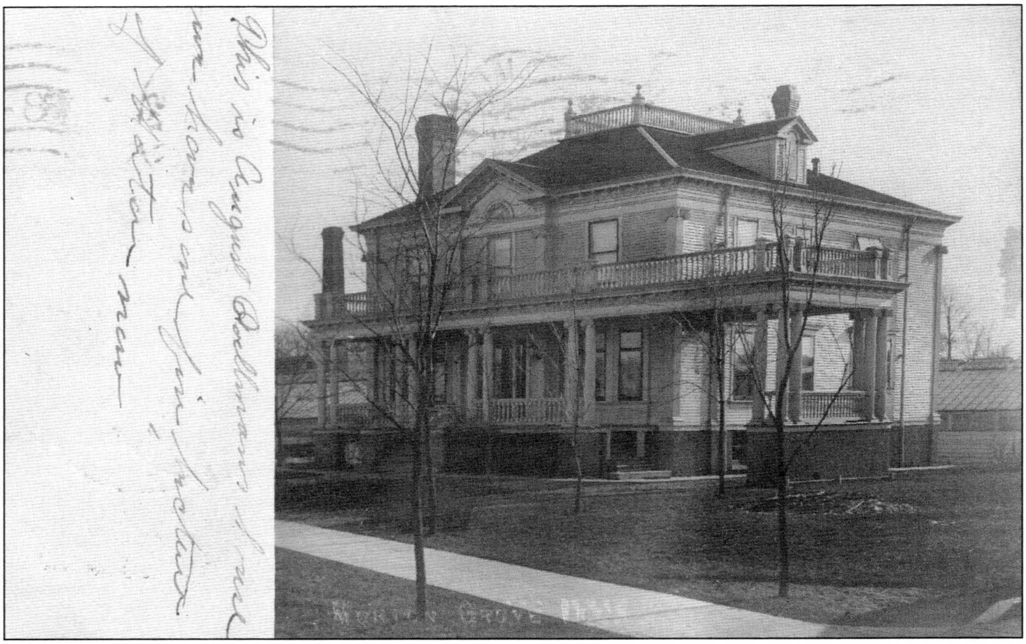

The home at 6249 Lincoln Avenue shown in this postcard was originally occupied by August Poehlmann, an early Morton Grove mayor and businessman. In 1946, the home was moved to Dempster Street to become Meyer's (now Simkin's) Funeral Home. It has since been modified and remodeled. Many other homes among the early housing section of Morton Grove have been moved and repurposed but remain as reminders of early settlement.

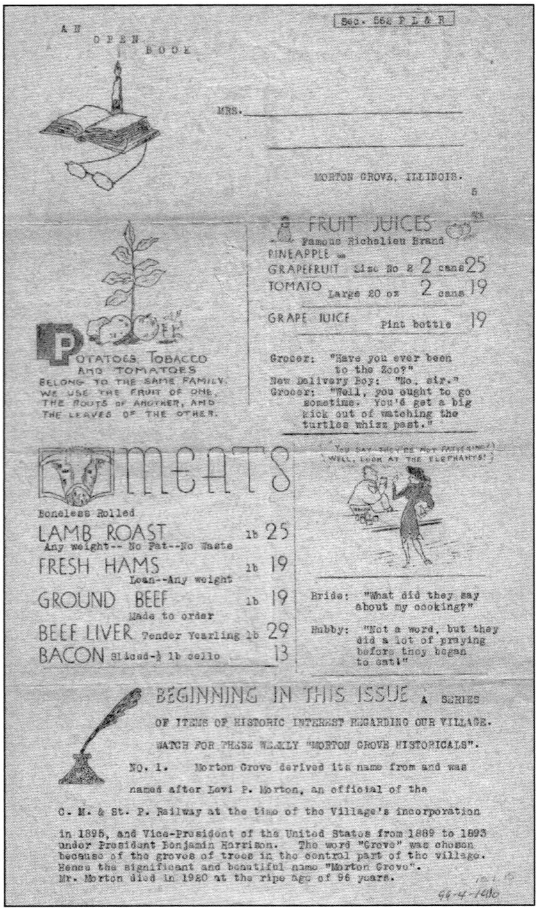

AN OPEN BOOK

Sec. 562 P L & R

MRS. ____________________

____

MORTON GROVE, ILLINOIS.

5

POTATOES, TOBACCO AND TOMATOES BELONG TO THE SAME FAMILY. WE USE THE FRUIT OF ONE, THE ROOTS OF ANOTHER, AND THE LEAVES OF THE OTHER.

FRUIT JUICES

Famous Richelieu Brand

PINEAPPLE
GRAPEFRUIT Size No 2 2 cans 25
TOMATO Large 20 oz 2 cans 19
GRAPE JUICE Pint bottle 19

Grocer: "Have you ever been to the Zoo?"
New Delivery Boy: "No, sir."
Grocer: "Well, you ought to go sometime. You'd get a big kick out of watching the turtles whizz past."

MEATS

Boneless Rolled
LAMB ROAST lb 25
Any weight-- No Fat--No Waste
FRESH HAMS lb 19
Lean--Any weight
GROUND BEEF lb 19
Made to order
BEEF LIVER Tender Yearling lb 29
BACON Sliced-½ lb cello 13

Bride: "What did they say about my cooking?"
Hubby: "Not a word, but they did a lot of praying before they began to eat!"

BEGINNING IN THIS ISSUE A SERIES OF ITEMS OF HISTORIC INTEREST REGARDING OUR VILLAGE. WATCH FOR THESE WEEKLY "MORTON GROVE HISTORICALS".

NO. 1. Morton Grove derived its name from and was named after Levi P. Morton, an official of the C. M. & St. P. Railway at the time of the Village's incorporation in 1895, and Vice-President of the United States from 1889 to 1893 under President Benjamin Harrison. The word "Grove" was chosen because of the groves of trees in the central part of the village. Hence the significant and beautiful name "Morton Grove". Mr. Morton died in 1920 at the ripe age of 96 years.

Along with advertisements for food specials, Loutch Brothers Foods fliers often featured a local history story, timeline, or other interesting facts. Arthur Loutsch, one of the four Loutsch brothers, collected Morton Grove history and prepared these fliers and other compilations of local history. Arthur was a significant personality in forming the Morton Grove Historical Society.

Board selects new acting village president, trustee

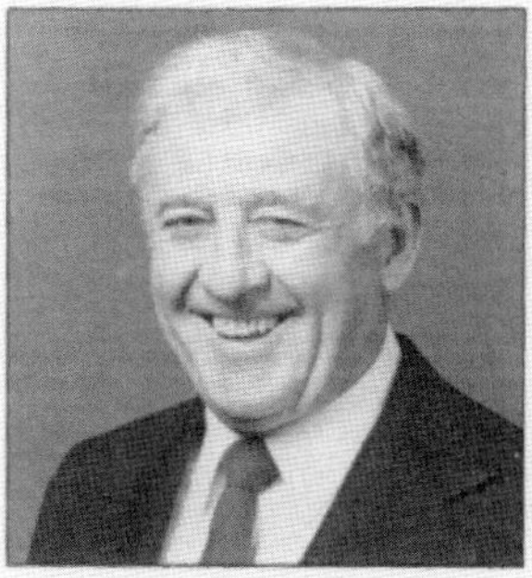

Richard P. Hohs
Acting Village President

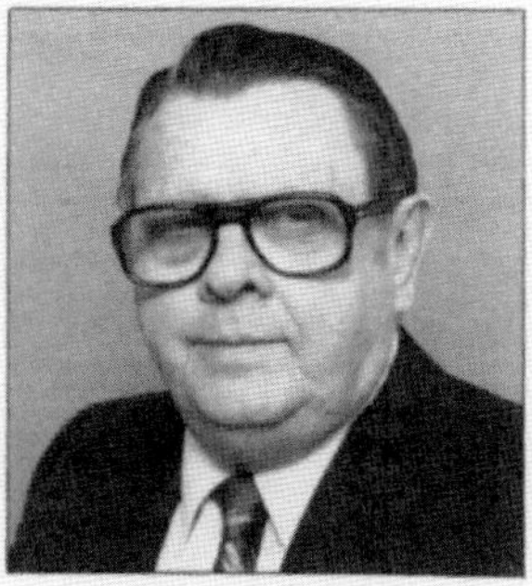

Daniel D. Scanlon
Village Trustee

Richard Hohs, 60, was appointed acting village president Monday Feb. 8 to serve the remaining 14 months of the late mayor Richard T. Flickinger's term.

Flickinger, 71, died Monday Feb. 1 after a long illness.

"Dick has the interest of this village at heart. He'll go to bat for any (cause) that seems right," said Trustee Lewis Greenberg.

"He's Mr. Integrity," said Cook County Circuit Court Judge Martin Ashman. Ashman is the village's former corporation counsel. "He exemplifies the hometown boy who makes good. There isn't a more worthy person in this village to take this position."

Hohs, a former volunteer fireman and lifetime resident of Morton Grove, has been a village trustee for 13 years. He serves on the Morton Grove Days Committee and was selected as Morton Grove VIP in 1987.

Hohs and his wife, Alice, have eight children and 20 grandchildren.

Daniel D. Scanlon, 63, a longtime resident of Morton Grove, also was unanimously appointed to fill Hohs' position as village trustee until the next April election in 1989.

"I think with a little help from the board, I can make a meaningful contribution," Scanlon said. "I feel honored to be serving as trustee."

Scanlon is a past president of the Electrical Inspectors Association of Northern Illinois and served as village electrical inspector from 1958 to 1969 and again from 1977 until his appointment.

He is a member of the American Legion Post #134 and a parishioner of St. Martha's Church. Scanlon and his wife, Betty, have seven children.

Richard P. Hohs was a lifelong resident of Morton Grove, served with the volunteer fire department, was an active member of the historical society and Morton Grove Days Committee, became the acting village president in 1988 with the passing of Mayor Richard Flickinger, and held that office until 1996. Daniel D. Scanlon filled the open trustee position and went on to become village president from 1996 to 2005.

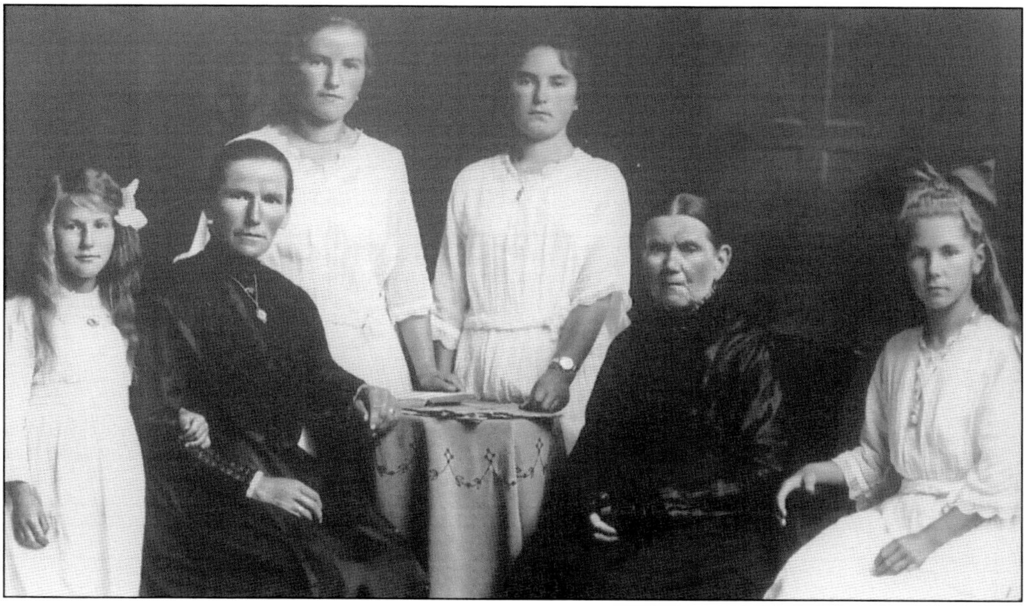

Lucia Klas (1905–2010) lived to be one of Morton Grove's oldest residents at the age of 105. She is pictured (third from left) with her family in Schwabisch Gmund, Germany, before traveling to America at age 17. She arrived at Ellis Island and traveled by steam locomotive to an aunt and uncle in Minnesota before seeking work in Chicago, meeting her husband, and settling in Morton Grove in 1946.

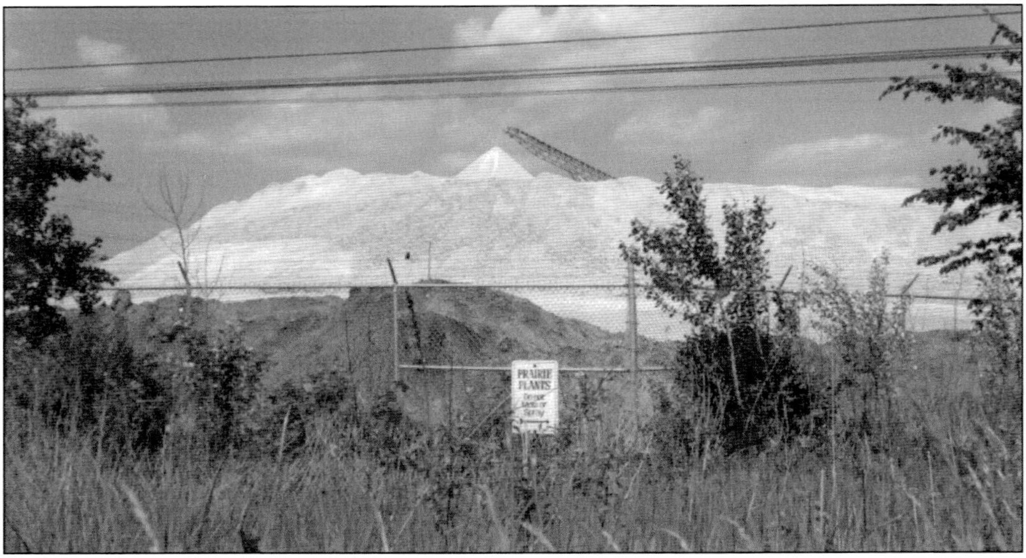

The Tunnel and Reservoir Plan (TARP), also called the Deep Tunnel Project, is an effort to improve local waterways and provide flood protection. Construction in Morton Grove of a tunnel nine miles long, up to 35 feet in diameter, and 250 feet underground began in 1992. This tunnel joined others that the Metropolitan Water Reclamation District of Greater Chicago (MWRDGC) began constructing in 1985. Morton Grove's section of the construction took place on forest preserve land west of the North Branch of the Chicago River south of Beckwith Road. The massive pile of limestone created as part of the excavation is shown, as well as the tunnel opening that remains in Linne Prairie.

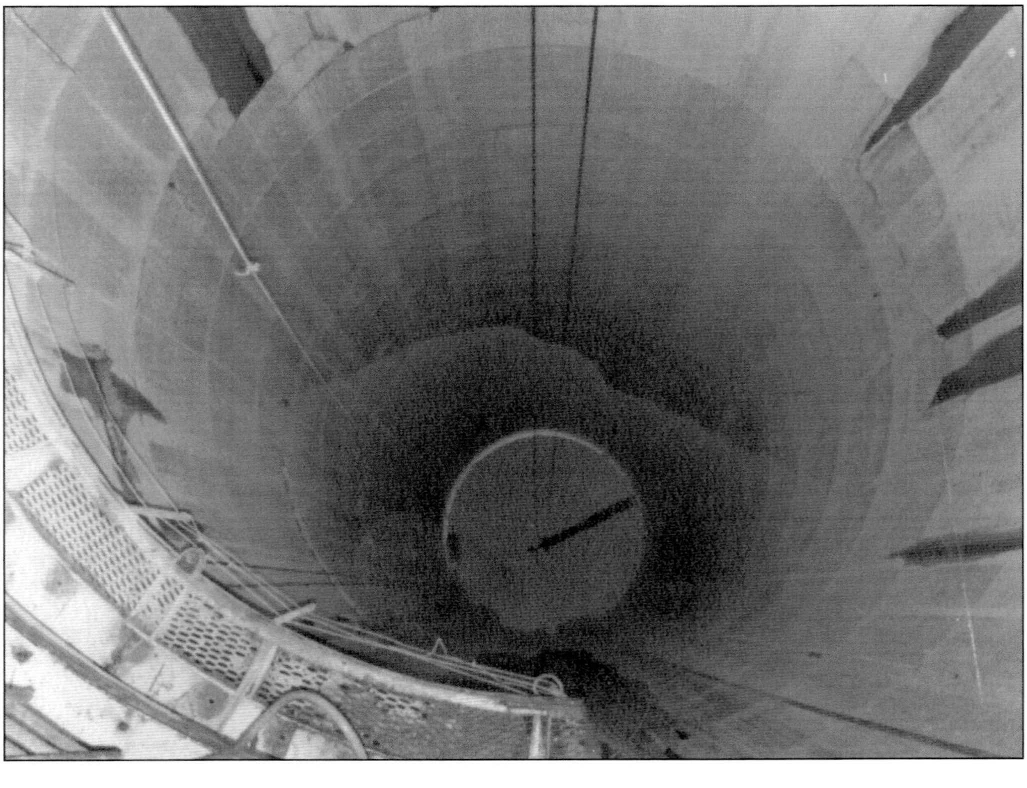

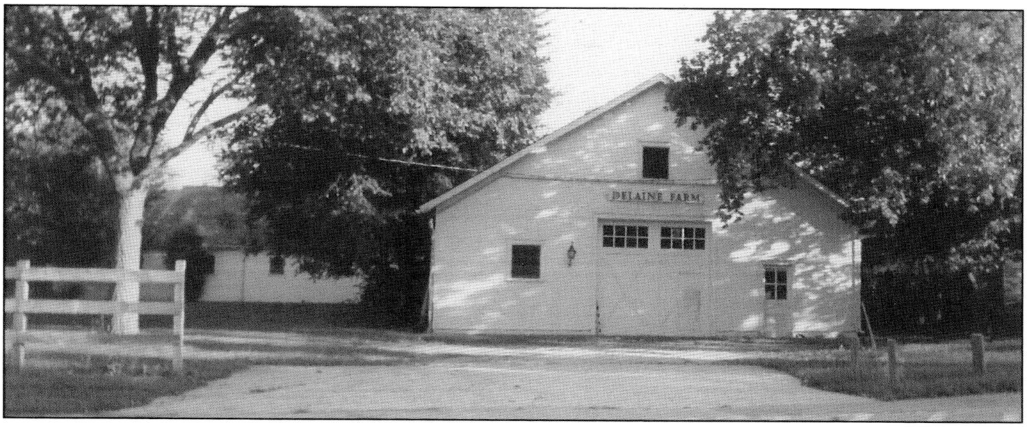

Delaine Farm, located at 6531 Beckwith Road, was founded by Hubert Silberman, who purchased land from Raymond Smith in 1932 and continued to purchase tracts of this historic Hoffman farm property over time. Silberman planned to graze sheep and so named his farm Delaine for the French word referring to a sheer wool or wool and cotton fabric, but horses became his main business. He won 14 medals in one season at Madison Square Garden riding their prize mount Something Wonderful.

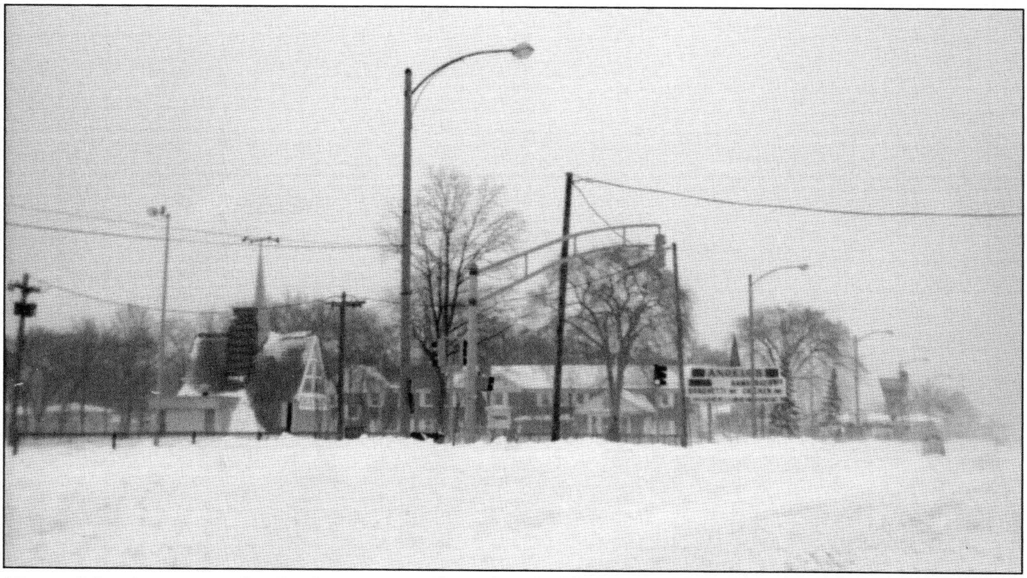

Grove Hamburgers, which also operated as the Golden Point on the 6100 block of Dempster Street, was a popular spot for families and teens, located adjacent to the Harrer Park pool. This photograph, taken looking east on Dempster Street from Harrer Park during the blizzard of 1967, shows the American Legion hall in the background.

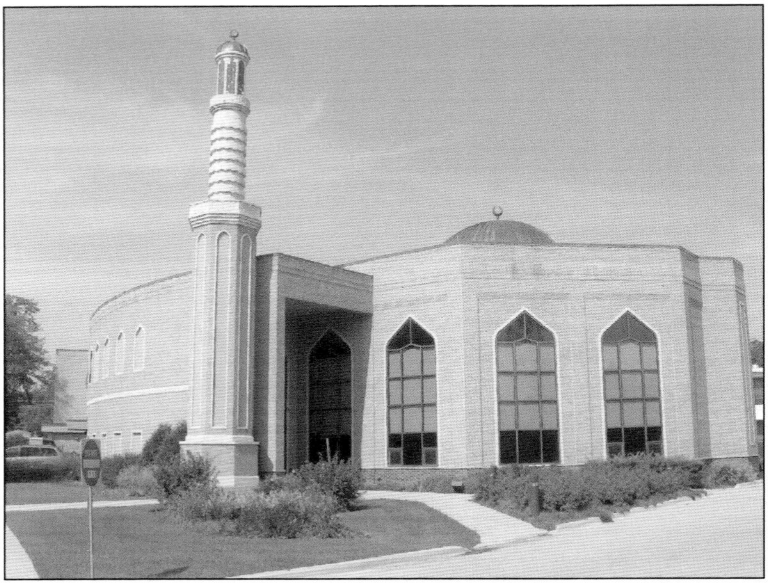

Blanche Borg School was built in 1965 at Menard and Park Avenues to accommodate a sharp rise in population. However, it was closed in the 1980s and sold in 1989. In 1990, Morton Grove's Muslim Community Center and Muslim Education Center's full-time school opened. The Muslim Community Center is pictured as it exists today.

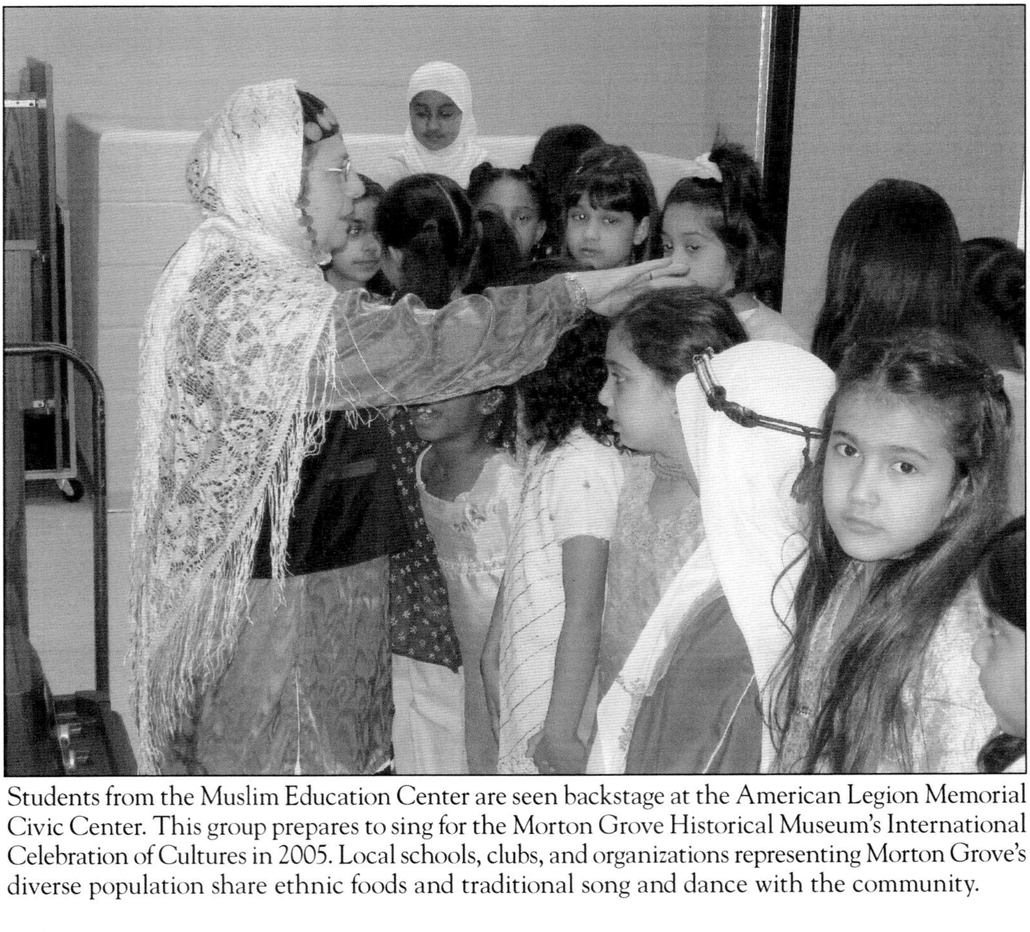

Students from the Muslim Education Center are seen backstage at the American Legion Memorial Civic Center. This group prepares to sing for the Morton Grove Historical Museum's International Celebration of Cultures in 2005. Local schools, clubs, and organizations representing Morton Grove's diverse population share ethnic foods and traditional song and dance with the community.

An Irish dancer from the Sheila Tully School of Dance is pictured with a young Indian woman in traditional dress. Performers representing the many groups of people who have settled in Morton Grove delighted participants with music and dance from around the world during the International Celebration of Cultures in 2005.

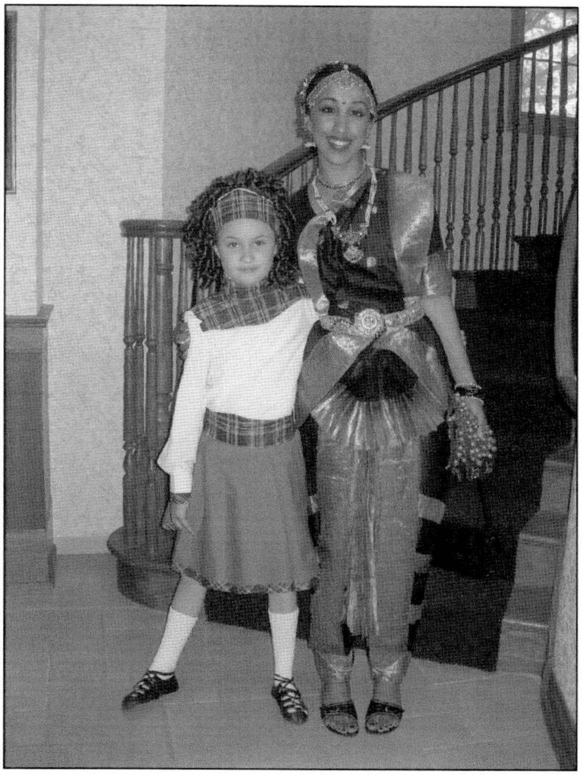

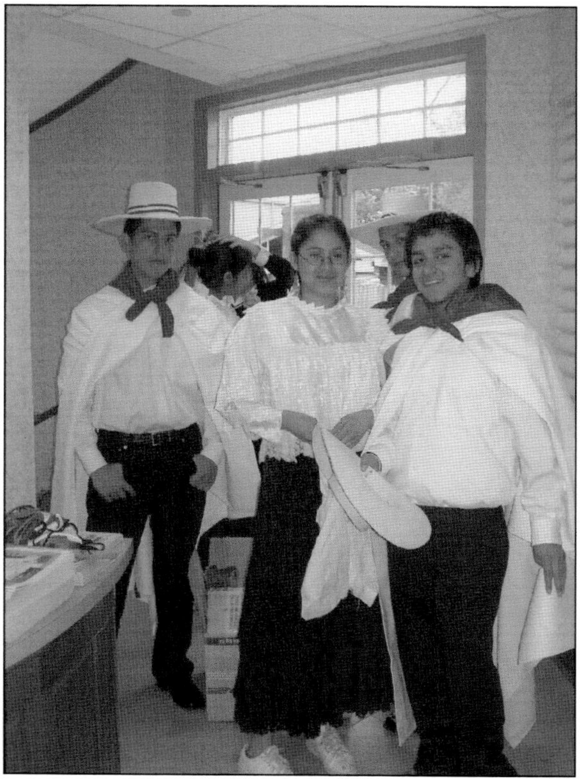

Members of the Latino club are pictured during performances at the American Legion Memorial Civic Center. Niles Township High School District 219 and Maine Township High School District 207 cultural clubs joined the Morton Grove Historical Museum's International Celebration of Cultures. Representing the cultures and languages spoken in the homes of Morton Grove residents at this time, Assyrian, Filipino, Chinese, French, Hellenic, Indo-Pak, Israeli and Korean clubs are a few of the extracurricular organizations that meet in our local high schools today.